6/23/15
$45.00

Mining Archaeology in the American West

Historical Archaeology
of the American West

Series Editors

Rebecca Allen
Annalies Corbin

Mining Archaeology in the American West

A View from the Silver State

Donald L. Hardesty

University of Nebraska Press
and the
Society for Historical Archaeology

© 2010 by The Society for Historical Archaeology
All rights reserved
Manufactured in the United States of America
⊚
Library of Congress
Cataloging-in-Publication Data
Hardesty, Donald L., 1941–
Mining archaeology in the American West :
a view from the Silver State / Donald L. Hardesty.
    p.   cm.
— (Historical archaeology of the American West)
Includes bibliographical references and index.
ISBN 978–0–8032–2440–7 (cloth : alk. paper)
1. Nevada—Antiquities.
2. Archaeology and history—Nevada.
3. Frontier and pioneer life—Nevada.
4. Mines and mineral resources—
Social aspects—Nevada—History.
5. Mines and mineral resources—
Nevada—History.
6. Mining engineering—Nevada—History.
7. Industrial archaeology—Nevada.
8. Social archaeology—Nevada.
I. Society for Historical Archaeology. II. Title.
F843.H25 2010
979.3′01—dc22
2009033169

Set in Quadraat & Quadraat Sans by Kim Essman.

Contents

List of Illustrations vii

List of Tables xi

Introduction xiii

1. Traveling into Nevada's Mining Past 1

2. The Archaeology of Mining Technology 29

3. The Social Archaeology of Mining 109

4. Conclusions
   *Understanding Variability and
   Change on the Mining Frontier* 179

References Cited 189

Index 203

Illustrations

Images

1. Miners at Cortez, early 20th century 2
2. Mining landscape, Bodie, California 9
3. Standard Mill at Bodie, California 13
4. Billie Mine Portal, Death Valley, California 14
5. Bullwheel at Bulwer Mill site, Bodie, California 16
6. An arrastra 17
7. Map of arrastra archaeological site 18
8. The Tenabo Mill in 1900 19
9. Lime kiln next to the Tenabo Mill........................... 19
10. The Mayflower Mine site, Bullfrog Mining District, Nevada ... 24
11. Hoist engine at the Pioneer Mine site,
    Bullfrog Mining District, Nevada 25
12. Virginia City, Nevada, from Cedar Hill, 1870s or 1880s 26
13. House site at Shoshone Wells 27
14. Mine waste dump and tramway at Arctic Mine,
    Cortez Mining District 30
15. Cyanide vats, Bodie, California 30
16. The Tenabo Mill site 32
17. The "Nevada Giant Ledge" in the Cortez Mining District 33
18. Placer deposits, Malakoff Diggings, California 34
19. The "glory hole" at the Montgomery-Shoshone Mine,
    Bullfrog Mining District 35
20. Lavender copper pit, Bisbee, Arizona 37
21. Abandoned dredge between Tok and Eagle, Alaska 39
22. "Giant" water nozzle used in hydraulic mining at
    Malakoff Diggings, California 39
23. Illustration of Burleigh mechanical rock drill 40
24. Air compressor at Caledonia Mine, Gold Hill,
    Comstock Mining District................................... 41
25. Mine shaft and collapsed headframe,
    Joshua Tree National Park, California 42

26. "Rat-holing" scene: miners, burro, and ore car 42

27. Underground workings at the
Consolidated Cortez Mine, 1920s 44

28. Adit at the Arctic Mine, Cortez Mining District 45

29. An 1876 lithograph by T. D. Dawes of square sets
on the Comstock Lode 46

30. Shrinkage stoping at Cortez, 1920s 47

31. Windlass at Rawhide, 1908 48

32. Underground at the Gold Bar Mine, 1905 48

33. Whim at Bodie 49

34. Gallows headframe at the new Gold Bar Mine, 1906 50

35. Gallows headframe at the Forman Shaft, Gold Hill,
Comstock Mining District 51

36. Hoisting cages, Bullion Mine, Gold Hill,
Comstock Mining District 52

37. Cornish pump at the Union Shaft,
Comstock Mining District, 1879 54

38. The Gold Bar Mine site 54

39. Horse whim at the original Gold Bar Mine, 1905 56

40. The original Gold Bar Mine site 56

41. Map of the original Gold Bar Mine 57

42. Blacksmithing feature at the original Gold Bar Mine 58

43. The new Gold Bar Mine in 1908 58

44. The new Gold Bar Mine site 59

45. Map of the new Gold Bar Mine 60

46. The Homestake Mine in 1906 61

47. The Homestake Mine site 61

48. Map of the Homestake Mine 62

49. Concrete machine pads at the Homestake Mine 63

50. The main shaft at the Homestake Mine 64

51. An arrastra, Joshua Tree National Park, California 65

52. An 1860s lithograph of a stamp battery at
Gould and Curry Mill, Comstock Mining District 66

53. Ruins of an 1870s stamp mill at Tuscarora, Nevada, in 1911 67

54. Illustration of a Blake rock crusher 68

55. Illustration of Krom rolls 68

56. Allis-Chalmers tube mill at Consolidated Cortez Mill,
Cortez Mining District, 1920s 69

57. Frue vanners at the Kinkaid Mill, Virginia City, Nevada.........71
58. Illustration of Fagergren flotation cells 72
59. Elevation and flow sheet of Black Hawk
    Flotation Mill, New Mexico 73
60. Patios at the 1864 Gould and Curry Mill,
    Comstock Mining District 74
61. Elevation of the Taylor Mill, Mineral Hill 75
62. Illustration of Wheeler amalgamation pan 77
63. Illustration of settler... 78
64. Interior of California Pan Mill,
    Virginia City, Nevada, in 1882................................ 79
65. Ruins of 1871 Monte Cristo Mill near Rawhide, 1914 80
66. Illustration of Bruckner cylinders 81
67. Illustration of Stetefeldt shaft furnace 82
68. Remains of leaching vats at the Tenabo Mill site 85
69. Bruckner cylinders and furnaces at the Tenabo Mill site 85
70. Butters Mill on the Comstock Lode, 1906 86
71. Interior of Butters Mill, showing agitation tanks 86
72. The 1909 Sanborn fire insurance map of
    Montgomery-Shoshone Mill, Bullfrog Mining District 87
73. Milling flow sheet for Montgomery-Shoshone Mill 88
74. Montgomery-Shoshone Mill site............................. 89
75. Illustration of Dorr thickening tank 90
76. Archaeological remains of Dorr thickener.................... 90
77. Illustration of Trent agitation tank 91
78. The Homestake-King Mill site, Bullfrog Mining District...... 92
79. The Homestake-King Mill in 1908 92
80. Map of the Homestake-King Mill 94
81. The Consolidated Cortez Mill site,
    Cortez Mining District 96
82. Consolidated Cortez Mill in the 1920s 96
83. Allis-Chalmers ball mill at the
    Consolidated Cortez Mill, 1920s 97
84. Agitation tanks at the Consolidated Cortez Mill, 1920s 97
85. Merrill slime press at the Consolidated Cortez Mill, 1920s..... 98
86. Oliver filter at the Queen Mill in Rawhide, Nevada, 1912 98
87. Bullion furnace at the Consolidated Cortez Mill 99
88. Map of the Consolidated Cortez Mill site 100

89. Tailings flow at the Consolidated Cortez Mill site............. 101

90. Consolidated Cortez Mill powerhouse in the 1920s........... 101

91. Fairbanks and Morse generators at the
    Consolidated Cortez Mill powerhouse........................ 102

92. The Consolidated Cortez Mill powerhouse site 102

93. Cyanide lid trash scatter at the
    Consolidated Cortez Mill site............................... 103

94. Richmond Consolidated Smelter, Eureka, Nevada 104

95. Assaying artifact: crucibles 106

96. Assaying artifact: cupels..................................... 106

97. Assay trash scatter at the Consolidated Cortez Mill site....... 107

98. Rhyolite, Nevada, in 1905 114

99. Map of settlements in Cortez Mining District 118

100. Town of Cortez, Nevada, in early 20th century.............. 119

101. Map of Shoshone Wells site 121

102. The Gold Bar Camp in 1908 126

103. Map of the Gold Bar townsite 127

104. The Gold Bar Camp in 1905 129

105. The Gold Bar Camp in 1906 129

106. The Gold Bar Camp in 1908 129

107. Residential locus at the Garrison Mine,
     Cortez Mining District 142

108. Chinese artifacts from Structure 22 150

Figures

1. Milling flow sheet for the Taylor Mill 76

2. Milling flow sheet for Russell process at the Tenabo Mill 84

3. Milling flow sheet for the Homestake-King Mill............... 95

4. Histogram of "purple" bottle glass
   assemblages at Gold Bar...................................... 131

5. Histogram of house-site floor areas at Gold Bar 160

6. Histogram of artifact assemblage sizes at Gold Bar 161

7. Histogram of artifact assemblage diversity at Gold Bar........ 164

8. Simple linear regression of assemblage diversity on
   assemblage size at Gold Bar 165

9. Histogram of ceramic percentages at Gold Bar 166

10. Histogram of bottle glass percentages at Gold Bar 166

Tables

1. Shoshone Wells house-site classification 123
2. Statistical description of Gold Bar "purple" bottle glass 132
3. Tin can assemblage from Gold Bar townsite. 133
4. Artifact assemblage from Wenban's house site 137
5. The 1900 household census for the Garrison Precinct 143
6. The 1900 household census for the Cortez Precinct 144
7. Shoshone Wells property owners with Chinese surnames 146
8. Artifact assemblage from Structure 22 149
9. Artifact assemblage from Structure 18. 151
10. Artifact assemblage from Structure 20. 154
11. Artifact assemblage from Structure 14. 157
12. Artifact assemblage from Structure 13. 158
13. Statistical description of Gold Bar house floor areas. 161
14. Statistical description of Gold Bar artifact assemblages 162
15. Statistical description of Gold Bar assemblage diversity 164
16. Statistical description of Gold Bar ceramics 167
17. Statistical description of Gold Bar bottle glass 167
18. Geographical origins of Cortez Store invoices, 1891–1893 172
19. List of suppliers to the Cortez Store, 1891–1893 173

Introduction

Mining and miners left an enduring legacy in the history and landscape of the American West (Smith 1987; Robbins 1994; Hine and Faragher 2000; Paul 2001; Isenberg 2006). Indigenous peoples mined minerals such as salt and turquoise in the region before the arrival of Europeans in the 1500s. Spanish explorers and settlers searched for the mythical El Dorado and opened mineral and metal mines in what is now the Southwest and Southern California. They introduced mining technologies and methods developed earlier in medieval Europe and other parts of New Spain. The discovery of gold in California in 1849 led to the first global mining rush in the American West (Holliday 1999). More mining rushes followed with gold strikes on the Fraser River in British Columbia and on Pikes Peak in Colorado in the late 1850s (Fetherling 1997). The discovery of the famous Comstock Lode in Nevada in 1859 spurred the industrialization of mining and revolutionized mining technology, society, and culture throughout the world (James 1998). Subsequent mining rushes took place during the next few decades in the Cariboo region of British Columbia; on Nevada's Reese River and Treasure Hill; in the Black Hills of South Dakota; at Bannack and Alder Gulch in Montana; at Leadville and Cripple Creek in Colorado; and at Idaho's Clearwater River, Boise Basin, and Owyhee Mountains, among other places. The end of the nineteenth century and beginning of the twentieth heralded the last of the famous global mining rushes in the American West: the Klondike Gold Rush in Alaska (Morse 2003) and the gold strikes at Tonopah, Nevada, in 1900 and at nearby Goldfield, Nevada, in 1902 (Elliott 1966; Zanjani 1992, 2002). Mining for base metals and minerals such as copper and iron played an equally prominent role in the history of the American West in the twentieth century (Hyde 1998).

Nevada's mining frontier is a microcosm of the western mining experience and is the focus of this book. Sporadic and small-scale mining took place in what is now Nevada before the expansion of the American state. In the late 18th century, Spanish Franciscan monks traveling on an old Spanish trail in what is now southern Nevada mined gold placers, silver lodes, and turquoise (Horton and Lincoln 1964:2). Mormon expansion out of the Salt Lake Valley in the late 1840s and 1850s also introduced some mining activity to Nevada in the aftermath of the California Gold Rush (Arrington 1958, 1979; Davies 1984; Owens 2002). In 1855 Mormons established a mission in the Las Vegas Valley at what is known today as Mormon Fort (Arrington 1979). Brigham Young sent a party of prospectors led by Nathaniel V. Jones in April 1856 to search for rumored silver and lead deposits (Arrington 1958:127–129; Lingenfelter 1986:60–61). They failed to discover a "silver mountain" but did find gold and lead deposits in the Spring Mountains of present-day southern Nevada. Young opted to develop the lead deposit at Potosi Spring close to the Spanish trail (Arrington 1958:127–129). By January 1857 the Mormon miners had "opened the mine, built a small smelting furnace, and produced over 9,000 pounds of lead" containing significant amounts of silver, giving rise to legends about Mormons using silver bullets (Lingenfelter 1986:61). The mine became unprofitable, however, and the group began to search for new lead deposits (Arrington 1958:127–129). Young called the Mormons back to Utah later that year (1857), bringing the search and the Las Vegas mission to an end. In 1861 non-Mormons discovered silver deposits near the Potosi lead mine, and the Colorado Mining Company built another smelter, along with the townsite of Potosi, about one-half mile from the mine (Paher 1970:265–266). William O. Vanderburg (1937:11) noted that the first systematic mining in present-day Nevada began in 1857 with the discovery of gold and silver deposits in the Eldorado Mining District on the Colorado River just west of Lake Mead.

Mormon emigrants discovered placer gold at the mouth of Gold Canyon on the Carson River in 1850, culminating in the discovery of the Comstock Lode in 1859, the subsequent "Rush to Washoe," and the global revolution of the mining industry. In 1860 prospectors found new silver deposits in the Esmeralda district in Mineral County and the Humboldt district in Humboldt County, soon leading to mining rushes in both places. The Reese River strike in 1862 and ensuing rush brought the mining industry to central Nevada, where production peaked between 1862 and the late 1880s (Abbe 1985). In 1867 excitement surrounding the Treasure Hill mines in central Nevada led to the establishment of the towns of Hamilton, Treasure City, and Shermantown as well as major British investment in the mines in the 1870s and 1880s (Jackson 1963). At one point, 200 mines and

23 mills operated on Treasure Hill. The Treasure Hill mines soon failed, however, with most closing down in the early 1870s. Eureka emerged in the 1870s and 1880s as a world-class smelting center for lead-silver ores mined in the region. Large-scale placer mining began in the Osceola district in northeastern Nevada during the 1880s and continued until 1900 through the use of hydraulic and sluicing mining technology. The Osceola Placer Mining Company constructed a large water conveyance system of ditches and flumes (Vanderburg 1936:168–169).

Tonopah and Goldfield emerged as early-20th-century centers of mining activity in Nevada in 1900 and 1901, respectively (Elliott 1966; Zanjani 1992, 2002). Secondary and short-lived booms also occurred in the Bullfrog district, Rawhide, and the Seven Troughs district (Ransome et al. 1910; Lincoln 1923:151, 216; Lingenfelter 1986). The western slopes of the Toquima Range were dominated by large-scale placer mining activities in the Round Mountain and Manhattan districts (Lincoln 1923:175). Using a variety of technologies ranging from hydraulic monitors to floating bucket dredges, both sites produced high yields of free gold between the first decade of the 20th century and the 1940s.

The purpose of this book is to explore the historical structure, characteristics, variability, and evolution of Nevada's mining frontier through the material remains of the technological systems, landscapes, and social formations associated with past mining activities. These physical expressions include standing buildings and structures, ruins and other archaeological remains, landforms, and historical documents. Toward this end, chapter 1 discusses how to travel into mining's past through the corridors of written and pictorial documents, landscapes, architecture, and the archaeological record and how to use these resources interactively to explore the Nevada mining frontier. Traveling through documents involves images of the past gleaned from personal diaries and letters, photographs, state and federal census records, tax assessments, company records, government publications, and the like. Mining landscapes are marked by images in landforms, vegetation patterns, land-use patterns, circulation networks, and cultural traditions. Another corridor passes through architectural images in the form of surviving buildings and structures associated with the extraction and processing of minerals and metals, mining infrastructures of transportation and communication, and the lifestyles and social organization of the miners. Traveling through the archaeological record of Nevada's mining past, one finds images of collapsed headframes and hoisting houses, foundations of pan amalgamation mills, remnants of arrastras, trash dumps, and the ruins of blacksmith shops and miner's residences.

Chapter 2 explores the archaeology of mining technology on Nevada's mining frontier. Miners and engineers developed technologies for exploration and extraction, processing, and building infrastructure. Extraction technologies included excavation, hoisting, ventilation, and drainage systems. Processing technologies involved mechanical crushing and grinding, simple collection, chemical methods for milling complex ores, and smelting. The technologies of mining infrastructure addressed transportation, power, and communication. Mining technologies have archaeological, architectural, and landscape expressions in mine waste-rock dumps, mill tailings, open pits and prospects, shafts and adits, mill foundations, concrete engine pads, tramways, hoist houses, air compressors, dredges, and headframes. Such remains reflect the tools, materials, operational sequences and skills, social coordination of work, and knowledge involved in the extraction and processing of metals and minerals, the key components of what has been called a "sociotechnical system." The chapter explores variability and change in the sociotechnical systems of mining.

Chapter 3 addresses the social archaeology of mining on Nevada's mining frontier in terms of settlement-systems, settlements, households, and the archaeology of gender, ethnicity, and class. Settlement-systems reflect the spatial arrangement of tools, operations, social formations, and coordination of work within mining-related sociotechnical systems. Such social relations are, in the words of Elizabeth Brumfiel (1992:551), "the composite outcomes of negotiation between positioned social agents pursuing their goals under both ecological and social constraints." Mining social systems can be conceptualized as a network of power relationships based on controlled access to resources like capital, ore deposits, labor, and water. Power relationships among individuals and groups are therefore situational: they are constantly being negotiated because of changing meanings or values of these resources. This chapter also explores local settlements as well as variability and change in households on the mining frontier. Local settlements formed the key nodes of mining-related settlement-systems, social networks, communities, and sociotechnical systems. They ranged from small social groups organized around mines or mills to large urban centers and company towns with a wide range of activities and diverse social structures. Chapter 3 focuses on Gold Bar, a short-lived early-20th-century camp in southwestern Nevada, and the late-19th-century settlement of Shoshone Wells in central Nevada. These mining settlements were organized around households—groups of people sharing domestic activities such as consumption and production who may or may not have lived together.

Chapter 4 considers the theoretical frameworks and evolutionary models used to understand Nevada's mining past. The principles of evolutionary theory and evolutionary ecology are applied to explore variability and change in the distinctive social and cultural characteristics of mining frontiers in the American West. Mining frontiers reflect the mechanisms and processes of evolutionary plays taking place in unique ecological theaters. How miners used coping strategies to adapt to the boom-bust cycles and island structures of the frontier is discussed in the chapter. They include opportunistic strategies (such as geographical expansion, resource intensification, and pooling) and resiliency strategies (such as finding new markets, cutting costs, and geographical contraction). The chapter concludes with the development of a coevolutionary model of adaptive change on mining frontiers and its application to the Comstock Mining District.

1. Traveling into Nevada's Mining Past

Exploring Nevada's mining past involves traveling through the historical corridors revealed by documents, landscapes, architecture, and the archaeological record. Each pathway follows an independent source of information that can be combined and used interactively with the others to construct models of the past (Deetz 1988). One source of information, like written documents, can provide a preliminary model of a mining technology, household, or community. The archaeologist or historian can derive hypotheses from the model and test them with data acquired from new research into the archaeological record, architecture, landscapes, or documents. The new information helps modify the preliminary model, leading to the identification of new hypotheses that can be tested and used to revise the model further. In this manner, the construction of mining's past from several independent sources of information is cyclical and continuously evolving.

Documentary Images

One corridor into Nevada's mining past is through written and pictorial documents (image 1). Community plats, cartographic sources, iconographic and pictorial material, company records, records of social service workers, professional and technical journals, consultants' reports, governmental publications, newspaper accounts, census records, and city directories are the most common documentary accounts of mining (Alanen 1979).

Townsite Plats

The Townsite Surveys of the General Land Office are one of the most important sources of plats for mining camps. Plats are available for several Nevada mining settlements, including Esmeralda, Aurora, Washoe City, Austin, American City, and Mineral City (Reps 1975). In addition, Sanborn fire insurance maps of several mining towns, including the Comstock towns of Virginia City, Gold Hill, Silver City, and Dayton, are available

1. Miners at Cortez, early 20th century. (Courtesy of Nevada Historical Society.)

for different time periods. The maps give important information about town layout and the use and construction of buildings. Sometimes included are maps of mines and mills in and around the town, such as the Montgomery-Shoshone Mine at Rhyolite.

Cartographic Sources

The maps produced by the U.S. Bureau of Mines and the Nevada Bureau of Mines and Geology are useful sources of information about ore deposits. Researchers can also turn to the township and mineral patent survey plats and notes in the Nevada State Office, Bureau of Land Management.

Company Records

The availability of written accounts kept by mining companies in the state of Nevada varies greatly. Some records are in the Nevada State Historical Society; the Nevada State Archives; the county historical societies, archives, and museums; and the university libraries at the Reno and Las Vegas campuses of the University of Nevada. For the most part, however, the records are scattered. The Churchill County Museum and Archive as well as Special Collections at the University of Nevada–Reno Library, for example, hold ledgers and invoices from the company store of the Cortez Mines Limited from 1889 to 1893. Ledgers and invoices for the company store of the Tenabo Mill and Mining Company for 1904, 1908, and 1909 are available elsewhere. The Adelberg and Raymond manuscript collection at the New York Public Library is another valuable source of company data, containing items like the 1865 report of the Manhattan Silver Mining Company in Austin, Nevada.

Diaries and Other Personal Reminiscences

Dan De Quille's (1876) *The Big Bonanza* is a newspaperman's account of the Comstock Mining District in its heyday. Mary McNair Mathews's (1985) *Ten Years in Nevada or Life on the Pacific Coast* is an account of 1870s Virginia City. Hubert H. Bancroft's (1889) multivolume series "Chronicle of the Kings" includes a biography of Simeon Wenban, a mine operator in Nevada. And John Ross Browne's (1871) *Adventures in the Apache Country: A Tour through Arizona and Sonora, with Notes on the Silver Regions of Nevada* is another classic.

Professional and Technical Journals

Two contemporary journals are the standard sources on mining technology and provide a wealth of information about the subject: the *Mining and Scientific Press* and the *Engineering and Mining Journal*. There are also several textbooks and handbooks, the most useful of which is Robert Peele's (1918) *Mining Engineers Handbook* (1st edition, with several later editions). Other key publications include Manuel Eissler's (1898) *The Metallurgy of Silver* (4th edition); Thomas Egleston's (1887) *Metallurgy of Silver, Gold and Mercury in the United States*; Carl A. Stetefeldt's (1895) *The Lixiviation of Silver-Ores with Hyposulphite Solution*; John Dorr's (1936) *Cyanidation and Concentration of Gold and Silver Ores*; William Storms's (1909) *Timbering and Mining*; Guido Kustel's (1863) *Nevada and California Processes of Silver and Gold Extraction*; and Thomas A. Rickard's (1901) classic *The Stamp Milling of Gold Ores*.

Government Records

Government records provide another important source of information about mining in Nevada. Chester Naramore and C. G. Yale's (1910) *Gold, Silver, Copper, Lead, and Zinc in the Western States and Territories in 1908* is a standard source, as are James Hague's (1870) mining reports in the U.S. *Geological Exploration of the Fortieth Parallel*. The *Information Circulars* of the

U.S. Bureau of Mines provide a wealth of geological and engineering information about the mines of Nevada and elsewhere, as do the bulletins of the U.S. Geological Survey and the bulletins of the Nevada Bureau of Mines and Geology. Couch and Carpenter's (1943) *Nevada's Metal and Mineral Production*, for example, is an extremely useful source. Many of these works contain key information about mining districts, such as J. M. Hill's (1912) *The Mining Districts of the Western United States* and Francis Church Lincoln's (1923) *Mining Districts and Mineral Resources in Nevada*.

Another key government source is the series Mineral Resources West of the Rocky Mountains, later renamed Mineral Resources of the United States. Several authors wrote the reports in this series, which the U.S. Treasury Department issued beginning in 1866; the most important were those by J. Ross Brown (1866–1867), Rossiter Raymond (1868–1875), and S. F. Emmons (1893). Several of the reports were published as annual reports of the U.S. Geological Survey between 1882 and 1893. Specific reports can be located through the *Checklist of U.S. Public Documents*, prepared by the superintendent of documents.

Whatever the political problems involved, Nevada's unique status of having 86% of its land in the public domain has created an unusually large body of written accounts. The Bureau of Land Management (BLM), which formed in 1812 as the General Land Office to administer public lands, maintains detailed records of land transactions. Jane F. Smith (1975:291) has classified these records into four groups, each of which contains different kinds of information: (1) *identification records*—mostly surveyors' field notes and plats containing information about topography, vegetation, and resources; (2) *status records*—tract books or ledgers and status plats giving a legal description of public lands and resources and detailing their ownership, size, purchase price, and use; (3) *case records* —land entry papers, especially related to homestead, desert land, and mineral claims, with information about dates, locations, and improvements to mining properties and settlements; and (4) *legal records*—mostly land patents and deeds. Many of these records are kept in the state and district offices of the BLM in Nevada, although some are located in the National Archives. Two categories of documents are especially important. After 1880 townsite survey files were separated from other land entry documents, and today they provide an important source of information about mining camps, both planned and actually built. Indeed, John W. Reps (1975) has made a case for early "urban planning" in western mining camps using the town plats from the Townsite Surveys, General Land Office, National Archives. And, second, the passage of the U.S. Mining Law in 1866 (Act of July 26, 1866, 14 Stat. 251) opened up public lands to mining and led to the "mineral entry" documents, which are located in the General Land Office section of the National Archives. The mineral entries contain field notes and plats, the bylaws of mining districts, records of litigation surrounding mining claims, mineral contest dockets, and much more (Smith 1975:302).

Historically, the Nevada Legislature has convened every two years and continues to do so. A published report of its activities appeared in the year following each session. From 1864, when Nevada was admitted to the union, to 1879, the "Biennial Report of the State Mineralogist of the State of Nevada" was included in an *Appendix to the Journals of the Senate and Assembly*. Each report contained detailed information about mining production in the state, usually arranged by county. The 1877 report, for example, noted that the Garrison Mine in the Cortez Mining District produced 492 tons of ore with a market value of $21,273.49 for the year 1875 (p. 197). And the 1873 report observed that the Cortez Mill was operating with 13 stamps (p. 67). From 1879 to 1911 the reports continued under the title "Biennial Report of the Surveyor-General and State Land Register of the State of Nevada." In addition to mining statistics, the reports included litigation. The 1891 report, for example, discusses the dispute between Lander and Eureka counties over the Cortez Mining District, which was bisected by the county line (pp. 106–110). Construction of a new mill by the Tenabo Mill and Mining Company in 1886 instigated a lawsuit by Eureka County to recover taxes paid by the company to Lander County. In a 22 September 1890 decision, the Nevada Supreme Court reversed a lower court decision and gave the new mill to Lander County. Since 1911 the reports have appeared under the title "Annual Report of the State Inspector of Mines."

The most important county records are those of the mining districts, which are usually stored in the vaults of the county recorder's office. Nye County, for example, has a large number of volumes on the Tonopah Mining District, including the Index to Mining Locations (26 volumes), the Index to Tonopah Mining District Records (2 volumes), the Tonopah Mining District Records (12 volumes), and Mining Locations (122 volumes) (Elliott 1966:315). Another important source of information about mining camps are the county tax assessment rolls, which are stored mostly in courthouses and administrative offices. (The Lander County rolls are currently stored in the Nevada State Archives in Carson City.) The rolls give especially good information about households. In the Cortez Mining District, for example, a detailed study of the rolls between 1865 and 1900 yielded several kinds of information. One kind is the estimated value of the household, including land, improvements, and personal possessions. The rolls between 1886 and 1888 show that the vast majority of the residents of Cortez had the same wealth, ranging from less than $100 to about $400; however, Simeon Wenban's household was valued at $2,000, and his total wealth, including mines and the mill, had grown from $20,000 to $30,000 by 1888. Another kind of information is the location and uses of buildings. According to the 1886 Lander County tax assessment rolls for Shoshone Wells, Antonio Montare owned the "stockade house at Shoshone Wells being opposite to the store of Yung Look, also a frame stable south and adjoining Young Look." And in 1899 Joe Frassetti was listed as owning a "stone cabin at Shoshone Wells, back of A. Montroses house," while Hing Wah and Company owned an "adobe house at Shoshone Wells known as Hop Sing's house."

Secondary Accounts

Researchers can consult several histories of mining in the American West for a general background. Of these, the best are Rodman Paul's (2001) *Mining Frontiers of the Far West, 1848–1880*; Otis Young's (1970) *Western Mining*; Mark Wyman's (1979) *Hard Rock Epic*; Douglas Fetherling's (1997) *The Gold Crusades*; Duane Smith's (1987) *Mining America*; Colleen Whitley's (2006) *From the Ground Up: A History of Mining in Utah*; and Ronald Brown's (1979) *Hard-Rock Miners: The Inter-mountain West, 1860–1920*. Others are more limited in scope, like Clark Spence's (1970) *Mining Engineers and the American West: The Lace Boot Brigade, 1849–1933*; Arthur Todd's (1967) *The Cornish Miner in America*; J. S. Holliday's (1999) *Rush for Riches: Gold Fever and the Making of California*; and Andrew Isenberg's (2006) *Mining California: An Ecological History*. Perhaps the best general history of mining in Nevada is Russell Elliott's (1966) *Nevada's Twentieth-Century Mining Boom*. Others include W. Turrentine Jackson's (1963) *Treasure Hill*; Eliot Lord's (1883) *Comstock Mining and Miners*; and Sally Zanjani's (1992, 2002) *Goldfield: The Last Gold Rush on the Western Frontier* and *The Glory Days in Goldfield, Nevada*. Two other useful sources on Nevada mining history are Myron Angel's (1881) *History of Nevada* and Don Ashbaugh's (1963) *Nevada's Turbulent Yesterday*.

Newspaper Accounts

Mining town newspapers, although often short-lived and sometimes prone to embellishment, provide the most detailed and current information about mining activities. They include the *Reese River Reveille* from Austin, the *Territorial Enterprise* and the *Virginia Evening Chronicle* from Virginia City, the *Gold Hill News*, the *Goldfield News* and the *Goldfield Daily Tribute* from Goldfield, the *Manhattan Post*, the *Wonder Mining News*, the *Bullfrog Miner*, the *Rhyolite Herald* from Rhyolite, and a large number of others too numerous to list here. In addition, accounts of mining in Nevada often appeared in the major San Francisco newspapers, including the *Chronicle*, the *Bulletin*, the *Alta California*, and the *Call*. The *Sacramento Union* is yet another source.

Census Records

Federal and state census records often provide key historical information about mining populations in the American West. The composition of some mining populations in the state of Nevada, for example, can be glimpsed through the federal census records of 1860, 1870, 1880, 1900, 1910, 1920, and 1930 as well as through the state of Nevada census of 1875. The federal census records through 1920 are now available on-line on the Nevada State Historic Preservation Office Web site (http://nevadaculture .org/shpo). Household data are especially useful. Census records list individual occupations, ethnicities, and places of birth as well as information on households—the names and number of household members, their age and sex composition, and the number of families. The records, however, are somewhat spotty. The census records for the Cortez Mining District are missing for 1880 and 1890, when it reached its peak population growth. And mining settlements often do not appear at all in the federal censuses. Many were so small that they were grouped together with other settlements in the district or simply overlooked. Thus, inhabitants of the mining camp at Shoshone Wells in the Cortez Mining District fell into the larger town of Cortez under the Cortez Precinct; they have no separate visibility. And many of the settlements had such short life spans that they grew up and died between censuses, becoming invisible in documentary history. The mining camp at the Gold Bar Mine in the Bullfrog Mining District, for instance, lasted from 1904 until 1909 (Hardesty 1987a), too early for the 1900 census and too late for the 1910 census.

Other documentary sources are too numerous and varied to be discussed in detail. Two additional ones, however, should be mentioned. Pictorial documents are quite common. Many illustrations of mining on the Comstock Lode, for example, appeared in *Harper's New Monthly Magazine* during the 1870s. The illustrations from the prospectus of the Gould and Curry Mill in Virginia City are another example. City directories give useful demographic information about the occupations and addresses of people and businesses.

Mining Landscapes

Another pathway into Nevada's mining past is through landscapes (Francaviglia 1997; Goin and Raymond 2004). Mining landscapes are among the most dramatic in the American West (image 2).

Some are "cut-and-pit" landscapes created by hydraulic mining and river diversion cuts, others large-scale open pits and strip mines. Deep industrial mining, like that on Nevada's Comstock Lode, as well as large-scale placer mining reservoirs and tailing systems form still other dramatic mining landscapes. Some are landscapes organized around "engineer-designed mine complexes" that integrate mines, processing plants, settlements, and transportation networks. Others reflect the ideology of corporate paternalism, such as company towns and outlying "satellite" settlements. The key components of mining landscapes are landforms such as mine waste-rock dumps, vegetation related to land use, buildings and structures, archaeological sites, transportation or circulation networks, boundary markers, and small-scale elements like mining claim markers (Noble and Spude 1992; McClelland et al. 1999). Mining landscapes are material expressions of the history of human-environmental interactions and reflect a wide variety of social, cultural, and environmental processes that include patterns of land use (like open-pit mining), ecological interactions, patterns of spatial organization, and cultural traditions.

Mining landscapes have variable boundaries. Sometimes the boundaries overlie those of mining districts, which are legal or quasi-legal organizations that regulate mining claims. The boundaries of mining districts reflect perceptions of the geological distribution of the metals or minerals being mined or social networks that regulate access to land. But mining landscapes are not necessarily the same as mining districts. In

2. Mining landscape, Bodie, California. (Photograph by author, 2007.)

some ways, the "real" boundaries are easy to identify; the cultural landforms created by mining activities such as mine waste-rock dumps, mill tailings, and open pits are often highly visible and mark where the lines should be drawn. Visual images or viewsheds drawn from paintings, photographs, or narrative descriptions are also useful in drawing culturally meaningful boundaries around mining landscapes.

The boundaries of mining landscapes typically reflect the geological distribution of metal or mineral deposits. But contemporaneous geological knowledge plays a key role in determining the relationship between geology and mining landscapes. Consider, for example, how preexisting ideas about the geology of ore bodies affected the perception of environment by prospectors searching for new discoveries. The discovery of the Comstock Lode led prospectors to search for "true fissure veins" within 500 feet of the surface for decades afterward, and the geographical pattern of mining settlements basically followed this model (Tingley et al. 2001). They completely overlooked precious metal deposits in nonvein silica ledges weathered to knobs. After the discovery in 1900 of this geological context at Goldfield in south-central Nevada, however, a new mining settlement pattern emerged during the following decades.

The boundaries of mining landscapes often contain more than just the place where the ore is mined. Mining landscapes must also include "outliers"—geographically separated places where mines, mills, settlements, and supply operations took place. The Comstock mines in Virginia City, Nevada, and its immediate environs defined a mining landscape on a local scale. The Comstock Lode, however, served as a control center for a much larger region. It encompassed the pinyon-juniper woodlands of the Virginia Range, the Carson River, woodlands in and around the Lake Tahoe Basin, and the farmlands of the Carson Valley—localities all several miles away from the Comstock mines. These local ecosystems, each with distinctive histories and ecologies, were linked together into a regional ecosystem by Comstock industrial mining. Mining landscapes are therefore often best understood at different scales with geographical boundaries that vary accordingly.

Mining landscapes can also be viewed as cultural representations that convey ideas and meaning through signs and symbols. As signs, the components of mining landscapes communicate messages, like the stone cairns that prospectors used to mark the boundaries of mining claims. Such markers

represent not only miners' knowledge of where ore bodies should occur but also legal concepts in mining law. The geographical distribution of settlements, buildings, and structures on mining landscapes reflects some combination of "ideal" concepts of settlement and community and "real" determinants, such as topography, water availability, transportation routes, and mine locations. Thus, miners coming from the eastern United States typically carried with them cultural concepts of settlements laid out in a grid pattern. (Hardesty and Fowler 2001:83–84)

As symbols, the components of mining landscapes "spontaneously and unintentionally evoke emotions deeply embedded within a specific historical and cultural context" (Hardesty 2001:23), bringing to mind culturally based images or past personal experiences. Ghost towns in the American West, such as Bodie, California (Delyser 1999), have this power, as do individual places or landforms in mining landscapes that have "traditional cultural properties" for particular tribal groups. Similarly, arsenic or mercury-contaminated mine waste or open mine shafts provoke a human survival response toward the "toxic" and "hazardous." Mining landscapes as places with signs and symbols may also have significant educational and market value as ecomuseums, outdoor museums of science and industry, sites for community-based archaeology, or cultural tourism.

Additionally, mining landscapes capture the ecological life histories of individuals or short-lived social units (like domestic households or companies) as networks or mosaics of microenvironments (Hardesty and Fowler 2001:80). Consider, for example, the evolution of the mining landscape associated with the Cortez Mining District (Hardesty 2006). Prospectors created the first microenvironment in 1863 in the Cortez Mountains after finding silver in what became known as the Nevada Giant Ledge. A few miles away, they added another microenvironment the following year in Mill Canyon by constructing a mercury amalgamation mill to process the ore from the ledge, later adding furnaces to heat the ore before processing. Significant environmental changes followed. Miners discharged mercury-contaminated sediments into the canyon and harvested wood from the surrounding pinyon-juniper forests to produce the charcoal necessary to fuel steam boilers and furnaces, creating a new microenvironment. Finally, yet another microenvironment became connected to the landscape with the extraction of salt from deposits in the Pleistocene-aged Lake Gilbert in nearby Grass Valley for use in the mill's amalgamation technology.

This network of microenvironments changed substantially about 15 years later with the construction of an innovative Russell leaching mill at the mouth of Arctic Canyon in 1886. Because it required lime for the leaching process, the mill was connected to a new limestone microenvironment nearby with an outcrop that could be quarried and processed into lime with kilns. Water for the mill came by pipeline from an aquifer seven miles away at the other side of Grass Valley. And as the demand for wood as fuel greatly increased, clear-cutting and thinning of the pinyon-juniper woodlands intensified. Wenban's mill closed in 1892, bringing the second episode of landscape transformation to an end.

The next mining episode began in 1908, when a new mining company refitted Wenban's abandoned mill with cyanide technology, enabling the extraction of low-grade ores and the reworking of old mill wastes. The new mill brought about a distinctive change in landform patterns. Cyanide technology continued to transform the landscape after the mill burned down in 1915. The Consolidated Cortez Silver Mines Company built and operated another cyanide and flotation mill further up Arctic Canyon from 1923 to 1929. Tailings from the mill eventually formed a large tailings flow downslope about one mile to the valley floor. Afterward, small-scale mining continued sporadically in the Cortez district until the 1980s, when high gold and silver prices once again reestablished large-scale industrial mining, this time as an open-pit operation that still continues.

Mining Architecture

Perhaps the most imposing material expression of mining's past comes from the surviving buildings, structures, and objects associated with technology, social formations, and culture (image 3).

The Historic American Engineering Record (HAER) of the National Park Service has played an important role in recent years in documenting many of these remains. In 1980, what was then the National Architectural and Engineering Record registered surviving buildings and structures as the Virginia City National Historic Landmark. Other mining-related HAER projects included the Kennecott Copper Mill in Alaska, the Bodie Standard Mill in California, the Wall Street Mill in Joshua Tree National Park, the Keane Wonder Mill in Death Valley National Park, and the Mariscal Quicksilver Works in Texas's Big Bend National Park.

The architectural expression of mining falls into the categories of extraction, beneficiation, infrastructure (related to transportation, power, and communication), residential, and social architecture. Extraction architecture includes buildings, structures, and objects used in the activities of mineral or metal exploration and extraction. Buildings associated with extraction include hoisting houses, storage warehouses, machine shops, offices, air compressor buildings, air ventilation buildings, water drainage, and powder houses for storing explosives. Structures and objects associated with extraction include headframes used for hoisting; bucket and dragline dredges; scoop trams (muckers); jammers; continuous miners (rock-cutting machines); air drills; pumps (like the Cornish pumps used on the Comstock); surface fans; minematic self-contained drilling machines; generators; lifts; and hydraulic nozzles, monitors, or "Giants." Miners used bulldozers, dump trucks, graders, wheel loaders, man-carriers, and locomotives for transportation and excavation activities. And dams, ponds, and ditches were some of the water conveyance and storage structures used in hydraulic and dredge mining of placer deposits.

3. Standard Mill at Bodie, California. (Photograph by author, 2007.)

By way of example, consider the architectural expression of extraction at the Billie Mine portal just outside the boundaries of Death Valley National Park in California (Hardesty 2007). Several buildings, structures, and objects associated with the underground extraction of borates deposits and their transportation to a processing facility mark the mine portal (image 4).

The cluster is dominated by the multiple-story headframe hoist and conveyor used to transport borates ore, miners, and supplies to and from the underground extraction chambers. Nearby is an escape hoist for use as an emergency manway. Other structures at the mine portal include a double drum skip hoist, loadout tower, headframe bin, fill-hole bin, hose station, water storage tanks, fuel storage tanks, stockpile area, mine-water holding pond (sump), waste dump, parking lot, and storage yard. Buildings at the mine portal include the headframe hoist house, escape hoist house, office, powerhouse, shop, warehouse, dry building, maintenance shop, compressor building, and guard house.

The architecture of beneficiation is another category of mining buildings, structures, and objects. Beneficiation is the process of upgrading the economic value of the extracted ore through mechanical or chemi-

4. Billie Mine Portal, Death Valley, California. (Photograph by author, 2007.)

cal methods. Buildings, structures, and objects are associated with mechanical crushing, concentration, and chemical recovery processes (like amalgamation, leaching, flotation, cyanide, chlorination, and smelting). Arrastras, stamp mills, ball mills, and rod mills are structures used in the mechanical crushing of hard rock ores. Concentration structures like Wilfley tables and amalgamation plates upgrade hard rock ores after crushing. The mechanical concentration of placer deposits with free gold particles involves the use of structures such as pans, rockers, Long Toms, and sluices. Structures used in the chemical recovery of ores include cyanide and lixiviation leaching vats, flotation tanks, Freiberg barrels, Washoe amalgamation pans, blast furnace smelters, and patios. Patios are rock pavements or rock-lined pits upon which crushed ore is mixed with salt, iron, and copper; stirred by burros walking around the pit; and heated with sunlight to transform silver sulphides into silver chlorides, which can be amalgamated, with silver removed by treating it with mercury. Other buildings and structures associated with the activities of beneficiation and recovery are assay houses, kilns (like those used to produce lime for the chemical process of lixiviation), foundries, and blacksmith shops.

The buildings and structures associated with the activities of transportation, power, and communication needed in mining operations comprise the architecture of mining infrastructure. Perhaps the most visible are roads and railroads such as the Virginia and Truckee Railroad from Reno to Virginia City, the Eureka and Palisade Railroad from Eureka to Central Pacific, the Nevada Central Railroad from Ely to Central Pacific at Battle Mountain, and the Geiger Grade Road on the Comstock. Associated railroad buildings and structures included depots, water towers, trestles and bridges, worker's houses, and warehouses. Other buildings and constructions involved in transportation include tipples and similar structures for loading and transporting extracted ores. Tramways—for example, the aerial tramways at the Keane Wonder Mine in Death Valley National Park—and funiculars like the one at Lake Tahoe, which transported wood from the basin up to the crest of the Carson Range and into flumes for transport down to Washoe Valley, are also a part of the transportation infrastructure. In order to produce and transmit electrical power, mining companies set up powerhouses, power substations, power lines (like Bodie and Cortez), and hydroelectric plants such as the Nevada-California Power Company facility near Bishop supplying Rhyolite. The production and transmission of steam power is also expressed architecturally at many mining operations in the form of boilers, fireboxes, and wood storage yards. Communications buildings and structures include telephone and telegraph lines and radio towers.

Residential architecture is expressed in dwellings such as boardinghouses, single-household buildings, duplex or multiple-household buildings, and bunkhouses. Other common buildings and structures in the category are cookhouses, privies, and wells. Social architecture is a category of buildings and structures associated with commercial, governmental, civic, and institutional activities in mining settlements (James 1994; Nicoletta 2000). It may include hotels and lodging houses, governmental buildings such as courthouses and post offices, fraternal organizations, stores and mercantile buildings, saloons and bars, warehouses, laundries, morgues, barber shops, banks, barns and stables, recreational facilities such as racetracks and baseball fields, cemeteries, churches, fraternal organizations, school houses, hospitals, and jails.

The Archaeological Record of Mining

The archaeological record offers another pathway to the mining past through the observation of things like the remains of buildings, trash

5. Bullwheel at Bulwer Mill site, Bodie, California. (Photograph by author, 2007.)

dumps, adits (horizontal passages into a mine), and machinery and their arrangement in three-dimensional space (image 5).

Observers can only view frontier social interactions indirectly, through the "morphology" or form of things that have been left behind. The morphology of the archaeological record is defined by (1) where the thing is found, (2) what is found next to or around it, and (3) its physical characteristics. All other information must be inferred. The strongest arguments regarding morphology do not stray far from these basic observations; indeed, simple inferences about time and activity are the most secure. For this reason, the analysis used here stays as close as possible to the most direct observations of the archaeological record's morphology. At the same time, it employs observations about morphology and activity in the documentary record. The description and analysis of feature systems is the cornerstone of this approach (Hardesty 1987c).

Feature Systems

A feature system is a group of archaeologically visible features and objects that are the product of a specific human activity. Constructing models of feature systems lie at the interface of history, archaeology, and ethnography. Identification of the feature system begins with documentary

6. An arrastra. (Egleston 1887, figure 104.)

and ethnographic accounts of the morphology and activity of mining. Roger E. Kelly and Marsha C. Kelly's (1983) description of the arrastra, for example, illustrates how a feature system is defined. The arrastra, a cheap and simple technology for grinding free milling ores, is a circular platform over which a heavy stone slab is pulled by animal or water power (image 6).

Introduced into the silver mines of Mexico from Spain in the 1500s, the arrastra was a staple of small-scale mining operations in the American West until the 1940s (Kelly and Kelly 1983:85,90; Van Bueren 2004). The documentary record of arrastra technology includes not only written accounts but also photographs. From these sources, the Kellys were able to construct a "historical model" of arrastra morphology and activity (Kelly and Kelly 1983:85–87). They then used the model to search archaeological sites for observable remnants of the arrastra mill, several of which they identified in the Lake Mead Recreation Area in Arizona (Kelly and Kelly 1983:90–92). Image 7 illustrates one of these arrastra sites.

The archaeological morphology of the arrastra feature system consists of several associated structural features—like the circular platform, the drag-stone pile, and the outlet trough—along with objects such as a perforated slab.

Feature systems may include archaeological features that are widely dispersed geographically. The Russell leaching technology first installed in 1886 at the Tenabo Mill site in the Cortez Mining District, for example, has an archaeological record that includes features placed over sev-

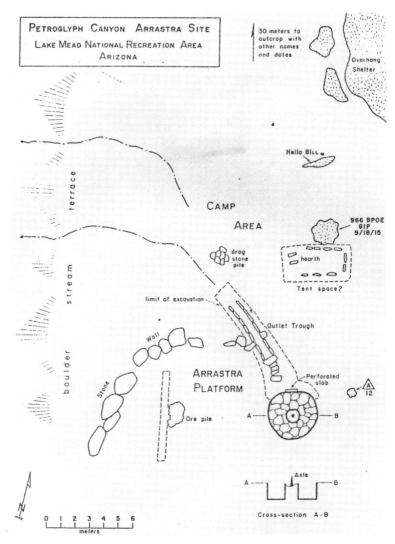

7. Map of arrastra archaeological site. (Reprinted from *Historical Archaeology* 17(1), figure 8.)

eral square miles (Bancroft 1889:16; Hardesty and Hattori 1982:7–10). Much of the feature system is clustered in and around the mill building (image 8), but the rest of the archaeological record of the technology is elsewhere.

The limestone quarry and kiln for making the lime needed for the Russell process were several hundred yards away (image 9). Workers gathered

8. The Tenabo Mill in 1900. (Courtesy of Nevada Historical Society.)

9. Lime kiln next to the Tenabo Mill. (Photograph by author, 1983.)

salt several miles distant at Williams salt marsh in upper Grass Valley, piped water from a spring seven miles across the valley, and manufactured charcoal for fuel in the timbered uplands above the mill site.

A single archaeological feature may play a role in more than one feature system. If both domestic trash and industrial waste are in a dump, the trash dump may be part of both a household feature system and an industrial technology feature system. The Consolidated Cortez Mill site in the Cortez Mining District, for example, includes a trash dump that contains not only domestic trash such as tin cans and glass bottles but also cupels, crucibles, and other waste from assaying. The implication is that the associated house site was used both for assaying and as a residence by the assayer. In addition, features and objects from more than one feature system may appear at the same site. The Tenabo Mill site consists of two separate feature systems: one including the archaeological remains of the original 1886 Russell Leaching technology, the other with the remains of the "new" cyanide leaching technology installed in 1908 (Weight 1950; Gilluly and Masursky 1965:98).

Mining Site Formation and Structure

At the grassroots level, mining sites are geographical clusters of building ruins, trash dumps, privies, roads, milling structures, and mines organized into feature systems. The feature systems, however, may come from different time periods. Mining and milling technologies, for example, were imported, used for a short time, and then dismantled, either replaced by a new technology or abandoned along with the district. Cycles of occupation and abandonment within the mining district created "layers" of feature systems. The layers, or "components," consist of one or more feature systems from the same time period.

The second distinctive characteristic of mining site structure is "horizontal stratigraphy." Site components are often separated horizontally rather than vertically. To take one example, trash dumps from different time periods are not piled on top of one another but are arranged geographically. And house sites typically do not show evidence of vertically stratified archaeological deposits, with each layer representing a different house occupation. More often, the buildings once placed on a house site were moved or torn down at the time of abandonment, and the next occupation then occurred at a different place. As a result, mining camps tended to be separated into geographical clusters, each representing a different time period or component.

The third characteristic of mining site structure is mutilation. Because of the typical mining cycles of occupation, abandonment, and reoccupation, later components tended to destroy partly the earlier components of mining sites. In many cases, only one or a few features, strata, or objects from the earlier feature system remain. For this reason, the "mutilation effect" must be taken into consideration. Furthermore, the "relic" features or strata may occur in any part of the site, either on the edge or in the center. Discontinuous surviving remnants of multiple occupations and feature systems, not a continuous accumulation of historic debris, define the structure of mining sites. As a result, it is essential to conduct good field searches for surviving feature systems as part of the survey and site evaluation plan; the approach is similar to searching for early man sites in "old dirt" rather than using a simple random sampling method.

Finally, the underground structure of mining sites must be reconstructed (Hardesty 1987c). In a sense the problem is similar to the one faced by geologists trying to understand the sedimentary history of large basins warped and twisted by mountain-building events. What remains is only an image of what actually happened, consisting of isolated fragments of sedimentary deposits. And it is precisely these fragmentary "clues" that geologists must locate and date in order to identify large-scale patterns and thereby reconstruct sedimentary history. New mining episodes have a similar kind of impact on the archaeological record of underground workings. Preexisting features, such as drifts, stopes, raises, and the like, are partly destroyed, reworked, or survive untouched, and new ones are created. The archaeologist observes the last image. But each successive image is actually a montage containing "warped and twisted" images of earlier mining episodes. The archaeologist can reconstruct every image in the montage from surviving "fragments"—drifts, stopes, raises, shafts, and other deeply buried features from the earlier mining episode. The actual reconstruction, of course, combines images from documentary history and surviving archaeological images of each mining episode.

Locating Mining Sites

Documenting the archaeological record of mining begins with the location of mining sites in the field. Perhaps the best place to start is with a simple "location model" that incorporates historical documents. The model gives preliminary information about what kind of archaeological sites are expected and where they are most likely to be located. Work on inventory models of several mining districts in Nevada has suggested that the best predictor of mining site pattern is the geographical distribution of the ore body, while secondary determinants are water, gravity centers such as towns and roads, and supporting resources like timber stands. In the Comstock Mining District, for example, documentary images provide evidence that land-use patterns mostly followed the location of ore-bearing faults, placer gravels, and water (Hardesty and Firby 1980; Rodman 1985). The two major faults in the district (the Comstock and the Silver City) and several minor ones had been mineralized during the late Miocene period. An erosional episode in the late Tertiary transported some of the ore-bearing rock downward to what is now the Carson River, creating placer gravel deposits in Gold Canyon, Six-Mile Canyon, American Flat, and the Carson River valley. How miners used the ore-bearing faults and placers varied from one time period to another, partly because of technological changes. They constructed mills in the two canyons near water sources, but after 1873 they also built them at the lower edge of Virginia City to take advantage of a new pipeline delivering water from the Carson Range. Gravity centers around settlements, roads, and railroads were focal points for domestic activities and those related to transportation.

Locating mining sites requires a combination of documentary and archaeological surveys. Any survey strategy should begin with a search for documentary accounts. Historical documents provide an important source of information about the possible locations of existing cultural resources and what activities took place there. Photographs, maps, newspapers, tax assessment rolls, and the like provide data that help build a documentary model of cultural resources. This model does not necessarily reflect historical reality. Newspaper and other accounts of local mining activity were often thinly veiled attempts to attract investors and get people to move to the mining area, not accurate reports. At the same time, historical models provide the takeoff point for conducting intensive searches for archaeological sites in the field. Researchers can use the places mentioned in written documents to define a set of "sampling strata" for archaeological surveys. The photographic record is also especially useful.

The first step in developing a field survey strategy involves the field identification of sites mentioned in historical documents. Some cultural resources are quite visible today but may not be mentioned in the written documents, however. These often include mine shafts, adits, prospects, roads, house sites, outhouses, and trash scatters, among other things. Most of these show up in aerial photographs and can be readily identified. The researcher can treat the archaeological evidence for each type of feature system, such as households or mines, as a separate sampling stratum and survey it accordingly. The second step in developing a field survey strategy, therefore, is the incorporation of these archaeologically visible features.

Between these sites of major activity is a "no man's land" with no clear documentary or archaeological visibility to guide the pedestrian surveys. These areas should be treated as separate sampling strata and surveyed with "random" methods. Probably the best approach is to divide the area into linear strips or transects, randomly select a percentage of these, and completely survey each transect selected. Scale is a key problem in doing archaeological surveys of mining sites, one that extends to industrial sites generally (Teague 1987:200–202). Mining features may cover a large geographical area, often well beyond the boundaries of a single site. Charles Zeier (1987), for example, found that the archaeological remains of charcoal ovens feeding the smelting mills in Eureka, Nevada, clustered around a single residential settlement. He could not have reconstructed the charcoal production system without an understanding of the large geographical area containing the remaining archaeological record. The Tenabo Mill in the Cortez Mining District is another example of the type of large-scale technological system likely to be encountered on the mining frontier. The system included not only the mill site itself and a nearby limestone quarry and kiln but also a salt marsh, a pipeline to a spring, and a sulfur mine several miles away (Hardesty and Hattori 1982). And railroads are linear transportation systems that may cover even greater distances.

Combining Multiple Images of Mining's Past

The study of mining's past is most effective when multiple images can be used. Consider, for example, the combined and interactive use of documentary, architectural, archaeological, and landscape images in studies of mining technology, the residential settlement, and the household.

Technology

Perhaps the most visible features in mining sites today are the remains of mining technology (image 10). Waste dumps from mines, mill tailings, shafts, adits, mill foundations, concrete engine pads, tramways, head-

10. The Mayflower Mine site, Bullfrog Mining District, Nevada. (Photograph by author, 1987.)

frames, and other structures are a part of the archaeological record that is often documented in written accounts (image 11).

Much of the documentary record of mining technology exists in technical and scientific journals and textbooks, especially the *Mining and Scientific Press*, the *Engineering and Mining Journal*, the *Information Circulars* of the U.S. Bureau of Mines, and the bulletins and professional papers of the U.S. Geological Survey. Otis Young's (1970) *Western Mining* is a good, basic introduction to mining technology but does not offer much detail. Textbooks tend to describe basic industrial processes and equipment without regard to the locally adapted technology that was actually used in many mines. The archaeological record does contain information about these adaptive variants. Much of the machinery, however, disappeared from mines because of traditional scavenging on the western frontier as well as the scrap metal drives during the Second World War. For this reason, the archaeological record of mining technology often seems rather impoverished.

Settlements

The mining camp or residential settlement is another point at which documentary and archaeological records overlap. For purposes here, the set-

11. Hoist engine at the Pioneer Mine site, Bullfrog Mining District, Nevada. (Photograph by author, 1987.)

tlement is the material expression of Murdock's (1949) "community," a group of people who live in the same place and interact daily with one another. As such, the settlement is a focal point of social information about the mining frontier. The social interactions that take place within the sphere find expression in the morphology and the activity of settlements. Combining documentary and archaeological records is the most effective approach to the study of mining camps. Small, short-lived settlements are most likely to be invisible in the usual documentary sources of demographic information, such as the federal population census, tax assessment rolls, and city directories. The size, age, and sex composition of such camps is more visible in the archaeological record. At the Original Bullfrog camp in Death Valley National Park, population size was estimated from the floor area of house sites (Hardesty 1981). Here, Cook's (1972:13–15) argument that no more than six people will live in a house with less than 350 square feet of floor space formed a key assumption. His calculation is important for the simple reason that many mining camp house sites have floor areas between 300 and 400 square feet. Archaeological indicators of age and sex, such as toys, cold cream jars, and a hair curler, were used to define the other demographic characteristics of the Original Bullfrog settlement.

12. Virginia City, Nevada, from Cedar Hill, 1870s or 1880s. (Courtesy of Special Collections, University of Nevada–Reno Library.)

John W. Reps (1975, 1979) illustrates how to use written records to understand mining settlements. Some townplats suggest that the growth of mining camps in Nevada followed a simple grid pattern. Virginia City was laid out in a grid on the steep eastern slope of Mount Davidson (image 12).

The main north-south streets through Virginia City were built on leveled terraces and were closely spaced; the east-west cross streets running up the slope were short, steep, and widely separated (Reps 1975:276–277). The town was famous for its hillside social stratification (De Quille 1876; Reps 1975:277). On the upper streets of the town were the large and luxurious houses of mine and mill owners and wealthy merchants. The commercial and governmental districts were on B and C streets just below, along with working-class residences. Below C Street in descending social and geographical order were the red-light district and Chinatown. And at the very bottom, scattered around the mill tailings, were the Native American residences.

Only the archaeological record shows the layout of most of the smaller mining camps on the Nevada frontier. And from these remains, it is clear that the grid pattern was not all that common. Many small settlements were linear strips along roads or convenience clusters around mills and

13. House site at Shoshone Wells. (Photograph by author, 1983.)

mines. The settlements with a lot of ethnic diversity were often partitioned into several "neighborhoods," each occupied by a different ethnic group and each with a somewhat different layout. Shoshone Wells in the Cortez Mining District, for example, has four or five visible clusters of house sites that may represent ethnic neighborhoods (image 13).

Excavations revealed Chinese material remains in the house sites in the ravine cluster and the road cluster; the hillside cluster provided some archaeological evidence of an Italian occupation; and the mine owner's family, representing a Victorian culture, occupied the Wenban cluster.

The Household

How the household should be defined has generated a lot of discussion and controversy among anthropologists and historians (Goody 1958; Buchler and Selby 1968; Laslett and Wall 1972; Hammel and Laslett 1974; Netting et al. 1984). Here, however, the household is considered to be a group of people sharing domestic activities such as consumption and production (Carter 1984:45; Wilk and Netting 1984:3). Such a definition does not require that the group actually live together under the same roof, although coresidence is a frequent characteristic of households. The least understood aspect of the household is the relationship between its morphology or form (such as size and geographical location) and its activities (such as reproduction or consumption) (Wilk and Netting 1984). Some authorities, though, view both the morphology and activity of households as controlled by a set of ideological rules or strategies that vary and change as part of a larger cultural process such as adaptation (Buchler and Selby 1968; Hammel 1972; Carter 1984).

Both documentary and archaeological images of the mining frontier household are strongly biased toward morphology. Census schedules, tax assessment rolls, and similar governmental records, for example, give information about household size, the sexes, ages, and occupations of its members, and the like. And the archaeological record of the household contains data on the location and size of house sites along with artifact assemblages that may include age and sex indicators such as toys and sex-specific clothing. But the identification of household activities is more difficult. The most consistent information probably arrives by reconstructing activities from the archaeological record of house sites. House site reconstruction gives indirect information about what were most likely coresidential groups: people who live under the same roof. "House-site groups," of course, are not necessarily households. Documentary sources may help considerably in understanding how house-site groups should be combined into mining households. Newspaper accounts of events at the Gold Bar Mine in Death Valley National Park, for example, identified bunkhouse, boarding house, and family households at the settlement.

Quite clearly, combining documentary and archaeological information is the most effective way of reconstructing households in mining camps. The activities that were most characteristic of the mining household were distribution and consumption. Production, reproduction, and inheritance, which are the important functions of most households, were not nearly as important to mining communities. Household morphology, however, varies for each of these activities.

2. The Archaeology of Mining Technology

Perhaps the most visible features in mining sites today are the remains of mining technology (images 14 and 15).

Documentary accounts of mining technologies and sociotechnical systems on western mining frontiers can be found in technical and scientific journals such as the *Mining and Scientific Press*, the *Engineering and Mining Journal*, the *Information Circulars* of the U.S. Bureau of Mines, and the bulletins and professional papers of the U.S. Geological Survey. Otis Young's (1970) *Western Mining*, Richmond Clow's (2002) *Chasing the Glitter: Black Hills Milling, 1874–1959*, and Eric Twitty's (2002) *Riches to Rust: A Guide to Mining in the Old West* provide historical overviews. Textbooks such as John Dorr's (1936) *Cyanidation and Concentration of Gold and Silver Ores*, Thomas Egleston's (1887) *Metallurgy of Silver, Gold and Mercury in the United States*, and Alfred Miller's (1900) *A Manual of Assaying* describe basic industrial processes and equipment used in mining. They do not detail the technologies that miners actually used in practice, but the archaeological record does contain information about these adaptive variants.

The technology of mining involves everything from simple hand tools to complex industrial machines. In all cases, however, the technology is used for locating, extracting, and processing metals or minerals from rock. The components include the tools and labor necessary for finding and removing the ore body, taking it to the mill, crushing the ore, removing the precious metals, and dumping the waste. Bruce Noble and Robert Spude (1992:12) note that this process consists of three steps: (1) the extraction of ore from the earth, which includes both exploration and development of mines; (2) beneficiation, or the upgrading of extracted ore with mechanical and chemical technologies to increase its economic value; and (3) refining, or the conversion of upgraded ore to "a state of purity suitable for industrial use, manufacturing, or for commercial exchange." In general, the process of mining can be understood and modeled as a "sociotechnical system." Several years ago, historian of technology Thomas Hughes developed this concept in his book *Net-*

14. Mine waste dump and tramway at Arctic Mine, Cortez Mining District. (Photograph by author, 1983.)

15. Cyanide vats, Bodie, California. (Photograph by author, 2007.)

works of Power (1983) to explain the emergence of electrical power in the United States. Brian Pfaffenberger (1992) applied the concept to a more general cross-cultural setting. In his model, the key components of a sociotechnical system are tools, materials, operational sequences and work skills involved in production, coordination of production work, social and cultural knowledge, and historical context. The model can be used as a hierarchical structure for formulating specific research questions. At the level of the system, for example, researchers can ask questions about the cross-cultural patterns of variability and change in the sociotechnical systems of mining or their landscape expression. At another hierarchical level, they can formulate research questions within the "problem domains" of individual system components, like tools or the coordination of work.

The components of mining sociotechnical systems are sometimes visible in documents describing the technological process as it was planned or as it actually worked at some time or another. They also may appear as a network of observable features and artifact assemblages in an archaeological site, ranging from mine shafts, headframes, and engine pads to mill foundations, crushing machines, mill tailings, and tramways. But an archaeological site consists not of the surviving remains of a single technological system or process but of several technologies that reflect how mining changed over time. The buildings and machinery from earlier processes may be left in place as new processes are added (Spude 1987:10). The Tenabo Mill in the Cortez Mining District in north-central Nevada is an example. The dry-crushing silver mill, built in 1886, was equipped with what was then a state-of-the-art Russell lixiviation technology (Bancroft 1889:20). But in 1908 the mill was completely overhauled and equipped with yet another new technology, a cyanide leaching plant capable of processing 100 tons of ore each day (Naramore and Yale 1910:220). Much of the original Russell-process equipment remained in place and was left idle. The archaeological site of the Tenabo Mill thus includes features from both the Russell and the cyanide processes (image 16).

How to inventory and understand the technology at a mining site most effectively is a substantial problem. One approach, and the one recommended here, is to first identify discrete steps or sub-systems in the process. Hoisting the ore out of the mine, for example, is one sub-system, and crushing the ore at the mill is another. The concept of the feature system, introduced earlier, is relevant. Each technological sub-system at

16. The Tenabo Mill site. (Photograph by author, 1983.)

a mine is most visible at the intersection between documentary and archaeological images of the process.

Islands of Gold and Silver: Geological Formations

The technology of gold and silver mining is closely related to the geology of the ore deposit. In general, geological formations containing base and precious metals, whether copper, iron, mercury, or gold, are found in seismically active regions where hot aqueous solutions from deep below the earth's surface intrude into rock fissures or porous rock. Most of the gold and silver deposits on the mining frontiers of the American West were distributed along the edges of large granite and related volcanic rock bodies called "batholiths" or the smaller "stocks" (Chadwick 1982:23). The batholithic geology of these precious metals reflects their hydrothermal origins (Gianella 1936; Bonham 1969; Chadwick 1982). Molten rock from the earth's interior welled upward, penetrating surface cracks and fissures often caused by faulting and other tectonic activities. The rock carried hot fluids charged with metals and other minerals in solution. Through cooling and lower pressure near the earth's surface, the fluids precipitated the minerals as a variety of compounds, including quartz and metallic sulfides (Bonham 1969:105; Chadwick 1982:23). Of these, argentite, or silver sulfide, is the most important source of silver. Still,

17. The "Nevada Giant Ledge" in the Cortez Mining District. (Photograph by author, 1983.)

only a very few batholiths on the mining frontier of the American West have yielded silver because hydrothermal activity was rarely substantial enough to precipitate precious metals.

The distribution of metal-bearing ore within a batholithic "island" depends on a complex set of geological circumstances. First of all, the minerals are vertically stratified simply because they precipitate at different temperatures and pressures (Chadwick 1982:22–24). The minerals that precipitate at higher temperatures and pressures are located closer to the batholith or intrusive volcanic rock than those that crystalize at lower temperatures and pressures. The "host" rock also controls how a metal-bearing ore is distributed. Tabular, and rather predictable, "vein" deposits were formed within fissures in granite or other volcanic host rock. The most common host rocks in the Comstock Mining District of western Nevada, for example, are andesites and rhyolites (Gianella 1936; Calkins 1944; Bonham 1969). Tectonic activity during the late Tertiary period created several cracks that were then mineralized by the intrusion of hot fluids. The "bonanza" ores of the Comstock came mostly from two mineralized fissures: the Comstock fault and the Silver City fault, both of which dipped about 45 degrees eastward. If the hot fluids found their

18. Placer deposits, Malakoff Diggings, California. (Photograph by author, 1995.)

way into chemically reactive rock such as limestone, however, the silver-bearing ores tended to be distributed as irregular, and unpredictable, "replacement bodies" (Chadwick 1982:23). In the Cortez Mining District of central Nevada, the "Nevada Giant Ledge" consists mostly of dolomite with highly irregular "blanket-and-pipe" replacement bodies and fissure veins (Emmons 1910:103–105; Gilluly and Masursky 1965:100; Roberts et al. 1967:72) (image 17). The veins and replacement bodies contain several metallic compounds, including argentite and silver chloride.

In addition to these "hard-rock" islands of gold and silver, the weathering and erosion of fissure veins and replacement bodies created secondary deposits of sediments called placers that sometimes contained precious metals (image 18).

Placers are predominantly loose, water-transported deposits that often occur close to the ground surface and which consist of unconsolidated gravels, sands, or other alluvium and colluvium. While gold-bearing placers are the most common, placers with silver do occur, as at Planchas de Plata in Arizona and Gold Canyon on the Comstock, where miners in the 1850s found silver in their sluice boxes.

Extraction

The first step in the mining process is extraction—the location and removal of precious metal-bearing ore from geological formations. Ex-

19. The "glory hole" at the Montgomery-Shoshone Mine, Bullfrog Mining District. (Photograph by author, 1987.)

traction takes place in two phases: (1) searching for ore bodies, and (2) extracting the ore body.

Searching for Ore Bodies

Miners searching for ore bodies or prospecting took a similar approach both to placers and to hard rock deposits, hand-digging holes or prospects in the ground in places suspected to have geological formations containing precious metals. Scattered prospect holes and associated waste-rock dumps typically mark the exploratory phase of mining landscapes. Mechanized prospecting emerged in the early 20th century and transformed the exploratory phase of mining landscapes into networks of power-shovel trenches, bulldozer cuts, and, after the 1950s, drill holes from truck-mounted drills. Other prospecting methods in recent years have included aerial photography, satellite imagery, and sound waves.

Extracting the Ore Body: Surface Mining

The technologies of ore extraction are considerably more varied. They include both surface mining and underground mining of placer and lode formations. Miners developed methods of surface mining to extract lode deposits when they outcropped and did not dip too steeply. If the ore body was narrow and dipped steeply, however, underground mining was required. The extraction of outcropping lode deposits began with simple hand shoveling to expose the veins and the creation of "glory holes" (image 19).

Large-scale open-pit mining using machines such as power shovels began in Minnesota's iron ranges in the 1890s. In the western United States, Bingham Canyon Copper Mine near Salt Lake City, Utah, began its open-pit operation in 1903. Today, at 2.5 miles wide and 0.5 miles deep, it is the largest open-pit mine in the world. Other large-scale open-pit operations in the West include Kaiser's Eagle Mountain Iron Mine in southern California; the Kennecott copper mine in Ruth, Nevada; Lavender copper pit at Bisbee, Arizona; and U.S. Borax mine at Boron, California (image 20).

Miners used open-pit, hydraulic, dredging, or bulldozing methods to extract surface or shallow placer deposits (Hovis 1992). Their extraction technologies included everything from small, "low-tech" hand-powered tools such as pans and bateas (wooden trays), rockers, sluices, Long Toms, and dry washers to large, "high-tech" mechanical hydraulic systems, dredges, power shovels, and scrapers (Vanderburg 1936). They employed both hand and mechanical methods in open-pit mining of placer deposits. The most common hand methods were sniping, sluicing, ground sluicing, and booming. Sniping is the hand shoveling of placers into sorting tools such as pans, rockers, or Long Toms. It does not involve the use of water. In dry washing, miners use fans or bellows to remove the matrix of sand and gravel from placer deposits with fans or bellows and trap the gold particles on strips (called riffles). The other hand methods required water. With sluicing, miners hand-shoveled placers into a constructed box with riffles arranged along the bottom and then channeled water through the box. The water washes away the lighter sand and other sediments and traps the heavier gold particles in the riffles. They sometimes placed mercury on the riffles to collect gold. Ground sluicing takes place not in constructed boxes but directly in streambeds or other placer deposits. Booming involves the storage in and periodic release of water from a reservoir to wash away the sedimentary matrix. Deserts have limited water, but placer miners in the Eagle Mountains of what is now Joshua Tree National Park in southern California constructed and used cement basins or reservoirs to catch winter rains for placer operations.

20. Lavender copper pit, Bisbee, Arizona. (Photograph by author, 1999.)

Mechanical methods of open-pit placer mining include the use of aerial scrapers as well as power shovels and draglines.

Dredging is another method that miners use to extract placer deposits. Dredges are floating excavation machines that come in three types: the bucket-line, dragline, and dry-land dredge. Bucket-line dredges consist of a continuous series of buckets on a cable that scoop up placers and transport the sediments to a washing plant inside the hull. In contrast, dragline dredges, or "doodlebugs," employ a single bucket on a line that swings horizontally and dumps the placer into a floating washing plant. Dry-land dredges operate without floating. Image 21 illustrates an abandoned dredge between the settlements of Tok and Eagle in the eastern boreal forest of Alaska.

Hydraulic mining employs a high-pressure stream of water directed at a placer deposit as a method of excavation (image 22). In Nevada large-scale placer mining began in the Osceola Mining District during the 1880s and continued until 1900 with hydraulic and sluicing methods. The Osceola Placer Mining Company constructed a large water-conveyance system of ditches and flumes (Vanderburg 1936:168–169). Large-scale placer mining activities in the Round Mountain Mining District and the Manhattan Mining District dominated the western slopes of the Toquima Range from the first decade of the 20th century to the 1940s. Mining in both districts produced high yields of gold through a variety of technologies, from hydraulic monitors to floating bucket dredges.

Extracting the Ore Body: Underground Mining

Underground mining technologies developed as a way of mining deeply buried, in situ mineralized cracks, fissures, replacement bodies, and secondary placer deposits. Again, the technology varies from "low-tech," hand-powered methods to large, standardized, and expensive industrial machines. The technology of underground mining is a response to the geology of the ore body as well as the engineering difficulty of gaining access to the ore body, removing it, and ventilating the mine (Young 1970:155; Twitty 2002). Underground miners used tools and techniques to open the mine either through vertical shafts (vertical or inclined passages that open to the surface of the mine) or through adits (horizontal passages or tunnels that open to the surface of the mine). They also used them to extract the ore through stopes, large openings in the ore body that were supported by a wooden, metal, or concrete frameworks. Hoist-

21. Abandoned dredge between Tok and Eagle, Alaska. (Photograph by author, 2003.)

22. "Giant" water nozzle used in hydraulic mining at Malakoff
Diggings, California. (Photograph by author, 1995.)

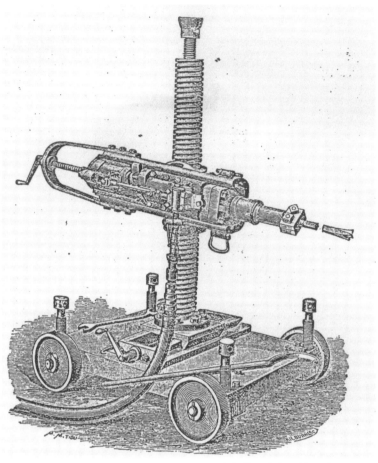

23. Illustration of Burleigh mechanical rock drill. (Drinker 1883:236.)

ing works built on top of shaft openings or rail systems running through tunnels transported ore, waste rock, miners, and supplies into and out of the mine. Ventilation systems, power plants, and drainage systems supported the underground workings. Drift mining—the excavation of deeply buried placer deposits—involved digging vertical shafts down to the bedrock underlying the placer deposit and then excavating horizontal underground tunnels or drifts that ran parallel to the placer.

Underground Workings

As described in written accounts, the tools of low-tech underground mining are simple. Miners used hammers and rock drills ("jacks") for making

24. Air compressor at Caledonia Mine, Gold Hill, Comstock Mining District. (Courtesy of Special Collections, University of Nevada–Reno Library.)

holes in the ore body, black powder for blasting, and picks and shovels for "mucking out" the loosened ore (Peele 1918; Young 1970; Wyman 1979; Paul 2001). They drilled into the ore face in one of two ways: the first, "single jacking," involved only one miner using a short hammer and a short drill; the second, "double jacking," required a team of two miners, one holding a long drill and the other driving with a long hammer. Until the 1870s, miners would place a charge of black powder into the hole, along with a Bickford slow-match fuse (Young 1970:212). The invention of dynamite in 1867 and the Burleigh mechanical drill in 1869, however, created a technological revolution in the mining industry (Raymond 1870:55, 489–496). Mechanical drills ran on compressed air, greatly reducing the labor requirements of mining (image 23). Air lines ran from the air compressor, which was usually installed outside the mine, to the drills used underground (image 24).

And dynamite, or "giant powder," as it was usually called in the West (after the Giant Powder Company, the Nobel licensee of dynamite that supplied the region), was safer and easier to control than black powder. As a result, only two-or three-dozen miners could work individual mines (Young 1970:214).

There were two methods of underground excavation: (1) the "rat-hole"

25. Mine shaft and collapsed headframe, Joshua Tree National Park, California. (Photograph by author, 2006.)

26. "Rat-holing" scene: miners, burro, and ore car. (Courtesy of Special Collections, University of Nevada–Reno Library.)

system, and (2) planned mining. (The best source of information about underground mining is the *Mining Engineer's Handbook*, edited by Robert Peele, which has several editions.) Still found in some small mining operations, the "rat-hole" system was one of the earliest methods used. Miners accessed and removed the ore body through a single shaft or adit (images 25, 26).

They mined the ore body through a maze-like network of drifts (horizontal passages excavated in, around, or parallel to the long axis of ore bodies), cross-cuts (horizontal passages running at sharp angles to the long axis of the ore body), winzes (shafts sunk downward in the mine's interior), and raises (shafts excavated upward to connect different levels of a mine's interior). The mining of deep ore bodies, however, demands better planning than the rat-hole system. For this purpose, miners developed a well-organized system of shafts and adits to access and remove the ore body and to provide for adequate ventilation in deep mines. They could only construct this system and begin mining with detailed knowledge about the shape of the ore body, which they obtained through exploratory drifts, each about 100 feet apart and at various mine levels.

The mining system used in the Cortez Mining District in the 1920s is typical (Hezzelwood 1930). Miners drove a series of adits into a long cliff face, which held an outcrop of the main ore body; they also drove inclined shafts from the footwall and then lateral drifts from these shafts into the ore body. Image 27 shows the underground workings of the Consolidated Cortez Mine in the 1920s.

The main adit from 1880 until the 1920s was the Garrison or Number 1 level at 7,055 feet above sea level; the most extensive mining took place at this level (Emmons 1910:103). Drifts, cross-cuts, and raises make up a total of 17 levels of underground workings at the Garrison Mine. In the early 1920s, the Arctic Tunnel, another adit, was driven almost 2,000 feet into the mountain at a level of 6,701 feet (image 28). From this adit, another significant ore body was mined through a network of drifts, cross-cuts, winzes, and raises.

Perhaps the most influential deep-mining system in the 19th century was developed in the Comstock Mining District in western Nevada. The heavily fractured country rock (the matrix within which the ore body was found) of the Comstock prevented miners from using the traditional support timbers or rock pillars to shore up the stopes (underground caverns left by excavating the ore body). In 1860 Philipp Deidesheimer solved the

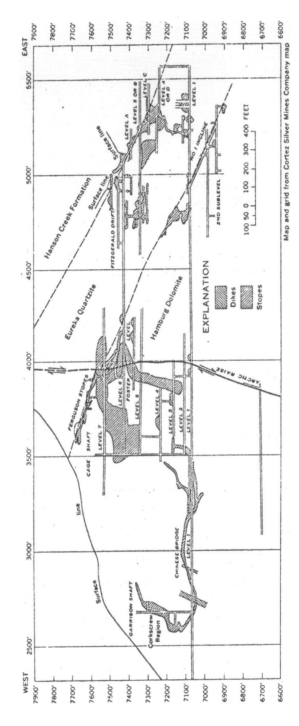

27. Underground workings at the Consolidated Cortez Mine, 1920s. (Gilluly and Masursky 1965, figure 15.)

28. Adit at the Arctic Mine, Cortez Mining District. (Photograph by author, 1983.)

problem by inventing a timbering system of cube-shaped modules that could be locked together (Young 1975). Such "square-sets" could be installed to completely fill the cavern left by mining the ore body (image 29).

The mined-out cubes were filled immediately with rock waste, so most of the ground weight was supported by rock fill rather than by timbers. Even so, the enormous weight exerted upon the cavity sometimes caused cave-ins. Square-sets were used only for stoping, not for other mine excavations involving shafts, cross-cuts, winzes, and raises.

With the development of milling technologies such as cyanide leaching for processing low-grade ores, however, the expensive system of square-set stoping was not practical. By the beginning of the 20th century, engineers had developed the "shrinkage" system of stoping to mine ore more cheaply (Peele 1918). The Arctic Mine in the Cortez Mining District, for example, used the shrinkage system of mining in the 1920s (Hezzelwood 1930). Here, miners excavated both a drift just below the ore body section to serve as a floor for ore cars and raises (called "manway raises") at each end of the ore body. The ore body was then laid out in sections of 100 to 125 feet. Next, they excavated, at 24-foot intervals, additional

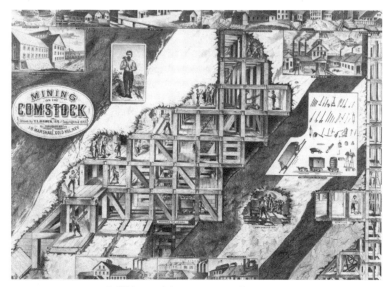

29. An 1876 lithograph by T. D. Dawes of square sets on the
Comstock Lode. (Courtesy of Nevada Historical Society.)

raises parallel to the manway raises. These "chuteway raises" were used
for dropping mined ore into the cars waiting on the floor below. The next
step was to excavate "working" drifts or sublevels parallel to, and about
15 feet above, the ore-car floor. At this point, the miners began stoping
(mining the ore body) by blasting slices from the top of the working drift
and allowing the loosened ore to fall through the chute raises into the
cars below. Rock waste was used to create a bottom cushion on which
the miners worked as the stope was carried upward. The shrinkage system of stoping is illustrated in image 30.

The archaeological record of underground mining is like an iceberg:
the vast majority of a site is buried far below the surface. Surviving drifts,
raises, stopes, and other features in underground mines are often closer
to being true "time capsules" than anything else encountered by archaeologists. In some instances, miners left behind tools, machinery, and re-
fuse in the underground caverns, and these can be used both to date and
to identify the activity associated with specific features in the mine. In
shrinkage stoping, for example, miners often employed machinery for
primary crushing of the ore underground before it went to the mill. With
this picture in mind, a three-dimensional image of the mine's chronology
and associated behavior can be constructed. Locating underground mine

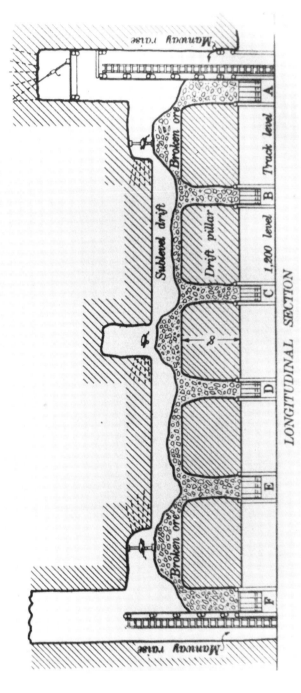

Ore in place

Manway raise

Broken ore

Sublevel drift

Broken ore

Manway raise

A

Track level

B

1,200 level

C

Drift pillar

D

E

F

LONGITUDINAL SECTION

30. Shrinkage stoping at Cortez, 1920s. (Hezzelwood 1930, figure 8.)

31. Windlass at Rawhide, 1908. (Courtesy of Special
Collections, University of Nevada–Reno Library.)

32. Underground at the Gold Bar Mine, 1905. (Courtesy of Nevada Historical Society.)

33. Whim at Bodie. (Photograph by author, 2007.)

features is not an easy task, for obvious reasons, and in no case should it be undertaken without assistance from mine-safety experts.

Hoisting Methods

Unlike surface mining, underground excavation requires a "hoisting technology" to get miners, waste rock, ore, and supplies in and out of the mine. The low-tech solution is manpower or animal power. Perhaps the simplest is carrying sacks of ore and waste rock by hand up and down a ladder. "Tump-lines" around the head were commonly used in Mexico and Peru for this purpose. Eliot Lord (1883:221–222) describes the miners at the Ophir Mine in the Comstock Mining District in 1863 "mounting the incline by a steep narrow flight of steps 400 feet in length, bearing flickering candles in a rational torchlight procession." Another common low-tech hoisting device was the windlass. Here, a hand-operated winch lowered and raised miners, ore, waste rock, and supplies in an iron bucket or similar container (images 31 and 32). The whim was a horse-powered variant (image 33).

Yet another solution was to use a small steam engine to pull ore cars up an inclined ramp. Small steam engines, in fact, are typically associated with small mining sites from the late 19th and early 20th centuries. The headframe hoisting system was one of the most common approaches in this period (image 34).

34. Gallows headframe at the new Gold Bar Mine, 1906.
(Courtesy of Nevada Historical Society.)

35. Gallows headframe at the Forman Shaft, Gold Hill, Comstock Mining District. (Courtesy of Special Collections, University of Nevada–Reno Library.)

Typically, the headframe is a "gallows"-like structure erected over the mine shaft. At the apex of the headframe is a drum or sheave over which a cable passes; an engine or another source of motive power pulls the cable to raise and lower miners, supplies, and ore. Until 1911, when the practice was outlawed, a building sometimes covered the headframe.

Deep mining requires an industrial, expensive, powerful, and energy-intensive solution to the problem of bringing the ore to the surface and moving it around (Peele 1918). By the mid-1860s in the Comstock district and Reese River district, for example, large steam engines had been installed to hoist miners, ore cars, and supplies in and out of the mines (Hardesty 1986a:60–62) (image 35).

In 1866 the 46 working mines on the Comstock used 44 steam engines adding up to about 1,000 horsepower (Lord 1883:227). Within 15 years, the Yellow Jacket mine alone had installed two 1,000–horsepower hoisting engines (Lord 1883:347). And these employed iron-frame "cages" rather than iron buckets (image 36).

Both the earlier cages—no more than open platforms—and later, enclosed versions were capable of traveling at speeds in excess of 700 feet per minute (De Quille 1876:228). The numerous cage-related accidents (Lord 1883:404) were reduced by the invention of the enclosed, "safety" cage. The invention of the flat-woven-metal cable, which replaced the earlier ropes, greatly increasing the speed, depth, and capacity of the cages and allowed for hoisting in the deep mines of the Comstock and elsewhere.

36. Hoisting cages, Bullion Mine, Gold Hill, Comstock
Mining District. (Courtesy of Nevada Historical Society.)

Ventilation Methods

Notwithstanding the ultimate purpose of mining, which was to locate
and remove ore, many mining features from the existing archaeological record relate simply to surviving underground. Ventilation is one of
these. The dangers of poorly ventilated mines are all too well illustrated
in mining history as well as in the modern world. Nineteenth-century
miners, for example, often carried canaries in cages into the mines to
serve as an early warning sign of foul air. If the bird died, the miner still
had time to get out.

On the Comstock, two methods of ventilation were used most commonly: (1) forcing air into the mine, and (2) creating an air draft (Hardesty 1986a:62–63). Archaeologists find tools and activities associated with
both approaches on the surface and in underground features. The contemporary journalist William Wright, writing under the pseudonym Dan
De Quille, describes some of the early forced air ventilation technology
used on the Comstock (De Quille 1876:385). Miners employed simple
blacksmith bellows, along with a number of other simple devices. Wind
sails, for example, were large cloth bags that filled with air and forced
it into a tube leading into the mine. None of these tools required much
capital or labor investment. But by 1865 mines were utilizing large industrial blowers or fans.

Draft ventilation worked much like a siphon. Lighter warm air from the inside of the mine would rise out of one shaft, drawing the heavier cool air from the outside down another shaft. Proper planning, however, was essential in using this kind of system. If all the drifts, raises, stopes, shafts, winzes, and so forth inside the mine were not connected, air could not circulate. In addition, the system is somewhat at the mercy of outside weather conditions and seasons. Outside air that is colder than air in the mine, for example, pushes air into the upper mine workings and out the lower. Just the reverse happens if the outside air is warmer than the inside: the air moves into the lower mine workings and out the upper. And under some weather conditions, the air does not move at all. If the draft system was properly planned, however, it was the most effective means of mine ventilation. The Bullion Mine in the Comstock Mining District, for example, was estimated to have 300,000 cubic feet of air flowing out of the mine every minute in 1877; with the exception of 10,000 cubic feet from air compressors and 30,000 cubic feet from air blowers, all of this air consisted of draft ventilation (Lord 1883:393). Many of the surviving shafts and adits leading outside of historical mines were used only for ventilation. What this suggests is that the proper identification of mine features requires the reconstruction of the complete mine technology, a point made often here.

Drainage Methods

Flooding was a common problem in underground mines, forcing the installation of a drainage-system. The most simple, and most common, method was the digging of adits into the hillside below the flooded mine. In the Comstock Mining District, workers had dug several drainage adits by 1863, including the 1,100–feet-long Union Tunnel that was intended to drain the Mexican, California, Central, and Ophir mines to a depth of 200 feet (Lord 1883:89, 231). The most famous of the Comstock drainage adits was the Sutro Tunnel, which, when completed in 1878, was over three miles long and intercepted the mines at a depth of 1,663 feet. Another low-tech solution was to "bail out" the mine by using the iron buckets on windlasses or whims to carry water. And yet another was to use a "water skip" that could be pulled up an inclined ramp, such as the one installed by Philipp Deidesheimer at the Ophir Mine in 1861 (Young 1975:364). Finally, as early as 1859, the Ophir Mine was using a small 15–horsepower,

37. Cornish pump at the Union Shaft, Comstock Mining
District, 1879. (Courtesy of Nevada Historical Society.)

38. The Gold Bar Mine site. (Photograph by author, 1987.)

steam-powered pump (Ophir Mine manuscript, Works Progress Admin-
istration, Nevada Historical Society, p. 1).

Deep mining, however, encouraged the development of high-tech solutions to draining mines. Once again, the Comstock Mining District
"wrote the book" on how powerful and expensive industrial technology
could be used to solve mining problems. After its installation in 1859, the

small pump at Ophir Mine was rapidly eclipsed by larger "Cornish" force pumps, and by the late 1860s and 1870s pumps generating hundreds of horsepower were common. In 1879, for example, the last Cornish pump in the Comstock district was installed at the Union shaft (image 37); it generated 540 horsepower and pumped two million gallons of water per day (Lord 1883:345).

The Cornish pumps, which used a single-action vacuum piston, eventually gave way to double-action pumps.

Extraction at the Gold Bar Mine

The Gold Bar Mine in southwestern Nevada was typical of small-scale mines of the early 20th century (image 38).

Situated in the Bullfrog Mining District just inside Death Valley National Park, the mine was worked mostly from 1905 until 1909. The recorded history of Gold Bar begins with the filing of a mining claim for a quartz outcrop on Bullfrog Mountain by Frank "Shorty" Harris in August 1904 (Ransome et al. 1910:122–123; Latschar 1981:897). The news of the discovery brought a rush of prospectors from the nearby towns of Tonopah and Goldfield to the newly organized Bullfrog Mining District. On 10 October 1904, two of these prospectors, Ben Hazeltine and N. P. Reinhart, located and filed new claims only two miles north of the original Bullfrog discovery (Latschar 1981:93). Early in 1905 they sold these claims to Goldfield promoters J. P. Loftus and J. R. Davis, who then organized the Bullfrog Gold Bar Mining Company (Latschar 1981:897). Mining began immediately.

The Original Gold Bar Shaft

The working shaft at the Gold Bar Mine was said to be the first in the Bullfrog district to use a horse whim rather than a hand windlass (Latschar 1981:99). A photograph from November 1905 shows the whim in action, along with the rest of the mine's superstructure: the headframe with an ore bucket, a blacksmith shop, an ore pile next to the shaft, and an ore car on a track presumably leading to the edge of the waste-rock dump (image 39).

It is unknown how long this shaft was in use, but by early January 1906, a new gasoline engine–powered hoisting plant had arrived (Latschar 1981:99). Apparently, the original Gold Bar shaft was abandoned when the new hoisting plant was installed. A photograph dated June 1906 shows

39. Horse whim at the original Gold Bar Mine, 1905.
(Courtesy of Nevada Historical Society.)

40. The original Gold Bar Mine site. (Photograph by author, 1987.)

the original shaft without a headframe and a new headframe over what
is here named Feature System 2, next to the remains of the Gold Bar mill
(Latschar 1981:102).

Images 40 and 41 show the remains of the original Gold Bar Mine
today.

Feature 1–1 is the original shaft at Gold Bar Mine. Features 1–2 and

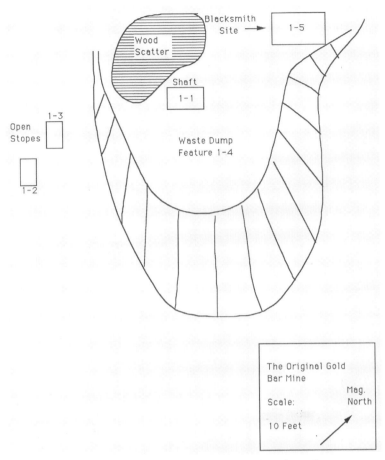

41. Map of the original Gold Bar Mine. (Drawn by author, 1987.)

1–3 are two open stopes at the base of the rock-waste dump. Feature 1–4 is the rock-waste dump associated with Feature 1. Feature 1–5 is probably associated with a blacksmith shop needed to sharpen rock drills and was most likely contained within the wooden frame building shown in the 1905 photograph (image 42).

The New Gold Bar Shaft

The new Gold Bar shaft is a second mining-feature system at the Gold Bar site. Documentary accounts suggest that it had a 28–horsepower Hercules gasoline hoist and a one-ton ore skip with automatic dumping capabilities (Latschar 1981:99). And the gallows headframe was 50 feet high

42. Blacksmithing feature at the original Gold Bar Mine. (Photograph by author, 1987.)

43. The new Gold Bar Mine in 1908. (Courtesy of Nevada Historical Society.)

(Latschar 1981:99). The Nye County tax assessment rolls for 1906 listed the hoisting plant, the gallows frame, a small engine house, a blacksmith shop, an office building, a boarding house, and four Lenox ore cars as improvements on the Gold Bar mining company property (Latschar 1981:105). Photographs taken in January 1908 show the gallows frame with skip, the ore bin, the engine house, and another building, probably the blacksmith shop (image 43).

44. The new Gold Bar Mine site. (Photograph by author, 1987.)

The boarding house and the office building are most likely the two structures in the photograph next to the Gold Bar Mill, just below the mine.

Three archaeological features are visible at the site of the new Gold Bar Mine (images 44 and 45).

Feature 2–1 is the shaft, with wooden ladder, shoring, and a steel track from the ore skip still intact. Feature 2–2 is the rock-waste dump associated with the shaft. Feature 2–3 is a concrete machine pad probably anchoring the hoisting engine contained within the engine house shown in the 1906 photo. Only a few timber fragments scattered on the ground around the shaft give evidence of the headframe and ore bin that once stood there. The site of the blacksmith shop is feature 2–6. Finally, features 2–4 and 2–5 are rock-waste dumps lying just southwest of the main waste dump, feature 2–2.

The Homestake Mine

Another mining feature system is the Homestake Mine. The first claims for the Homestake Mine were made in early 1905 (Latschar 1981:124). After buying the claim in September of the same year, the Homestake Consolidated Mining Company started the first shaft at the mine. A 15–horsepower hoisting engine arrived on 5 January 1906 and was installed shortly thereafter. A photograph taken in June 1906 shows a corrugated metal

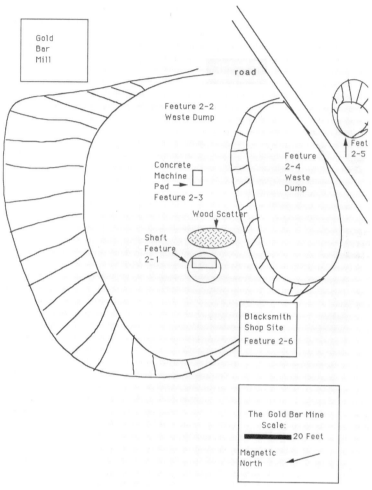

Inside map:

Gold
Bar
Mill

road

Feature 2-2
Waste Dump

Feature
2-5
Feet

Concrete
Machine
Pad →
Feature 2-3

Feature
2-4
Waste
Dump

Wood Scatter

Shaft
Feature
2-1

Blacksmith
Shop Site
Feature 2-6

The Gold Bar Mine
Scale:
20 Feet

Magnetic
North

45. Map of the new Gold Bar Mine. (Drawn by author, 1987.)

building housing the hoisting engine, a small headframe, a surface tram, and an open cut on the hillside above the shaft (image 46).

Two additional shafts were started in 1906, but they were not well documented. The underground workings of both, however, are situated so as to suggest that the Homestake Mine was "sniping" on Gold Bar Mine property (that is, mining the ore body that extended onto the Gold Bar claim). By 29 March 1907, a 40–horsepower hoisting engine was installed at the main shaft, along with an air compressor for running air drills (Latschar 1981:129, 131). Another 6–drill air compressor had been added

46. The Homestake Mine in 1906. (Courtesy of Nevada Historical Society.)

47. The Homestake Mine site. (Photograph by author, 1987.)

by May 1908 (Latschar 1981:137). The Homestake-King Mine was closed on 19 April 1909, along with the mill. Miners conducted some additional exploration work in 1912 but discovered no new ore bodies (Latschar 1981:153). The mine was not worked again until the 1930s. In 1937 it had been equipped with a gas hoist, air compressor, and machine drills, and was being worked by 14 men (Latschar 1981:154). From 1940 until 1942,

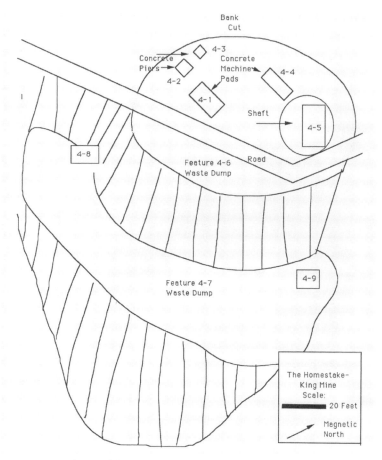

Bank
Cut

Concrete
Piers

4-3
Concrete
Machine
Pads

4-4

4-2

4-1

Shaft

4-5

4-8

Feature 4-6
Waste Dump

Road

Feature 4-7
Waste Dump

4-9

The Homestake-
King Mine
Scale:
20 Feet

Magnetic
North

48. Map of the Homestake Mine. (Drawn by author, 1987.)

the mine was again worked, but there is no further evidence of its productivity until it became part of what is now Death Valley National Park
in the 1970s (Latschar 1981:155).

What is visible today at the Homestake-King Mine is typical of early-
20th-century mining sites. No hoisting engines, air compressors, or other
equipment remain on the surface, nor are there standing buildings or
headframes (images 47 and 48).

The Feature System includes 13 features. Features 4–1, 4–2, 4–3, and
4–4 are concrete machine pads next to the main shaft, Feature 4–5 (image 49).

All of these appear to be associated with the corrugated metal hoist

49. Concrete machine pads at the Homestake Mine. (Photograph by author, 1987.)

house shown in the June 1906 photograph of the Homestake Mine. It is likely, however, that two of the four pads belong to air compressors and the others to two separate hoist engines installed at the site at different times—the smaller 15-horsepower engine in 1906 and the larger 40-horsepower engine in 1907. It is also possible that some of these features are associated with the 1940–1942 mine occupation. No diagnostic artifacts help clarify time placement. Feature 4–5 is the mine shaft shown in the same photograph, associated with a simple headframe, ore bucket, and surface tram that are no longer visible. Much of the wooden shoring is still intact, but the shaft entrance has partially collapsed (image 50).

A 1978 photograph of the shaft shows part of the collapsed headframe, but this structure is now gone (see Latschar 1981:164). Feature 4–6 is a rock-waste dump at the same level as features 1 through 5, while Feature 4–7 is a related rock-waste dump just below Feature 4–6. Features 4–8 and 4–9 are two other mine shafts associated with the lower rock-waste dump, Feature 4–7. Feature 4–10 (not shown) is a rock-waste dump associated with an adit just east of Feature 4–7. And, finally, Features 4–11, 4–12, and 4–13 are rock-waste dumps in the ravine just below the Homestake Mine and above the Gold Bar Mine. None of these features are associated with diagnostic artifacts, but historical documentation, especially photographs, helps identify their time period and use.

50. The main shaft at the Homestake Mine. (Photograph by author, 1987.)

Beneficiation

The minerals extracted from mines are typically impure. The process of upgrading ore to increase its economic value is called "beneficiation" (Noble and Spude 1992:11). Metal beneficiation includes a wide variety of techniques ranging from the mechanical treatment of ores through crushing and concentration to smelting and chemical processes like cyanidation. The process of beneficiation depends on the kind of metal being extracted, how easily it can be separated from its rock matrix ("free milling"), and whether it is in complex metallic compounds. In all cases, however, metal beneficiation begins with mechanical crushing and grinding of the ore. Miners accomplished crushing with a variety of machines, the most common of which were jaw crushers, stamps, and rollers. Free-milling ores required relatively little crushing and grinding to separate the metal from the "gangue" (rock containing no ore). Miners could then collect the free-metal particles easily through a variety of devices, such as copper plates or tables covered with a thin film of mercury. The mercury amalgamated with the copper to form a coating, and particles of gold and silver passing over the coated plate then were caught and amalgamated. Ores that were not free milling, however, required more elaborate and expensive milling methods—more crushing and grinding, the use of complex chemical processes to wrestle the metal from the rock before collection could begin, and more complicated collection methods.

51. An arrastra, Joshua Tree National Park, California. (Photograph by author, 2006.)

Mechanical Crushing and Grinding Methods

Crushing the rock ore is the first stage of beneficiation. Several steps are usually involved, starting first with breaking up the ore with rock breakers and then either stamping, grinding, or both to reduce the ore to "sands" (a coarse fraction) or "slimes" (a fine fraction). The amount of crushing depended on the particle size needed in the rest of the milling process. Crushing either took place underground in the mine, in the top level of the mill, or in a separate building. The earliest, simplest, cheapest, and most widespread crushing technology in small-scale gold operations in the American West was the arrastra (Van Bueren 2004) (image 51).

Arrastras were used widely in the small mines of Nevada during the entire mining period, usually in one- or two-man operations. Rock breakers and stamp mills were the industry standard throughout the last half of the 19th century (Rickard 1901). By the 1910s, however, the stamp-mill technology had given way to ball, tube, and rod mills, which could produce much smaller and more uniform particle sizes. Cyanidation and flotation, two beneficiation technologies designed to recover metals from low-grade ores, required "slimes," or smaller particles. But by the late 20th century, milling technology such as heap leaching did not require grinding to slime-size particles.

52. An 1860s lithograph of a stamp battery at Gould and Curry Mill, Comstock Mining District. (Courtesy of Nevada Historical Society.)

Stamp Mills

The first stamp mills for crushing rock ores in Nevada were introduced into the Comstock Mining District from the California gold fields. Stamp mills were used widely during the 19th century, reaching their peak in size and efficiency on the Comstock and in the Black Hills of South Dakota in the 1880s and 1890s (Rickard 1901:75–101). The stamps crushed ores to sand-sized particles with the up-and-down action of several heavy stamps connected by a camshaft (image 52).

Each of the stamps fell upon what was sometimes a wooden or concrete but most often an iron anvil ("die") installed in a mortar box (Rickard 1901:2). The ore was crushed between the anvil and the iron head of the stamp, a process that separated large free-metal particles from the matrix rock in much the same way a nutcracker separates the kernel from the shell. Either a dry or wet process was used to feed the ore to the stamps. In dry-crushing stamp mills, the ore was heated in a roaster or kiln before or sometimes after being introduced to the stamps, which converted silver sulfides into chlorides. In wet-stamp mills, water was piped into the mortar boxes. The falling stamp not only crushed the ore but also created pulsations, forcing the ore and water mixture or "pulp" out through the open front of the mortar box onto amalgamating plates or other collecting devices (Rickard 1901:2–3). "Sizing" screens covered

53. Ruins of an 1870s stamp mill at Tuscarora, Nevada,
in 1911. (Courtesy of Nevada Historical Society.)

the opening, keeping ore that was too large inside the mortar box for more
crushing. The archaeological record of stamp mills is typically limited
to foundations and a few scattered parts of machinery; however, early-
20th-century photographs of the ruins of 19th-century stamp mills, such
as the 1911 photograph of a dry-crushing 10–stamp mill site at Tuscarora
in eastern Nevada (image 53), give a more complete image. The picture
shows a revolving furnace or cylinder in the mill ruins.

Rock Breakers

Before ores went to the stamps, miners often broke them up into smaller
pieces with heavy, nutcracker-like mechanical crushers placed near the
top level of the mill, below the ore bin. The most commonly used rock
breaker in late-19th-century Nevada was Blake's jaw-crusher (image 54),
although comparable machines, like Dodge's and Krom's jaw crushers,
were used as well (Eissler 1898:41–46).

In the early 20th century, most of the jaw crushers had given way to
the more effective gyratory crushers, such as the Allis-Chalmers gyratory
crusher used at the Consolidated Cortez Mill in 1925 (Heikes 1927:2335).
Gyratory crushers have a "fixed crushing surface, in the form of a frustum of an inverted cone, around the axis of which gyrates a movable
crushing surface, having the shape of a conical frustum in erect position" (Peele 1941:28–04).

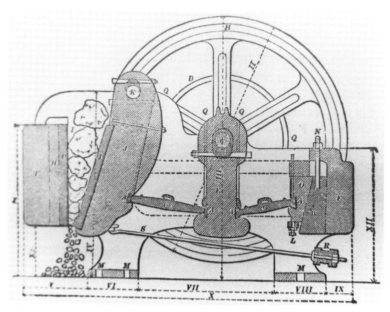

54. Illustration of a Blake rock crusher. (Eissler 1898, figure 3.)

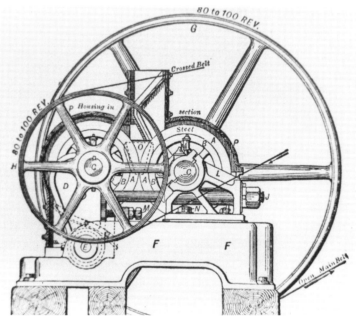

55. Illustration of Krom rolls. (Eissler 1898, figure 76.)

56. Allis-Chalmers tube mill at Consolidated Cortez Mill, Cortez Mining District, 1920s. (Courtesy of Mackay School of Mines, University of Nevada–Reno.)

Grinding Mills

In order to recover very small metal particles from low-grade ores in the beneficiation process, ores had to be crushed to a clay-like "slime" with uniformly sized particles, something stamp mills could not do. For this reason, grinding mills such as Krom rolls were introduced into Nevada in the late 19th and early 20th centuries (image 55).

Chilean mills, which worked something like arrastras but were set up in a vertical position, were also used occasionally to grind ores even more, as at the Montgomery-Shoshone Mill at Rhyolite, Nevada, which operated between 1907 and 1911. By 1910, however, ball-and-tube or rod mills were standard in the "all-slime" mills that dominated the Nevada frontier (Elliot 1966:157–158; Spude 1987) (image 56).

These mills were large rotating cylinders containing stone or steel balls or rods. Ore put into the cylinder was ground to the desired size by the jostling and cascading movement of the balls or rods.

Classifiers

Rock-breaking and grinding machines were linked into a system that included classifiers, screen-like devices for sorting ore by size. The first in line was the grizzly, a grate that allowed small pieces of ore from the mine to go directly into an ore bin for stamping or grinding. Ore that was too large to pass through the grizzly was conveyed to the rock breaker for crushing and then returned. The earliest classifiers, Trommels, were cylindrical screens placed along ore chutes to keep larger rock from jamming the mill machinery. Later, sorting screens, such as the Dorr classifier, became part of a series with the stamps and grinding mills. These screens raked oversized particles uphill and out one end for regrounding and washed slime-size particles downhill and out the other end.

Simple Collection Methods

Miners could process free-milling ores simply by crushing the rock into sand and then collecting the metal particles that were released. Most of the simple collection methods of the 19th and early 20th centuries used amalgamating tables or plates and "concentrators" that separated the metal from the gangue. The concentrate was then shipped to smelters. Flotation was introduced in the early 20th century as another way of concentrating metal compounds. Here, finely ground rock ores are "frothed" with air and oil or other reagents; the metal compounds float to the surface with the air bubbles and are collected by the oil. Miners did not need much technical expertise to operate most of the simple collection processes. Furthermore, the methods were cheap and could be used on a large scale. Simple collection, however, could not be used for low-grade ores with very small metallic particles.

Plate or Table Amalgamation

Many of the stamp mills of the 19th century recovered free gold and silver by passing the "pulp" (crushed ore mixed with water) over an "apron" of copper plates covered with a thin film of mercury. Amalgamating plates usually are described in documents by number of feet; the Homestake-King Mill in the Bullfrog Mining District, for example, had 12 feet of copper amalgamating plates in 1908 (Latschar 1981:136). Workers often added mercury to the ore during the grinding stage, however, because that made it possible for mercury and ore to be in contact for a longer period of time to form an amalgam. The amalgam that formed was collected at frequent intervals and taken to the assay shop, where the mercury was removed by means of a retort (Young 1970). A variant of the amalgamation table is the "blanket table," a sluice-like device covered with blanket strips. Pulp is allowed to flow over the table, with the blanket trapping the heavier metals and washing away the lighter sands.

57. Frue vanners at the Kinkaid Mill, Virginia City, Nevada. (Courtesy of Special Collections, University of Nevada–Reno Library.)

Concentrators

Concentrators use a shaking, vibrating motion to separate metals from gangue. The most common concentrators were jigs, buddles, vanners, Embrey tables, and, in the early 20th century, Wilfley tables. Jigs are sieve-like machines that vibrate up and down in water, causing the crushed ore on the sieve to stratify; the heavier metals settle at the bottom, next to the sieve, while the lighter gangue stays on top. The buddle, which Cornish miners introduced onto the mining frontier of the American West along with the jig, is a circular table swept by brushes that rotate around a center pivot. Buddle tables are either concave or convex, inclining toward the center or the outer edge. Pulp flows slowly through baffles onto the table and down the inclined sides. The heavier metals work their way to the bottom, leaving the lighter gangue on top. Vanners, the best known of which is the Frue vanner (image 57), are table-mounted endless belts that shake or vibrate side to side.

The pulp flows onto the belt surface, where the shaking motion vertically separates the metals and the gangue; the heavier metals settle at the bottom, and the lighter gangue stays near the top and is washed away. Embrey tables differ from vanners only in that they have belts that shake end to end, not side to side. And Wilfley's tables are similar to both but

58. Illustration of Fagergren flotation cells. (Dorr 1936, figure 56.)

have vibrating solid plates instead of endless belts. In effect, the concentrators transformed lower-grade ore into a higher-grade concentrate, which was then shipped by railroad to smelters in San Francisco, Salt Lake City, or Denver.

Flotation

In the early 20th century, flotation was developed as yet another method of separating metal compounds from gangue. The process involved the use of "frothing" machines like Fagergren cells (image 58) to create air bubbles in a liquid solution of finely ground ore.

Air bubbles together with flotation agents such as pine oil carried metal compounds to the surface, where they could be skimmed off. In order to mill complex ores containing some combination of silver, lead, and zinc, miners often combined the flotation process with other milling methods that lost more silver than gold, such as cyanidation. Image 59 illustrates a

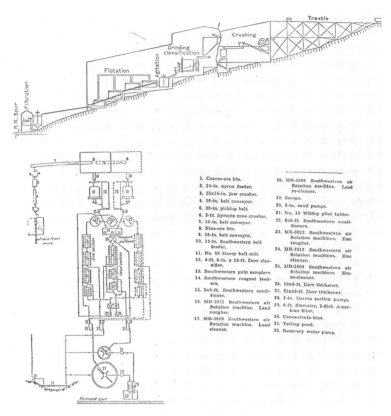

1. Coarse-ore bin.
2. 24-in. apron feeder.
3. 15x24-in. jaw crusher.
4. 16-in. belt conveyor.
5. 30-in. picking belt.
6. 3-ft. Symons cone crusher.
7. 16-in. belt conveyor.
8. Fine-ore bin.
9. 16-in. belt conveyor.
10. 16-in. Southwestern belt feeder.
11. No. 65 Marcy ball mill.
12. 4-ft. 6-in. x 18-ft. Dorr classifier.
13. Southwestern pulp samplers.
14. Southwestern reagent feeders.
15. 5x5-ft. Southwestern conditioner.
16. MB-3012 Southwestern air flotation machine. Lead rougher.
17. MB-3008 Southwestern air flotation machine. Lead cleaner.
18. MB-3006 Southwestern air flotation machine. Lead re-cleaner.
19. Sumps.
20. 2-in. sand pumps.
21. No. 13 Wilfley pilot tables.
22. 6x6-ft. Southwestern conditioners.
23. MB-3012 Southwestern air flotation machines. Zinc rougher.
24. MB-3012 Southwestern air flotation machines. Zinc cleaner.
25. MB-3008 Southwestern air flotation machines. Zinc re-cleaner.
26. 10x8-ft. Dorr thickener.
27. 22x10-ft. Dorr thickener.
28. 2-in. Dorrco suction pumps.
29. 6-ft. diameter, 3-disk American filter.
30. Concentrate bins.
31. Tailing pond.
32. Recovery water pump.

59. Elevation and flow sheet of Black Hawk Flotation Mill, New Mexico. (Wright 1930, figures 1 and 2.)

typical 1920s silver flotation mill with an elevation and a flow sheet, this one from the Black Hawk Consolidated Mill in New Mexico.

Chemical Methods for More Complex Ores

The milling of ores that contain complex metallic compounds like argentite (silver sulfide) required more than simple collection methods. These ores necessitated the development of chemical methods that rapidly left behind the old "fly by the seat of the pants" mill workers and opened the era of the highly trained mining engineer (Spence 1970). The principal chemical milling methods were chlorination and lixiviation or leaching, both expensive but exceptionally effective, recovering 70 to more than 90 percent of the metals. The chemical processes required finely ground ores, which also brought about a revolution in the tools used to crush ores.

60. Patios at the 1864 Gould and Curry Mill, Comstock Mining District. (Courtesy of Nevada Historical Society.)

Patios

One of the earliest chemical methods used in Nevada was patio amalgamation (image 60).

The patio process was discovered in Mexico in about 1540 and worked best under the hot sun. After crushing, the ore was mixed with water, salt, mercury, and copper sulfate, usually by having animals or mill workers walk through the mixture or "pulp." The pulp was then spread out on a rock pavement or patio. Heating by exposure to the sun started a chemical reaction, combining silver with mercury to form an "amalgam"; additional heating could then drive off the mercury.

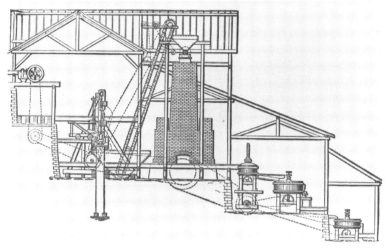

61. Elevation of the Taylor Mill, Mineral Hill. (Eissler 1898, figure 58.)

Pan Amalgamation

The key catalyst in the chemical reaction from the patio process was the heat of the sun. Long, cold winters on the Comstock and elsewhere in northern Nevada greatly limited the effectiveness of the patio process, which just took too long. The invention of large metal tubs or pans that were artificially heated with steam overcame this obstacle. Pan amalgamation, as the process was called, was used widely in Nevada and spread throughout the mining West during the 19th century. The Washoe Process and the Reese River Process were its two main variants (Egleston 1887; Eissler 1898; Oberbillig 1967). The only difference between the two processes was that the Reese River mills roasted the crushed ore in a furnace (which converted the ore to a more manageable silver chloride) before amalgamation, while Washoe mills did not.

Image 61 illustrates the elevation of the Taylor Mill in Mineral Hill. It was a typical 1870s Reese River pan mill with a Stetefeldt furnace that roasted the ore after it was crushed with stamps. Figure 1 shows a reconstructed milling flow sheet.

The mill was excavated into a hillside to take advantage of gravity when transporting materials between milling steps. At the top level of the mill, ore brought from the mine was dumped into a grizzly. Small

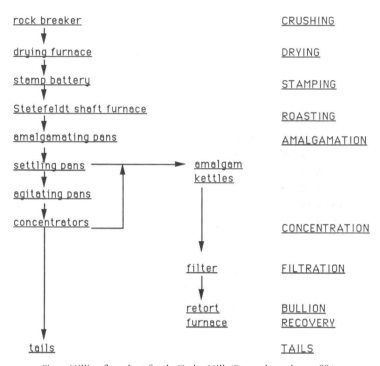

Fig. 1. Milling flow sheet for the Taylor Mill. (Drawn by author, 1988.)

pieces of ore dropped through the grate onto the floor below, where they were put into drying kilns. (Instead of a kiln, earlier mills often used a drying floor in which heat from a furnace passed through flues beneath the floor.) Pieces that were too large to pass through the grizzly were sent to a rock crusher. From there, the crushed ore passed down to the kiln floor for drying. In Reese River mills, workers dried the salt that would later be mixed with the ore for roasting in the same kilns as the ore. After drying, both ore and salt were fed into a battery of stamps for fine crushing. In most mills, the stamp batteries were on the same floor as the drying kilns. Stamps produced so much noise and dust, however, that they were often installed in a separate building. After stamping, the ore and the salt in Reese River mills passed through the drying kilns once again and were then mixed mechanically before being roasted in a furnace. The Taylor Mill used a Stetefeldt shaft furnace for this purpose, as illustrated

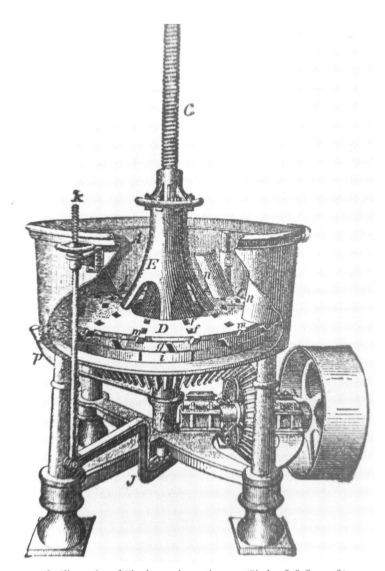

62. Illustration of Wheeler amalgamation pan. (Eissler 1898, figure 18.)

in the elevation. Next, the roasted ore was taken out of the furnace and put onto a cooling floor. From here, the ore was moved by railroad car to amalgamation pans (image 62).

Into these metal tubs was put the "pulp"—a mixture of ore, water, salt, sulfate of copper, and mercury. The pulp was finely ground and heated in the pans, which were equipped with both a rotating muller and a steam

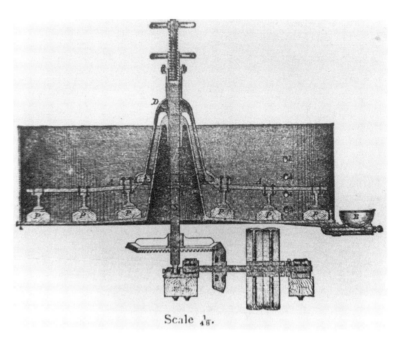

Scale $\frac{1}{48}$.

63. Illustration of settler. (Eissler 1898, figure 27.)

chamber. During this step, silver in the ore combined chemically with the mercury to form an amalgam, with salt and copper sulfate assisting in the process. Next, the pulp from the amalgamating pans was discharged into settlers (image 63) on the floor below.

Settlers are large tubs with rotating stirring arms used to separate the amalgam from the rest of the pulp. The heavier amalgam and free mercury settled to the bottom of the tub, where it was drawn off into kettles. The collected amalgam was taken to a retort furnace where the mercury was vaporized, condensed, and then reused. What remained was silver bullion, which was sent to a refining furnace for casting into bars. The lighter liquid in the settlers was drawn off into large wooden tubs called agitators on the floor below. Here, rotating stirring arms, as in the settlers, mixed the remaining pulp further and continued the "settling out" process. Amalgam that settled to the bottom of the tubs was again collected, and the recalcitrant solution discharged into a variety of mechanical concentrators, like blanket tables, for a final attempt at amalgamation. Workers moved the exhausted sediments remaining after concentration outside the mill and dumped them as tailings.

64. Interior of California Pan Mill, Virginia City, Nevada, in 1882. (Courtesy of Nevada Historical Society.)

Image 64 is an 1882 photograph of the interior of the Washoe Process California Pan Mill in Virginia City on the Comstock, showing both pans and settlers.

This pan mill, which was quite far down Six-Mile Canyon from an associated stamp mill, had 44 pans and 20 settlers (Eissler 1898:93–94). The tailings were then treated in an unknown number of agitators and passed over two sets of blanket sluices, each of which had six 300–feet-long tables, before leaving the mill. Existing archaeological remains of pan mills typically do not include the pans, settlers, or agitators. Image 65, however, illustrates what was left in 1914 of the 1871 Monte Cristo Pan Mill in Rawhide; some of the pans were still there, if not in place.

Chlorination

Another early chemical technology for milling complex ores was the "chlorination process," developed in Prussia in 1848 by Karl Friedrich Plattner to extract gold from mill tailings (Egleston 1887:596–598; Clow 2002:82–94). The process involved exposing crushed gold ore to chlorine gas and then leaching the ore in a water solution to produce gold chloride. Adding ferrous sulphate to the solution precipitated the gold, which could then be filtered out. The most common method was "barrel chlorination," in which bleach powder and acid were added to a cylinder

65. Ruins of 1871 Monte Cristo Mill near Rawhide,
1914. (Courtesy of Nevada Historical Society.)

containing the crushed ore. By the 1870s, however, pressurized chlorine gas was inserted into a rotating metal barrel. In the United States, the first use of the chlorination process in gold mills occurred in 1858 in California. Shortly thereafter, the Ophir Mill on Nevada's Comstock Lode experimented with the expensive process (Lord 1883:122–123). But chlorination on the Comstock, and on the Nevada mining frontier generally, was soon dropped in favor of the cheaper pan amalgamation technology, which was used on a large scale. Still, chlorination was quite common in other areas, including the Appalachian gold fields in the 1870s and, in the very late 19th century, the Black Hills of South Dakota and the Cripple Creek region of Colorado (Clow 2002:82–94). By 1902, the year of the Goldfield discovery in Nevada, the cyanide process had replaced chlorination, though even in the late 20th century some gold operations in the American West were using a greatly improved version of the chlorination process.

Von Patera and Russell Lixiviation

By the 1880s several mills in the western United States were employing the Von Patera "lixiviation," or leaching, technology (Stetefeldt 1895; Eissler 1898). The process began by roasting ores with salt to create silver chloride, which was then dissolved in a solution of sodium or calcium hyposulfite. Silver could then be precipitated from the solution by adding an alkaline sulfide such as sodium sulfide or calcium sulfide (Eissler 1898:281). Perhaps the best-documented Von Patera mill is the Bertrand Mill near Eu-

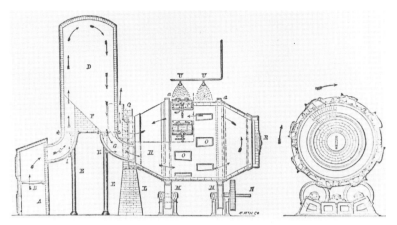

66. Illustration of Bruckner cylinders. (Eissler 1898, figure 61.)

reka, Nevada, which used seven milling steps (Egleston 1887:487–515). The first three were quite similar to pan amalgamation: crushing, drying, and roasting. The ore, however, was not finely ground with stamps but crushed with Krom rolls. Krom rolls were cheaper to buy, less expensive to maintain, and did not require a separate building. The Bertrand Mill, moreover, used Bruckner cylinders (image 66) for roasting the ore, rather than the Stetefeldt shaft furnaces so commonly used in other Reese River mills (image 67).

Each of the four firebrick-lined horizontal cylinders, which rotated on rollers inside a furnace, had a diameter of 7 feet, a length of 19 feet, and held a charge of 5 tons. The charge was fired for 8 to 11 hours. Throughout the mining West, the Bruckner furnace replaced the Stetefeldt furnace because it was portable and less costly.

After roasting, the Von Patera mills used methods quite different from the pan amalgamation mills. At the Bertrand, the roasted ore was dumped into a set of 24 wooden leaching vats, each of which was 6 feet in diameter and 3 feet deep. The ore was then given a water bath to separate base metals (including lead, zinc, aluminum, and antimony) from gangue. After drawing off the bath water from the vats, mill workers added a solution of sodium hyposulfite. The silver chloride in the roasted ore changed chemically into sodium silver hyposulfite after leaching in the vats for 6 to 20 hours.

The silver solution from the leaching vats was then pumped into boiler

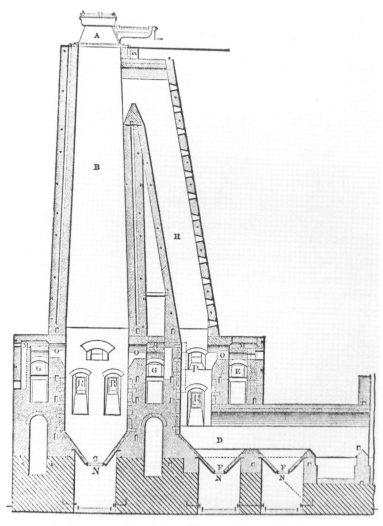

67. Illustration of Stetefeldt shaft furnace. (Eissler 1898, figure 59.)

iron precipitation tanks, which were 8 feet in diameter and 12 feet deep. Workers shoveled any sediments remaining in the leaching vats into cars and dumped them outside the mill. They added calcium sulfide to the silver solution in the precipitation tanks, creating silver sulfide as a precipitant. The silver sulfide was allowed to accumulate in the bottom of the tank for about 15 days. Then the sludge was drawn off through a stopcock and poured onto cloth filters. The Bertrand Mill used 30 filters, each of which was a 2.5–foot square frame over which sackcloth had been stretched. The silver sulfide that collected on the filters was removed and taken to a furnace for roasting. Roasting drove off the sulfur, leaving a gray metallic mass that was refined more and cast into bullion bars.

The Von Patera method, however, did not work on ores that contained significant amounts of lead. Leaching with sodium hyposulfite dissolved both silver and lead, creating a silver and lead sulfide that was extremely difficult to refine into pure silver. Furthermore, the process did not remove silver from any ores that were not changed to silver chloride during roasting. The recovery of silver, accordingly, was not as high as it might have been. In the 1880s E. H. Russell solved both problems in experiments at the Mount Cory (Nevada) and Ontario (Utah) mills (Eissler 1898:282). The "Russell process" removed lead from the silver solution in the precipitation tanks by adding sodium carbonate or soda ash, which formed lead carbonate as a precipitant. And the recovery of silver could be improved by adding an "extra" solution of cupreous hyposulfite to the leaching vats (Stetefeldt 1895:2–3). During the latter part of the 19th century, Russell mills appeared in several places throughout the western United States and Mexico, including the Marsac Mill at Park City, Utah; the Yedras Mill in the state of Sinaloa, Mexico; and the Blue Bird Mill at Butte, Montana (Stetefeldt 1895:5–6).

One of the earliest Russell mills in the United States was the Tenabo Mill at Cortez, Nevada. Built in 1886, the mill was described in some detail by Hubert H. Bancroft (1889:20). According to his account, the mill operated much like the Bertrand Mill but with a number of modifications that made it unique and state of the art. The Russell process at the Tenabo Mill is shown in the flow sheet in figure 2.

In 1908, however, a new cyanide leaching technology was installed in the mill, making the existing archaeological site a combination of the two technological feature systems. The wooden leaching vats from the 1886 mill are still visible in the archaeological record (image 68), as are the Bruckner furnaces (image 69).

Cyanide Leaching

During the last decade of the 19th century, cyanide leaching mills rapidly replaced both the Von Patera and Russell lixiviation and pan amalgamation mills. In cyanidation, a compound of cyanide (first potassium

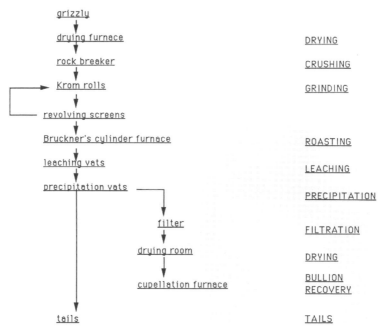

Fig. 2. Milling flow sheet for Russell process at
the Tenabo Mill. (Drawn by author, 1988.)

cyanide and later sodium cyanide) in solution dissolved silver and gold
from the crushed ore. Workers added zinc shavings to precipitate a silver-
gold sludge, which they then refined into bullion. The history of cyanide
leaching technology begins with the granting of a patent in England to
three Scottish chemists in 1887 (Dorr 1936:2–3). In 1889 miners in New
Zealand built the first full-scale cyanide mill. And in 1891 the first cyanide
mills were constructed in the United States. Cyanidation of silver ores,
however, did not take place until later. The first experiments suggested
that silver chlorides and sulfides could not be leached with cyanide, but
in 1900 engineers at the Sirena Mine in the state of Guanajuato in Mexico proved this was untrue (Dorr 1936:4). Within the next few years, cyanidation was almost universally used for milling silver and gold ores. In
Nevada, Professor Robert Jackson of the Mackay School of Mines first employed the cyanide process in 1896 to treat old mill tailings at Washoe Lake
(Elliott 1966:157). The first successful large-scale cyanide mill in Nevada

68. Remains of leaching vats at the Tenabo Mill site. (Photograph by author, 1983.)

69. Bruckner cylinders and furnaces at the Tenabo
Mill site. (Photograph by author, 1983.)

70. Butters Mill on the Comstock Lode, 1906. (Courtesy of
Special Collections, University of Nevada–Reno Library.)

71. Interior of Butters Mill, showing agitation tanks. (Courtesy
of Special Collections, University of Nevada–Reno Library.)

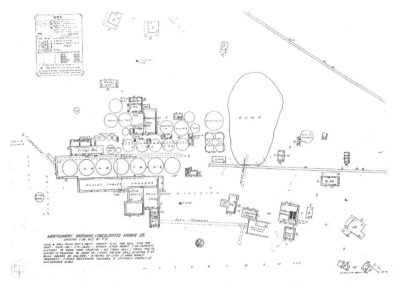

72. The 1909 Sanborn fire insurance map of Montgomery-Shoshone Mill, Bullfrog Mining District. (Courtesy of Nevada Historical Society.)

was the Charles Butters Mill in the Comstock Mining District, erected in Six-Mile Canyon in 1901 (Elliott 1966:157) (images 70, 71).

How a cyanide mill worked is illustrated by the Montgomery-Shoshone Mill at Rhyolite, Nevada, which operated from 1907 until early 1911 and had a daily capacity of 200 tons of ore. The layout and operation of the mill are described amply in contemporary written accounts, including a 1909 Sanborn fire insurance map (image 72) and a 1910 flow sheet from the *Engineering and Mining Journal* (Van Saun 1910:217–219) (image 73).

Image 74 shows the remains of the mill in 1987.

Workers brought the ore from the mine by elevated tram to an ore bin at the top of the mill, where they fed it into a Blake's rock crusher and then sent it through a grinding system that included three rolls and two Chilean mills. Two mechanical classifiers sorted what came out of the grinding system into sands and slimes. The sands were fed directly into a concentration system that included 7 Wilfley tables, but the slimes, mixed with water, were delivered first to a battery of 6 settling tanks and then to 10 vanners for concentration. Afterward, both concentrates (in effect, high-grade ore) were collected, leaving the "tailings" that contained very small metal particles. The sand tailings and the slime tail-

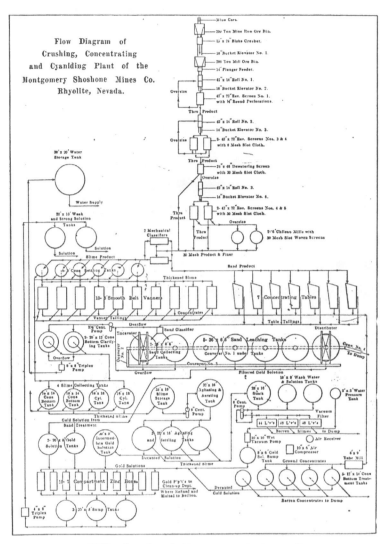

73. Milling flow sheet for Montgomery-Shoshone Mill.
(*Engineering and Mining Journal* 22 (January 1910):218.)

ings then entered two different cyanidation systems that would recover the metal. In the case of sand, the tailings were sent to two sand collection tanks, which, when full, were discharged by conveyor belts into a series of two sand leaching tanks. An alkaline solution of sodium cyanide, lime, and lead acetate was allowed to percolate through each of the leaching tanks for a total period of 10 or 11 days. The sodium cya-

74. Montgomery-Shoshone Mill site. (Photograph by author, 1987.)

nide solution, which had "leached" out gold and silver particles from the sands, was then collected at the bottom of the tanks, where it was pumped into two gold solution tanks. From there, the solution entered a series of 10 zinc boxes, where zinc shavings were added to precipitate the gold and silver. The precipitant was collected with filters and then sent to the smelting room, where it was refined and melted into bullion. Workers transported what was left in the sand tanks after leaching outside the mill to the tailings dump.

The slime tailings were sent through a somewhat different system. First, a series of four collecting tanks, somewhat similar to the Dorr thickening tank shown in image 75, received them for concentration or "thickening."

Image 76 shows the archaeological remains of a Dorr thickener.

The thickened tailings then went to a slime storage tank. From there, they were pumped into an agitation and aeration tank, where they were mixed with a cyanide solution and stirred with large rotating arms (image 77).

The purpose of agitation was to keep the tailings in suspension long enough for them to be dissolved. Next, the solution was transferred to

75. Illustration of Dorr thickening tank. (MacFarren 1912, figure 2.)

76. Archaeological remains of Dorr thickener. (Courtesy of Philip Wilke.)

three tanks for further agitation, after which it was allowed to settle for 15 hours. The tanks were then "decanted." Solution at the top of the tanks was pumped into a gold-solution tank and then the zinc boxes for precipitation. The slime tailings settling to the bottom of the tanks were conveyed to a vacuum-filter room, where 140 filter "leaves" removed the precipitated gold and silver. For both sand and slime the precipitant was taken to the smelting room for refining into bullion. The slime tailings

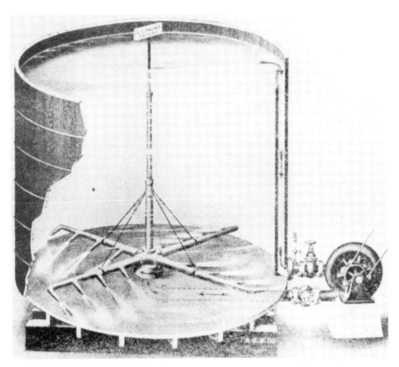

77. Illustration of Trent agitation tank. (MacFarren 1912, figure 10.)

left in the tanks were conveyed outside the mill to the dump, as were the sand tailings. The concentrates, which had been separated from the tailings at the concentration tables, were conveyed to a tube mill, where they were ground for 20 hours in a cyanide solution. Then the solution was pumped through a series of five tanks for agitation and settling. The tanks were decanted, sending the solution to the zinc boxes for precipitation and the settled tailings outside the mill to the dump.

Another contemporary but smaller cyanide mill in the same district was the Homestake-King Mill (image 78).

Completed on 20 June 1908, the mill building, which was 103 feet wide and 231 feet long, had concrete foundations and a steel framework covered with corrugated metal sheets (Latschar 1981:136–138) (image 79).

The equipment installed in the mill in 1908 included eighteen different components: (1) two settling tanks, each 30 feet in diameter and 6 feet deep; (2) cyanide tanks; (3) 3 tube mills; (4) a 25–stamp battery; (5) a 75–ton ore bin; (6) a 350–ton bin to hold the crushed ore; (7) a 50,000–

78. The Homestake-King Mill site, Bullfrog Mining
District. (Photograph by author, 1987.)

79. The Homestake-King Mill in 1908. (Courtesy of Nevada Historical Society.)

gallon water tank; (8) a Dorr classifier; (9) a grizzly; (10) a McCully gyratory crusher; (11) 12 feet of copper amalgamating plates; (12) a 40–frame Butters filter; (13) gold storage solution tanks; (14) two 17–feet-long agitators; (15) stock slime tanks; (16) zinc boxes; (17) two sand leaching tanks, each 20 feet in diameter and 5 feet high; (18) and, finally, five electric motors (two 30–horsepower, two 10–horsepower, and one 20–horsepower) (Latschar 1981:134, 136).

After starting up on 20 June 1908, the mill ran three shifts daily until September, when it shut down for a short period of time. The mill resumed operations toward the end of September and continued until 19 April 1909, when both the mill and the mines closed down (Latschar 1981:148). The history of the mill's decay is only partly known. Its equipment was sold in pieces, so that by 1914 only 15 stamps remained. The same 15 stamps were still reported as late as 1921, but the Nye County tax assessment list from 1930 suggests that all the mill's equipment had disappeared by that date (Latschar 1981:154).

Not surprisingly, the Homestake-King Mill site is the most imposing in the Gold Bar area today. The site is a series of seven levels or floors of concrete building foundations and walls arranged on a steep slope (image 80).

Visible archaeological features include several concrete machine pads, tank supports, chutes, and other equipment-related features inside the mill; the mill tailings; and trash scatters such as firebrick and timbers. Feature 5–1 is the mill tailings flowing from the lowest floor level of the mill down to the valley floor; Features 5–2, 5–3, 5–4, and 5–5 are associated with floor 1; Feature 5–2 is a concrete pier for anchoring machinery; Feature 5–3 is a shallow recess in the floor next to the pier; Feature 5–4 is a set of chutes through which the tails were exhausted from the mill; Feature 5–5 is a pile of firebricks and construction bricks; Feature 5–6 is a group of concrete piers piled together on floor 3; Feature 5–7 is a concrete wall and pier separating floors 4 and 5, with bolts set into the wall for anchoring machinery; Feature 5–8 is a wooden and concrete platform and support for what were probably leaching tanks on floor 5; and Feature 5–9 is a wooden chute or deck support on floor 7, which may be associated with the ore bin.

No time-or use-diagnostic artifacts are associated with the mill site, other than a few cupel fragments on the first floor. None of the milling equipment has survived; the Nye County tax assessment list implies that

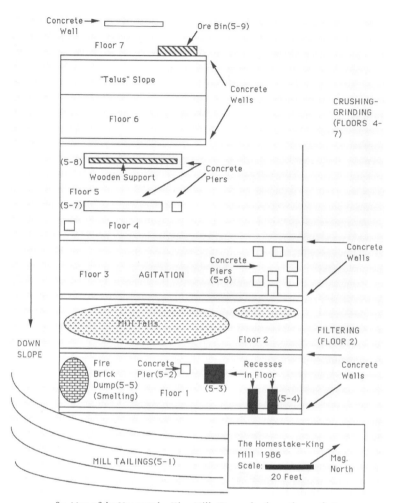

80. Map of the Homestake-King Mill. (Drawn by the author, 1987.)

it had disappeared by the 1920s. Figure 3 is a milling flow sheet for the Homestake-King Mill, reconstructed from documentary and archaeological records.

The Consolidated Cortez Mill site in the Cortez Mining District is a particularly good example of what is likely to be archaeologically visible from a later, 1920s cyanide mill (image 81).

Completed in 1923 (Lincoln 1923:86), the mill was operated continuously until 1930 (Roberts et al. 1967:68) (image 82).

V. C. Heikes (1927:2335) gave a list of equipment in the mill in 1925

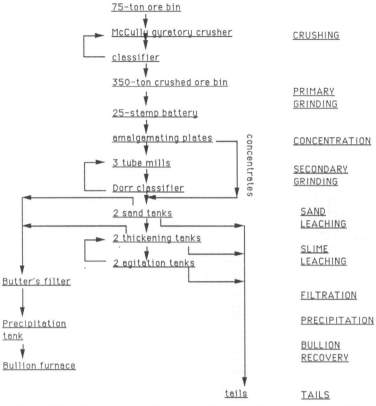

Fig. 3. Milling flow sheet for the Homestake-King Mill. (Drawn by author, 1988.)

that suggests how the mill operated before 1927. A set of annotated photographs taken sometime between 1923 and 1927, and now located in the Mackay School of Earth Sciences and Engineering (formerly the Mackay School of Mines) at the University of Nevada, Reno, provides more information (Hardesty and Hattori 1982:17). The ore was first fed into an Allis-Chalmers Type 4N gyratory crusher, in line with a Bunker Hill screen for sorting. Next, the ore was conveyed to the grinding department (image 83), where it was ground into a slime, first by an Allis-Chalmers ball mill to 40 mesh and then by an Allis-Chalmers tube mill to 100 mesh.

A single Dorr duplex drag classifier that was connected to the tube mill

81. The Consolidated Cortez Mill site, Cortez Mining
District. (Photograph by author, 1983.)

82. Consolidated Cortez Mill in the 1920s. (Courtesy of Mackay
School of Mines, University of Nevada–Reno.)

83. Allis-Chalmers ball mill at the Consolidated Cortez Mill, 1920s.
(Courtesy of Mackay School of Mines, University of Nevada–Reno.)

84. Agitation tanks at the Consolidated Cortez Mill, 1920s. (Courtesy
of Mackay School of Mines, University of Nevada–Reno.)

85. Merrill slime press at the Consolidated Cortez Mill, 1920s. (Courtesy of Mackay School of Mines, University of Nevada–Reno.)

86. Oliver filter at the Queen Mill in Rawhide, Nevada, 1912. (Courtesy of Nevada Historical Society.)

87. Bullion furnace at the Consolidated Cortez Mill. (Courtesy of Mackay School of Mines, University of Nevada–Reno.)

circuit sized and classified the ore. After tube milling, the ore passed over eight Deister concentration tables before entering a system of five Dorr thickening tanks and three Dorr agitation tanks (image 84).

Two Merrill clarifying presses (image 85) that were linked into this system removed suspended particles.

After precipitation, two Oliver filters recovered the silver precipitate (image 86).

The precipitate was then taken to the furnace in the bullion recovery building (image 87).

In 1927 the Con Cortez was converted to an oil flotation concentration plant (*Engineering and Mining Journal* 124[5]:188; Hezzelwood 1930:2). Engineers designed the flotation process around Fagergren flotation cells and pine oil; the plant was probably arranged somewhat like the Black Hawk Mill mentioned earlier. In 1929 the Con Cortez flotation mill employed 60 workers, processed 125 tons of ore each day, and shipped the concentrate by rail to smelters in the Salt Lake Valley in Utah (Hezzelwood 1930:1).

Archaeologically, six geographically distinct activity loci are visible at the site of the mill (image 88).

The most imposing locus consists of the remains of the concentration and cyanide mill. Ore arrived at the upper level of the multistory building by means of a tram from the Arctic Tunnel, while exhausted mill tailings flowed out the lower level of the building and down the canyon. Most of

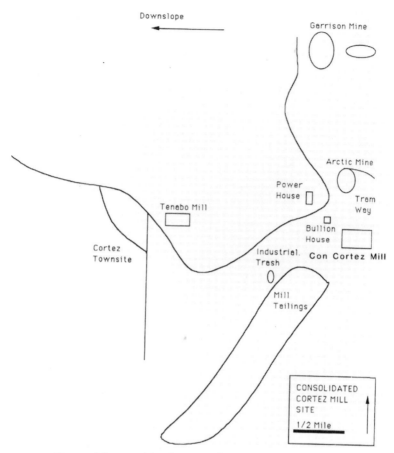

88. Map of the Consolidated Cortez Mill site. (Drawn by author, 1983.)

the equipment is gone. The archaeological record of the building is limited mostly to the foundation; scattered construction-related artifacts such as nails, bolts, and window glass; the remains of an Oliver filter; and the bottoms of several agitation tanks.

The mill's tailings flow is the second activity locus (image 89), and it has a postdepositional history somewhat different from that of the mill itself.

Weathering and erosion has changed the flow structure. But there is no documentary or archaeological evidence that the flow has been changed by removal and reworking at a later time like the effluent from nearby Tenabo Mill.

The tram system is the third activity locus, extending from the Arc-

89. Tailings flow at the Consolidated Cortez Mill site. (Photograph by author, 1983.)

90. Consolidated Cortez Mill powerhouse in the 1920s. (Courtesy of Mackay School of Mines, University of Nevada–Reno.)

91. Fairbanks and Morse generators at the Consolidated Cortez Mill powerhouse. (Courtesy of Mackay School of Mines, University of Nevada–Reno.)

92. The Consolidated Cortez Mill powerhouse site. (Photograph by author, 1983.)

93. Cyanide lid trash scatter at the Consolidated
Cortez Mill site. (Photograph by author, 1983.)

tic Mine adit to the mine waste-rock dump and the concentration building's upper level. Mostly only the grade of the surface tram remains, but
rails and ties are still intact in a few places. No documentary information has been located about the tram.

Support buildings for power, storage, and the bullion furnace make up
the fifth activity locus (image 90). Documentary accounts of these buildings are quite good and include photographs of the equipment inside the
powerhouse (image 91). Notes on the photographs reveal that the power
plant had two 200–horsepower, semidiesel engines, at least one of which
was manufactured by Fairbanks and Morse, along with three fuel oil–
burning air compressors, one of which was a Sullivan angle-compound
type (Hardesty and Hattori 1982:17). The archaeological record of the locus, however, is limited mostly to the wooden frame of the powerhouse
(image 92) and the still standing bullion recovery buildings; the equipment has been removed from all the building sites.

Finally, the sixth activity locus at the site of the Consolidated Cortez
Mill is a cluster of industrial trash scatters next to the tailings flow. The

94. Richmond Consolidated Smelter, Eureka, Nevada.
(Courtesy of Nevada Historical Society.)

scatters may or may not be primary deposits. One consists entirely of cyanide can lids (image 93); another is a mixed deposit of cupels, crucibles, slag, and domestic trash such as tin cans and glass bottles. The latter feature is unquestionably associated with assaying.

Smelting

The precious metal ores that are perhaps most difficult to process are lead, copper, or iron compounds, which require smelting in "blast" furnaces at high temperatures to separate. The smelting process involves heating crushed ore with a "flux," an added substance such as limestone that combines with impurities in the ore to form a liquid slag, which can be poured off. What remains is a "matte," a mixture of gold or silver and base metals like lead that can then be separated by further refining. Smelting was used extensively throughout the American West in the late 19th century. (Richmond L. Clow [2002:95–112] offers a history of smelting in the Black Hills region of South Dakota.) Smelters in the Eureka Mining District in central Nevada were the earliest to experiment with and develop an appropriate technology for lead-based ores (image 94).

In 1869 Major W. W. McCoy built the first effective smelter at Eureka by modifying a cupola blast furnace to increase its firing temperatures (Molinelli 1879:15). A contemporary article gives a technical description, adapted here, of the K. K. Consolidated smelter in Eureka (Molinelli 1879:29–33). After being crushed at the top of the gravity-flow mill, the ore was mixed with charcoal (and flux) and fed into the blast furnaces. Made out of sandstone blocks, the furnaces were 10 to 12 feet high. Each had a fuel hole for inserting the ore "charge," tweer (tuyere) lines for carrying air from blowers, and a sump at the bottom for collecting the melted ore. From the sump, the melted ore flowed by means of a groove or canal out into a basin placed in front of the furnace. The components of the liquid ore settled out in the basin into layers, with the heavier lead-gold-silver compounds sinking to the bottom and the lighter slag (mostly iron oxide and sand) floating on top. Slag was drawn off continuously, leaving only the crude lead-based bullion.

More documentary information about the Eureka smelters comes from a 1907 article by Walter R. Ingalls (1907:1054, 1057–1058). At the time of his description, only the Matamoras Mill furnace remained standing. The sandstone furnace had a shaft with a square cross-section and was covered by a brick-lined, sheet-iron "dust catcher." Steam and air were piped in from the bottom of the dust catcher, which was shaped like an inverted pyramid; a large hole about 18 inches in diameter in the top of the structure allowed gases to pass through while dust settled inside.

The archaeological record of the Eureka smelters is unique in two ways. First, not much is visible today at the mill sites other than large slag dumps. Second, smoke ditches are visible on the hillsides surrounding the town of Eureka. The smoke ditches once contained large pipes that carried smoke from the smelters well up the hillsides in the hope that the gases would disperse at the higher altitude.

Assaying

Assaying was a way of monitoring both mining and milling processes. Silver and gold ore assaying in the late 19th century worked as follows (Miller 1900; Rhead and Sexton 1902; Zeier 1986:64–66). The first step was to crush the ore into a powder. This powder was then mixed with a flux in a fire clay or porcelain crucible (image 95), melted in a furnace, and poured into a cast-iron button mold. After cooling, the glassy slag outer surface was chipped off, leaving a silver-lead "button." The button was cold-hammered into a cube, put into a bone-ash cupel (image 96), and heated in a muffle furnace.

Upon melting, the lead oxidized, becoming a lead oxide that was then

95. Assaying artifact: crucibles. (Photograph by author, 1983.)

96. Assaying artifact: cupels. (Photograph by author, 1983.)

97. Assay trash scatter at the Consolidated Cortez
Mill site. (Photograph by author, 1983.)

absorbed by the bone-ash, leaving free silver or gold. The same assaying
process had been used at least since the time of Agricola in the 1400s.
Miners usually built assay houses close to the mill or mine site but far
enough away so that vibrations would not be a problem. The archaeological record of an assay house site is quite distinctive, with a scatter of crucible and cupel fragments the most visible element (image 97).

The artifacts collected from an assay house site usually include crucible and cupel fragments; slag and charcoal; and nails, window glass,
and lumber fragments related to architecture. In addition, the site may
contain a concrete pad used to support the assaying scales.

3. The Social Archaeology of Mining

The archaeological record also reflects the social organization of mining. Mining households, local settlements, regional settlement-systems, and global networks were social manifestations of mining that left an imprint on the archaeological landscape of Nevada (Hardesty 1992, 1998; Knapp et al. 1998).

Mining Settlement-Systems

Settlement-systems reflect the spatial arrangement of tools, operations, and social formations as well as the coordination of work within mining-related sociotechnical systems. Such social relations are, in the words of Elizabeth Brumfiel (1992:551), "the composite outcomes of negotiation between positioned social agents pursuing their goals under both ecological and social constraints." Mining social systems can be conceptualized as a network of power relationships (Hardesty 1998:82). However, power relationships among individuals and groups based on controlled access to resources (such as capital, ore deposits, labor, and water) are situational, constantly being negotiated because of changing meanings or values of the resources. Four key power networks connect individuals into social groups: ideological, economic, military, and political (Mann 1986:1–2). Individuals and groups negotiate power relationships within these networks with methods that range from violence to ideology and politics. Mining-related social networks sometimes approximate hierarchical organizations, as in company towns, but typically are much more flexible, situational, and changing organizations that Carole Crumley (1994a:186–187) refers to as "heterarchical."

Such social networks underlay the formation of mining communities. The concept of "community" is quite expansive. It includes not only social groups that regularly engage in social interaction but also those that share a common place-space and life experiences. And it encompasses the idea of cultural identity—individuals who think of themselves as belonging to the same group. Community is a concept that has multiple scales in time and space (Canuto and Yaeger 2000; Hall and Silliman 2006). Hine (1980) has examined the concept of the western mining community from an historian's perspective, and Nash (1979) and Godoy (1985, 1990) have looked at modern mining communities from an anthropological perspective. All these studies have stressed the unique demographic and social features of mining societies. The 19th-century mining camp in the American West, for example, emerges as a place mainly inhabited by adult males with high mobility, cosmopolitan origins, and a poorly developed sense of community dominated by laissez-faire individualism (Hine 1980; Paul 2001; Young 1970). Social and demographic variability, however, is the norm. As a working model, variability in mining communities in the American West is related to ecology, technology and the workplace, ethnicity, social class, and laissez-faire individualism (Hine 1980). The archaeological record of mining sites helps reveal the variability among mining communities from a broad comparative and chronological perspective. The key problem in the archaeological study of the mining community is relating the "settlement," which is directly visible in the archaeological record, to social networks and community, which are more abstract concepts that must be understood by combining the documentary record, oral testimony, and archaeological sources.

Settlement-systems in the Cortez Mining District

The Cortez Mining District in north-central Nevada provides one example of a mining-related social network embedded within a distinctive sociotechnical system. In the fall of 1863, a party of nine prospectors led by Andrew A. Veatch organized the Cortez Mining District after the discovery of several ore veins on Mount Tenabo (Bancroft 1889:11; Cassell 1863). George Hearst was a major investor in the first mining company formed in the district, the Cortez Joint Stock Company (Bancroft 1889:12–13). By 1864, 60 or 70 men were in the district (*Reese River Reveille* 3 May 1864:1). The mining camps of Cortez Camp, St. Louis, and Shoshone Wells had been established as well by this time (Hattori et al. 1984:47), along with the Cortez Gold and Silver Mining Company (CGSMC) Mill near Cortez Camp in Mill Canyon (*Reese River Reveille* 7 May 1864:1). Simeon Wenban, a member of the original discovery party, was the mill superintendent.

Washoe pan amalgamation technology was installed in the CGSMC Mill but did not work because the Cortez ores were not free milling (Bancroft 1889:12). In 1865 workers added four reverberatory roasting furnaces to the mill technology, changing it to the Reese River process (*Reese River Reveille* 8 July 1867:1). In 1867 the mill contained 13 stamps, 4 furnaces, and 4 Varney pans (*Reese River Reveille* 3 January 1867:1). Despite several changes in technology, the mill failed and closed in 1868, along with most of the mining operations in the district (Raymond 1869:82). The Tenabo Mill and Mining Company (TMMC) purchased the mill, probably in 1869 (Whitehall 1875:47). Wenban owned the company, which was mining several claims on the Nevada Giant Ledge on the west slope of Mount Tenabo and shipping the ore to the new mill by mule train.

The discovery of an important ore body at the Garrison Mine led to the construction nearby of a new mill by the TMMC in 1886 (Bancroft 1889:16). Installed with Russell process equipment, the mill was one of the first on the mining frontier to use the new leaching technology (Bancroft 1889:20). It included Krom rolls for grinding ore, Bruckner's cylinders and an O'Hara furnace for roasting ore, and a short-line railroad (Bancroft 1889:20; *Mining and Scientific Press* 1920:803–804). A pipeline transported water for the new mill from a spring seven miles away, providing the stimulus for the formation of a new settlement named Cortez next to the mill. In 1888 the TMMC was transferred to a holding company in London under the name Cortez Mines, Ltd. (*Reese River Reveille* 5 March 1888:1). Between 1889 and 1891, the TMMC mining operation was leased to the Bewick-Moering Syndicate of London (Lincoln 1923:86). The mining operation was returned to Wenban in 1892, but the mill closed in the same year. All mining in the district would stop by 1895 (Weed 1922:1173). Wenban retained ownership but apparently moved to San Francisco, where he died in 1901 (*San Francisco Chronicle* 1901:8). Afterward, the Cortez Mining District was worked mostly by lease on a small scale until 1919 (Lincoln 1923: 86). In 1908, however, a new cyanide leaching technology capable of treating 100 tons of ore per day was installed in the TMMC Mill (Naramore and Yale 1910:220). No mining took place during this period, but old mill tailings and mine dumps were reworked.

In 1919 mining began anew with the discovery of a new ore body at the Arctic Mine, just above the old TMMC Mill. The Consolidated Cortez Silver Mines Company (CCSMC) purchased the Cortez mines in that year. In 1923 the company finished building a large cyanide leaching mill with a daily capacity of 125 tons of ore next to the Arctic Mine (Lincoln 1923:86). It refitted the mill with oil flotation technology in 1927 (Hezzelwood 1930; Vanderburg 1938). By 1928 the CCSMC operation in the Cortez

Mining District was the top silver producer in the state of Nevada, but the company crashed in 1929 when the price of silver dropped to 48.7 cents an ounce (Weight 1950:11). After the CCSMC went into receivership in 1930, the district was worked only sporadically and on a small scale. William O. Vanderburg (1938:22), for example, described a small cyanide leaching mill in Mill Canyon with a daily capacity of 20 tons of ore that was being operated by the Roberts Mining and Milling Company in the late 1930s. Open-pit mining began in the district in the 1960s, and its operators established a new heap-leaching mill in neighboring Crescent Valley in 1969. The open-pit operation has continued to the present and is currently under the management of Cortez Gold Mines.

Four mining settlements in the district served as "gravity centers" around which human residential and domestic activities clustered (Hardesty and Hattori 1982:1–23, 32; Hattori et al. 1984:47–49). Of these, the Cortez Company Camp, Saint Louis, and Shoshone Wells appeared in written accounts by 1864. The Cortez Company Camp, which was usually called "Cortez" in the 1860s and the 1870s, was established in Mill Canyon next to the Cortez Company Mill. In 1864 it had a large stone and wood mill, a stone blacksmith shop, a stone ore house, a stone machine shop, and two or three "palisade" log buildings used as boarding houses, bunkhouses, store houses, and offices (*Reese River Reveille* 7 April 1864:2, 5 May 1864:1). The full history of the camp is unknown, but it was apparently occupied well into the 20th century; the 1938 U.S. Geological Survey Cortez Quadrangle, for example, shows 14 standing buildings at the site. Another camp called "Cortez City" was planned in 1864 for construction at the mouth of Mill Canyon (*Reese River Reveille* 7 May 1864:1); however, there is no documentary or archaeological evidence to suggest it was actually constructed. Early accounts mentioned Saint Louis in association with the St. Louis Mine on the western slope of Mount Tenabo (*Reese River Reveille* 3 May 1864:1).

Shoshone Wells was the third early mining settlement in the Cortez Mining District (*Reese River Reveille* 7 April 1864:2, 30 April 1864:3). By 1864 it included six houses (*Reese River Reveille* 1864:2). Established across the valley from St. Louis, Shoshone Wells was also known as "Mugginsville" in the early years (Cassel 1863: 25, 257) and later as "Lower Cortez" (*Reese River Reveille* 10 November 1888:1). The latter name seems to have emerged shortly after 1886, when the modern settlement of Cortez grew up less than a quarter mile away around the newly constructed Tenabo Mill.

Yet another mining settlement without a name is visible in both the documentary and archaeological records of the Cortez Mining District. At the Garrison Mine is a nucleated cluster of house sites arranged upon a series of terraces. The small settlement has not been documented archaeologically, but preliminary field observations suggest a Chinese occupation. In the federal population census schedules for 1900 and 1910, the Cortez district was divided into two precincts, separated by the county line between Eureka and Lander counties. The Eureka County portion of the district was known as the Garrison Mine Precinct and included a cosmopolitan population of Chinese, Italian, Canadian, British, and other European immigrants as well as American-born workers. Virtually all these settlers were identified as "mine laborers." The Cortez Precinct in Lander County, by contrast, also held a cosmopolitan population but one that was mostly identified as "mill laborers," presumably employees of the Tenabo Mill.

Settlement-Systems in the Bullfrog Mining District

Another settlement-system developed in the Bullfrog Mining District in southern Nevada (Hardesty 1987b). Mining activities began with the first discovery of ore deposits on August 1904 by Frank "Shorty" Harris at what later became known as the Original Bullfrog Mine (Rhyolite Herald, Special Pictorial Edition, 1909:4). The district was organized officially on 30 August 1904 (Lingenfelter 1986:209). In early 1905 strikes were made at the Denver claim on Bonanza Mountain, the National Bank claim on Ladd Mountain, and the Montgomery-Shoshone claim between Montgomery and Rainbow Mountain (Ransome et al. 1910:12; Myrick 1963:456; Lingenfelter 1986:208). Other significant mines soon followed, including the Gold Bar about four miles north of the Original Bullfrog and the Mayflower Mine in the far northern or "Pioneer" section of the district (Ransome et al. 1910:104–125). After the original strike, mining activity in the district proceeded at a rather slow pace, in large part because of a lack of adequate transportation. By the spring of 1906, for example, only the Original Bullfrog mine, the Denver mine on Bonanza Mountain, and the Montgomery-Shoshone Mine had shipped ore (Weight and Weight 1970:1, photo caption; Lingenfelter 1986:212). Furthermore, the Montgomery-Shoshone Mine, the most promising ore body in the district, was in the midst of litigation (Ransome et al. 1910:12). The dispute soon was settled, however, and the mine was sold in February 1906 to Pittsburgh

98. Rhyolite, Nevada, in 1905. (Courtesy of Nevada Historical Society.)

steel magnate Charles Schwab, who then organized the Montgomery-Shoshone Consolidated Mining Company (Lingenfelter 1986:215). The mine and the district developed at a rapid pace thereafter.

Several mining camps grew up around these mines. The first was the Original Bullfrog, a tent camp that expanded next to the original Bullfrog claim, followed rapidly by Amargosa City about one-half mile away (Ransome et al. 1910:12; Weight and Weight 1970:7–8; Lingenfelter 1986:209). In addition, Gold Center and Beatty, both of which had been established in 1904 as ranching settlements in the upper Amargosa valley, emerged as supply centers for the new mines (Weight and Weight 1970:13–14; Lingenfelter 1986:209). But the movement of mining activity eastward from the Original Bullfrog into the Ladd Mountain and Bonanza Mountain area by early 1905 caused a population shift. The town of Bonanza was established just south of Ladd Mountain. In February 1905 the town of Rhyolite was laid out, and it rapidly became the largest camp in the district (image 98).

The entire town of Bonanza then moved to Rhyolite. In mid-March 1905 the *Tonopah Sun* reported that 40 people lived in Bullfrog, 160 in Amargosa City, 200 in Rhyolite, and 300 in Beatty, and that 20 tents remained in Gold Center (Weight and Weight 1970:7). In the same month, the old Bonanza townsite was incorporated into yet another new town also called Bullfrog, to which the entire population of Amargosa City moved (Ransome et al. 1910:12; Weight and Weight 1970:7–8; Lingenfelter

1986:209). By mid-1905, then, the nuclei of the Bullfrog Mining District settlement pattern included Rhyolite, Bullfrog, Beatty, and Gold Center (Myrick 1963:466–67). The year 1906, however, brought about several changes, culminating in the complete dominance of Rhyolite as the population center. Bullfrog had lost virtually all its population to Rhyolite by late spring 1906, and Gold Center was abandoned later in the same year. The town of Transvaal, which emerged in the spring of 1906 and reached a population of 700, died about the same time (Lingenfelter 1986:229–230). Of the original population nuclei, Beatty was the only one that remained other than Rhyolite. In addition, there were several small settlements, including those at the Gold Bar, Homestake, and Mayflower mines. The written accounts, however, are scanty, and most of the information about the camps must come from the archaeological record.

In late 1906 the Las Vegas and Tonopah Railroad reached the district, making possible effective ore transport to Salt Lake City and then to Goldfield. Within a few months, two other railroads had been completed. The Bullfrog Goldfield was finished in mid-1907, and the Tonopah and Tidewater by late 1907 (Ransome et al. 1910:13; Myrick 1963). During the next two years, the Bullfrog district mines reached peak production. The Montgomery-Shoshone Mine built the largest mill in the district in 1907. Several other mills also were erected during this period, including the 25–stamp Homestake-King Mill at Gold Bar (Hardesty 1986b) and a 15–stamp mill at the Mayflower Mine (Legislature of the State of Nevada, Report of the State Inspector of Mines, *Appendix to the Journals of the State Senate and Assembly, 25th Session* 1911[2]:54–57). The Tramps Consolidated Mining Company worked several mines on Bonanza Mountain, including the Denver, the Tramp, the Eclipse, and the Hobo (Ransome et al. 1910:90–91). By 1910 the Eclipse Development Company was working these properties and had also started a mill (Legislature of the State of Nevada, Report of the State Inspector of Mines, *Appendix to the Journals of the State Senate and Assembly, 25th Session* 1911[2]:54–57). In 1907 the Pioneer Mine, just across from the Mayflower in the northern section, was established. The Bi-Metallic Mine at Pioneer struck rich ore in November 1908, and by February 1909 there were 2,500 people in the associated town of Pioneer, along with nearly 300 buildings and 2 newspapers (Myrick 1963:514–515; Lingenfelter 1986:230–231). Moreover, a five-stamp mill was started at the Mayflower in March 1909 and was enlarged to 15 stamps (Lingenfelter 1986:231–233). A power line built by the Nevada-

California Power Company supplied electricity to the district until 1916. And pipelines were constructed to transport water from springs several miles away to the mines and the towns of Rhyolite and Bullfrog. The population of the district probably peaked during this period, although few specific data could be found. Richard E. Lingenfelter (1986:239) estimates the population of Rhyolite at this time to be 4,000, to which can be added the boomtown of Pioneer, which had 2,500 people. There is also data for several smaller camps in the district, including Gold Bar, which had a population of 100 to 150 people (Hardesty 1987a).

The end of the Bullfrog Mining District's most prosperous period was signaled by the *Engineering and Mining Journal*'s comment on 8 January 1910 that the district was "generally inactive" during 1909 (p. 102). By the summer of 1909 the Pioneer boom had died in a series of litigations (Lingenfelter 1986:232–233; Legislature of the State of Nevada, Report of the State Inspector of Mines, *Appendix to the Journals of the State Senate and Assembly, 25th Session,* 1911[2]:54–57). In December 1909 the Mayflower Mill was shut down (Lingenfelter 1986:233). The Montgomery-Shoshone Mill, which treated 6,000 tons per month for the first six months of 1909, greatly reduced production during the second six months. By the end of March 1911, both the mine and the mill had closed (*Engineering and Mining Journal* 1911:683). At Gold Bar, the Homestake-King mine and mill closed on 19 April 1909 (Latschar 1981:148). The impact on the Bullfrog mining towns was devastating. In the 1910 federal census, the population of Rhyolite had dropped to about 500. (Lingenfelter 1986:239 gives a population of 611, but that includes a number of people living outside the town in Indian Springs, Mud Springs, and the Original Bullfrog.) And a note on a fire insurance map prepared for Rhyolite by the Sanborn Map Company ascribes a population of 900 to the town a short time earlier (Nevada Historical Society, Nevada in Maps Collection). The last train left Rhyolite in July 1913, and the post office closed in November of the same year (Lingenfelter 1986:241). And in 1916 the Nevada-California Power Company turned off power (Lingenfelter 1986:241).

During the next decade, mining activity in the Bullfrog Mining District was limited to two places: the northern or Pioneer section and Bonanza Mountain. The Tramp Mine on Bonanza Mountain operated a mill in 1912 and, after reorganization as the Sunset Mining Company, continued to do so from 1914 to 1916 (Lincoln 1923:162–163; Kral 1951:28–40). Apparently, the Tramp Mine was worked at least until 1918 (Legislature of the State of Nevada, Report of the State Inspector of Mines, *Appendix to the Journals of the State Senate and Assembly, 29th Session* 1919[1]:60). During this period, active mines in the Pioneer section included the Mayflower, which by 1911 was again operating its 15–stamp amalgamation mill, and the Pioneer, which built a 10–stamp mill in 1913 and ran it until 1917 (Lincoln 1923:162–163). The Mayflower Mill was enlarged in 1918–1919 by the addition of a ball mill and some tables (Kral 1951:37–39).

During the 1920s and 1930s, the district was mostly deserted, with the exception of the Mayflower and the Pioneer mines (Kral 1951:37–39; Legislature of the State of Nevada, Report of the State Inspector of Mines, *Appendix to the Journals of the State Senate and Assembly,* 30th through 37th sessions, 1921–1935). Mining was rejuvenated in the late 1930s. Work at the Original Bullfrog Mine, now known as the "Burm Ball Mine," and at the Montgomery-Shoshone Mine began again in 1938 (Legislature of the State of Nevada, Report of the State Inspector of Mines, *Appendix to the Journals of the State Senate and Assembly, 39th Session* 1939[1]:34). Ore from the Burm Ball was treated at a new 25–ton amalgamation, concentration, and cyanidation mill in Beatty (Kral 1951:36). The Senator Stewart Mine on Ladd Mountain opened in 1939 or 1940 (Legislature of the State of Nevada, Report of the State Inspector of Mines, *Appendix to the Journals of the State Senate and Assembly,* 40th Session 1941[1]:54; Ritchie 1940:15–16). Development work at the Tramp Mine, the Homestake Mine, and the Pioneer Mine recommenced in the late 1930s and early 1940s (Ritchie 1940:15–16; Legislature of the State of Nevada, Report of the State Inspector of Mines, *Appendix to the Journals of the State Senate and Assembly,* 41st Session 1943[1]:96). In addition, the old mill tailings at the Mayflower were reworked in 1938–1940 by the addition of leaching tanks (Kral 1951:37–39). And in 1938 workers constructed a 100–ton custom flotation mill at Beatty on the Amargosa River (Kral 1951:40).

Mining was suspended again during the Second World War. After the war, a few of the mines in the Bullfrog district once again resumed activity. During his visit to the district, Victor E. Kral (1951) recorded work at the Pioneer and the Senator Stewart, and post-1950s work is evident in the archaeological record at the Montgomery-Shoshone, the Senator Stewart, and the Mayflower mines, among others. Open-pit mining in the district began in 1989 near the town of Rhyolite, and these miners established a new heap leaching facility. The mining operation continued until 1998 and is currently inactive.

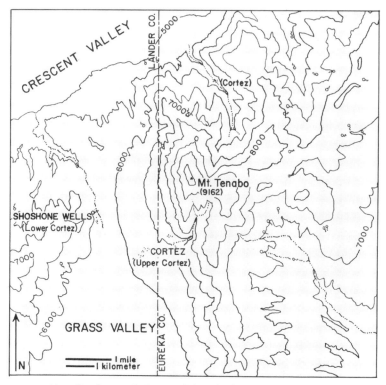

99. Map of settlements in Cortez Mining District. (Drawn by author, 1983.)

Mining Settlements

Local settlements form the key nodes of mining-related settlement-systems, social networks, communities, and sociotechnical systems. They range from small social groups organized around mines or mills to large urban centers and company towns with a wide range of activities and a diverse social structure.

Shoshone Wells

One of the first mining camps established in the district, Shoshone Wells (image 99) appears in the original mining-claim record book for the district as "Shoshone Wells or Mugginsville" in 1863 (Cassel 1863:25, 257).

In 1864 a newspaper said the camp had 6 houses (*Reese River Reveille* 7 April 1864:2). Shoshone Wells grew up around a well across the valley from the Nevada Giant ore body on Mount Tenabo. The water-bearing locality seems to have been used earlier by Western Shoshones who

100. Town of Cortez, Nevada, in early 20th century.
(Courtesy of Nevada Historical Society.)

lived historically in Grass Valley, thus accounting for the name. Simeon
Wenban, the owner of the largest mining company in the district, built
a large house at the settlement, probably in 1884. Shoshone Wells was
the largest camp in the Cortez district before the construction of the new
Tenabo Mill and Mining Company Mill in 1886 (Hardesty and Hattori
1982, 1984). The settlement was ethnically diverse, including what appear
archaeologically to be geographically distinct Chinese, Italian, Anglo-
European, and possibly Mexican "neighborhoods" (Hardesty and Hattori
1982, 1984). After 1886 the old settlement was rapidly eclipsed by "Upper
Cortez," which grew up around the new Tenabo Mill as the commercial
center of the Cortez Mining District (image 100).

Shoshone Wells, however, continued to be occupied by the Chinese
community until 1902, along with several Italian immigrants who stayed
a few years longer.

Documentary records for Shoshone Wells and the Cortez Mining District in general are especially difficult to evaluate. Both the 1880 and 1890
federal population schedules are missing, and the district has a complex
legal history that makes written accounts hard to locate. The district is
situated exactly on the border between what is now Lander and Eureka
counties. Eureka County was not created until 1873, however. For this
reason, the 1870 federal population schedules for the Cortez district are
found under Lander County, as are state and county documents such as

tax assessment rolls and the state mineralogist reports. After 1873 the Cortez records are split between the two counties. The federal population census schedules for 1900 and 1910, for example, group the Cortez households into two precincts, each of which is in a different county: the Cortez Precinct in Lander County and the Garrison Precinct in Eureka County. Unfortunately, other documents are not classified the same way. Thus, the biennial reports of the state mineralogist (before 1879) and the surveyor general (after 1879) list the Cortez Mining District only under Eureka. County tax records for the Cortez district, however, are found only under Lander County. The report of the surveyor general of the state of Nevada for 1888 and 1889 explains part of the problem (Legislature of the State of Nevada, *Appendix to the Journals of the Senate and Assembly* 1891:106–110). After the construction of the Tenabo (TMMC) Mill in 1886, Eureka County sued Lander County to recover the taxes that Simeon Wenban had been paying to Lander County. On 22 September 1890, the Nevada Supreme Court reversed a lower court ruling and gave the mill to Lander County.

Another problem with written accounts of the Cortez Mining District is that they do not specifically identify the settlement of Shoshone Wells but lump it in with other settlements. For example, the federal population schedules do not separate households from Upper Cortez and Lower Cortez (Shoshone Wells). The 1900 census listed 11 Chinese households, 6 Italian households, 2 Mexican households, 2 Black households, 3 Anglo-American households, 1 Canadian household, and 2 British households. However, it is unclear whether these were located in Upper or Lower Cortez. In addition, several people lived in a boarding house that is known to have been at Upper Cortez. The 1910 census listed no Chinese but Italian, Portuguese, Black, and Anglo-American households in the Cortez Precinct.

Settlement Layout

The existing archaeological site of Shoshone Wells consists of 50 house sites along with several trash scatters, wells, roads, and unidentified rock alignments (image 101).

Most of the house sites are arranged into five geographical clusters with distinctive archaeological features, suggesting that the settlement of Shoshone Wells had a "neighborhood" structure. In each of the neighborhoods lived a group of people who participated in a distinctive world

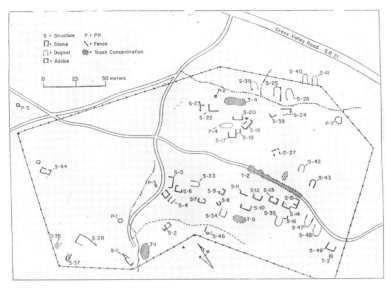

101. Map of Shoshone Wells site. (Hardesty and Hattori 1984:35.)

system or "interaction sphere." The neighborhoods thus formed the so-cial links between the households, local settlements, settlement-systems, and the world systems.

The "road cluster," the first neighborhood, is a linear scatter of 22 adobe, dugout, and wooden-frame house sites arranged along a road running parallel to a deep ravine on the valley floor. The artifact assemblages as-sociated with the house sites suggest two social groups: an Anglo-Euro-pean or Anglo-American population and an ethnic Chinese population. Between the ravine and the road is a nucleated group of seven mostly adobe houses that form the "bottomland cluster." The houses are asso-ciated with the archaeological record of another Chinese population, probably dating between 1872 and 1910. The "ravine cluster" is a linear scatter of eight mostly dugout houses built along and in the stream chan-nel of the valley bottom. Although the houses have not been excavated and could not be associated definitively with any ethnic group, there is some archaeological evidence of a Chinese occupation. The "hillside clus-ter" is a dispersed group of four stone houses on the hillside above the other house clusters; it appears to have been occupied by Italian wood-cutters mentioned in written documents. The archaeological record—especially Italian bitters bottles and outdoor earth ovens found with two of the houses—also indicates an Italian presence. Finally, the "Wenban cluster" encircles Simeon Wenban's house site (Structure 29). It includes four house sites, a well, and a trash dump. The archaeological record of these features suggests not only a high-social-status household but also participation in a "Victorian" interaction sphere with ties to the American and European urban middle class.

Both the documentary and the archaeological records suggest that a large group of immigrant Chinese miners lived at Shoshone Wells in the 1870s and 1880s. The settlement was one of at least three that have been identified in the Cortez Mining District, the others being at the Garrison Mine and at Upper Cortez. Shoshone Wells was apparently the earliest, but the other two settlements replaced it after the construction of the Tenabo Mill in 1886. The Chinese residents of Shoshone Wells lived in adobe, dugout, and wooden-frame houses spread out in two adjacent "neighborhoods." One of the neighborhoods was clustered around what may have been a "joss house" (temple); the other was arranged linearly along a main road in the settlement, perhaps in houses constructed earlier by Cornish miners. As reflected in the Shoshone Wells archaeological record, the material culture of immigrant Chinese miners on the rural Nevada mining frontier was dominated by imported Chinese ceramics, as elsewhere, but also included a substantial number of glass bottles and other items of Western origin.

Construction Variability

Settlers used several construction methods to build the houses at Shoshone Wells (table 1).

Excavations revealed adobe houses, dugouts, dry-set stone houses, and wooden-frame houses.

1. Stone Buildings. At Shoshone Wells, dry-set stone was used to build 10 houses, most of which are associated with the hillside "neighborhood." The stone houses were constructed with a variety of techniques, but especially with undressed angular cobbles of native volcanic rock caulked with small stones and mud. While most of the stone houses have only one room, multiple-room buildings with common walls are present, including two that have integrated stone fireplaces. No roofs remain, but it is likely that most were gabled with a central beam and wooden shingles. Window openings were small and high on the wall, and the few re-

Table 1. Shoshone Wells house-site classification

Structure	Architecture	Cultural Affiliation	Date
1	Stone	Euroamerican/Italian	Early 20th century
2	Stone	Italian	Late 19th century
3	Wood frame	Euroamerican	Early 20th century
4	Wood frame	Euroamerican	Late 19th century
5	Wood frame	Euroamerican	Late 19th/early 20th century
6	Wood frame	Euroamerican	Late 19th/early 20th century
7	Stone dugout	Euroamerican	Unknown
8	Rock chimney	Euroamerican-Chinese?	Late 19th century
9	Adobe	Unknown	Late 19th century
10	Stone	Chinese	Unknown
11	Wood frame?	Chinese?	Unknown
12	Stone	Euroamerican?	Unknown
13	Adobe	Chinese	1890–1910
14	Wood frame	Chinese	1880–1910
15	Rock annex	Chinese	Unknown
16	Stone (small)		
17	Stone	Chinese?	Unknown
18	Adobe (?)	Chinese	1890–1910
19	Stone	Chinese?	Unknown
20	Adobe (?)	Chinese	1870–1890
21	Unknown	Unknown	Unknown
22	Wood frame	Chinese	1895–1905
23	Wood frame	Chinese?	Unknown
24	Dugout	Chinese?	1870–1890
25	Dugout	Chinese?	Late 19th century
26	Dugout	Chinese?	Late 19th century
27	Wood frame	Chinese?	Early 20th century
28	Terrace	Euroamerican	Unknown
29	Wood frame	Euroamerican (Wenban)	1880s-1890s
30	Rock wall	Unknown	Unknown
31	Stone	Euroamerican	Unknown
32	Stone/frame	Euroamerican	Unknown
33	Dugout	Euroamerican	Late 19th century
34	Dugout	Unknown	Unknown
35	Dugout	Chinese	Unknown
36	Walk-in well	Unknown	Unknown
37	Walk-in well	Euroamerican	Unknown
38	Wood frame	Unknown	Unknown
39	Dugout	Chinese?	Unknown
40	Dugout	Chinese	Unknown
41	Dugout	Unknown	Unknown
42	Dugout	Chinese	Late 19th/early 20th century

(continued)

Table 1. Shoshone Wells house-site classification (*continued*)

Structure	Architecture	Cultural Affiliation	Date
43	Adobe	Chinese	1894–1915
44	Stone	Euroamerican	20th century
45	Dugout	Euroamerican	Unknown
46	Dugout/rock fireplace	Euroamerican & Chinese	Unknown
47	Dugout	Chinese	Late 19th century
48	Dugout	Euroamerican	Late 19th century
49	Dugout/stone lined	Euroamerican & Chinese	Early 20th century
P4	Dugout	Chinese	Unknown

maining doorsills were wooden, with one clay-brick exception. Dry-set stone buildings are a common feature of mining camps on the Nevada mining frontier, probably because of the readily available volcanic rock, the lack of wood, the difficulty of moving stone buildings, and their good preservation. Adobe, dugouts, and dry-set stone methods, for example, appear to have been much more common than wooden-frame construction in the mid-19th century, probably a reflection of the poor development of the lumber industry on the frontier. But the actual percentage of stone buildings varies tremendously, in part because of unique local conditions as well as the date of the camp. By the turn of the century, wooden-frame buildings were used almost exclusively.

2. Adobe. Five buildings at Shoshone Wells were constructed out of adobe blocks, and all are in the ravine and the road clusters. The adobe structures are badly decomposed, but some have remnants of plaster and whitewash on the interior walls. The buildings typically used two noninterlocking wythes of adobe bricks laid upon a low rock foundation. The bricks were usually about 12 inches long, 6 inches wide, and 4 inches thick. Excavations revealed both single-room and multiple-room adobe houses. Builders used adobe bricks as early as 1864 in the nearby Reese River Mining District, relying on "numerous" adobe brickyards (*Reese River Reveille* 1 May 1864:1). The prevalence of adobe-brick construction in the 1860s in Nevada is further suggested by its use at Fort Churchill and some Pony Express stations. And although there is a tendency to associate adobe-brick houses with ethnic Mexicans, there is little evidence to support such a conclusion on the mining frontier. Indeed, people who did not have Spanish surnames occupied the early adobe-brick houses in the Reese River District (*Reese River Reveille* 1 May 1864:1). Furthermore, the adobe-brick houses at Shoshone Wells are most often associated with ethnic Chinese artifact assemblages, although the 1900 census records for the Cortez Mining District lists people with Mexican origins. Adobe-brick construction on the Nevada mining frontier, therefore, is probably best interpreted as a mid-19th-century time marker.

3. **Dugouts.** The most common house construction method at Shoshone Wells was the dugout, with 17 examples. Most of the dugouts are archaeologically visible as trenches dug into a hill slope, though a few were dug into level ground. The largest group of dugouts is associated with the ravine house cluster, including one in the stream channel. Several, however, are included in the road cluster. Dugout houses at Shoshone Wells are true pit houses; they apparently had little or no wall exposed above the ground, but the open end was enclosed by a wooden or stone wall and door. The roof was flat, covered with branches, dirt, flattened tin cans, corrugated metal sheets, and almost anything else that could be used for the purpose.

4. **Wooden-frame houses.** Wooden-frame house construction could not be directly observed at Shoshone Wells because no wooden-frame houses are standing today. Twelve examples were identified based on remains at the house site. Most commonly, the house site is visible as a leveled platform or terrace, on which sometimes stands a low rock foundation. Several wooden-frame buildings that are still standing at the Cortez townsite about a mile away may have been moved from Shoshone Wells. Relocation and lumber scavenging are probably the most common post-occupational processes responsible for the archaeological invisibility of wooden-frame house sites on the Nevada mining frontier.

Gold Bar

Gold Bar (image 102) has a documentary and archaeological record that is typical of small mining settlements from the early 20th century.

The following reconstruction of Gold Bar depends on both documentary and archaeological sources of information (Latschar 1981:93–165; Hardesty 1986b, 1987a). The settlement lasted only a short time, from the fall of 1905 until the spring of 1909. And only about 100 people lived in the camp. Documentary information about the camp is mostly limited to a few newspaper accounts in the *Rhyolite Herald*, the *Rhyolite Daily Bul-*

102. The Gold Bar Camp in 1908. (Courtesy of Nevada Historical Society.)

letin, and the *Bullfrog Miner* as well as several contemporary photographs. Gold Bar was born, lived, and died between the federal censuses of 1900 and 1910, making its population largely invisible in documentary history. The archaeological record of the camp includes trash dumps, privies, and about 30 house sites (image 103).

Bottle hunters dug most of the privies, and there are no standing buildings. Yet what survives gives a good archaeological profile of a very thin "time slice" of life on the early-20th-century Nevada mining frontier.

In the fall of 1905 the camp at Gold Bar had a bunkhouse housing 14 miners, a boarding house, and the beginnings of a bungalow for the superintendent (*Rhyolite Herald* 1905:1). Within a few months, a new boarding house for 60 miners was under construction. The Homestake Consolidated Mining Company began the construction of a new bunkhouse for its miners in late 1905; the building was presumably at the Gold Bar campsite, but this could not be confirmed. A saloon was established about the same time "near the mine," and this may have also been at the Gold Bar campsite. In February 1907 the newly formed Homestake-King Consolidated Mining and Milling Company began constructing another bunk house and a boarding house, again presumably at the Gold Bar campsite. In late 1907 it built yet another bunk house to hold an additional 15 men who had been hired to work on the Homestake-King Mill.

The size of the settlement can only be estimated. By the end of July 1906, the Gold Bar Mine employed 25 men. By February 1907 the Homestake Company employed 21 men, and it would add another 15 men in late

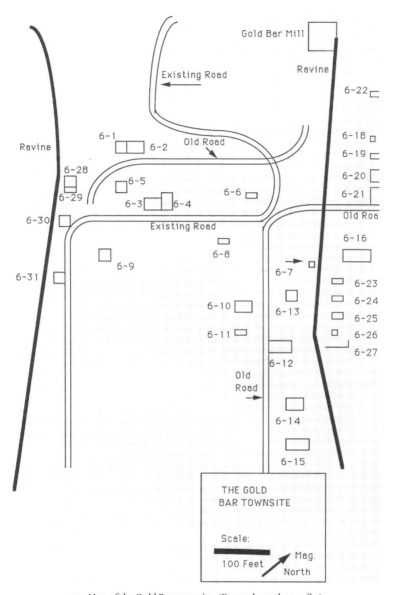

103. Map of the Gold Bar townsite. (Drawn by author, 1987.)

1907. The same company had a work force of 63 men by the end of April 1908. In the fall of 1908 it was reported that 18 school-age children lived at the camp (Latschar 1981:145). And, finally, when the Homestake-King Mill closed on 19 April 1909, reportedly 30 miners and millmen prepared to move on (Latschar 1981:148). All of this suggests that the settlement may have had a maximum population of around 100 in early 1908.

Settlement Layout

The Gold Bar settlement is separated into two geographical clusters. On the southwestern edge of the site, around the road to the Gold Bar Mine, is the "Gold Bar camp." At the opposite, northeastern edge of the site is the "Homestake camp," a larger cluster of house sites formed around the roads to the Homestake Mine and Mill. Chronologically, the two camps have somewhat different histories. The Gold Bar camp most likely pre-dated the Homestake one by a very short period of time; a November 1905 photograph, for example, shows several tents erected in the area of Gold Bar camp but nothing in the area of the Homestake camp (image 104).

By June 1906, however, both tents and signs of wooden-frame buildings had appeared at the Homestake camp site (image 105).

Photographs show clearly that by 1908 the Gold Bar camp had shrunk to a small cluster of wooden-frame buildings but that the Homestake camp has grown much larger (image 106).

Certainly, the construction of the Gold Bar Mill in early 1908 just above the Homestake camp and the completion in June 1908 of the Homestake-King Mill further to the northeast did much to stimulate settlement growth in this area. At the same time, the four-year life of the settlement renders the archaeological record insensitive to the slight time differences between the two camps. Time variability over a few months could not be detected in the artifact assemblages.

The Gold Bar Artifact Assemblage

From an archaeological perspective, the Gold Bar settlement is rare because of its short period of occupation from 1905 to 1909. The artifact assemblage, therefore, is potentially valuable as a way of cross-dating house sites for which no documentary record exists. Glass bottles, tin cans, and nails are used as time indicators for three reasons: (1) their abundance at mining camps, (2) the rapid technological changes that took place in each of the industries during this time, and (3) the relative abundance of documentary information on each of the three industries.

104. The Gold Bar Camp in 1905. (Courtesy of Nevada Historical Society.)

105. The Gold Bar Camp in 1906. (Courtesy of Nevada Historical Society.)

106. The Gold Bar Camp in 1908. (Courtesy of Nevada Historical Society.)

Technological changes in the glass bottle industry in the late 19th and early 20th centuries have been discussed in detail by a number of researchers (Hunt 1959; Lorrain 1968; Jones 1971; Toulouse 1971; Wilson 1981; Miller and Sullivan 1984; Jones and Sullivan 1989). The period saw the emergence of mass production technology using semiautomatic and automatic bottle-blowing machines. George Miller and Catherine Sullivan (1984:88–89) estimate that by 1917, between 90 and 95% of all glass bottles and jars in the United States were made in this manner. Other significant changes during this time included the introduction of the crown top, first patented in 1892, and, from 1880 to 1917, bleaching glass with manganese oxide, which changes the bottle into an amethyst or "purple" color when it is exposed to sunlight. All these changes are visible on the bottles, making it possible to use well-dated archaeological sites to study the rate of technological diffusion into households on the mining frontier.

The Gold Bar camps were occupied for less than a four-year period between 1905 and 1909, a critical time for bottle glass technology. The Owens automatic bottle machine was patented in 1903. By 1909 46 of these machines were blowing glass bottles, and the number jumped to 103 by 1911 (Miller and Sullivan 1984:85–86). By 1917 50% of all the glass containers in the United States were being blown on 200 Owens machines. Semiautomatic machines blew most of the rest, with only 5 to 10% being handblown in molds. How rapidly the new technology was reaching the consumer is suggested by the Gold Bar data. Of the 50 bottles that were identified by finish technology, 70% were handblown and 30% machine-blown.

The Gold Bar data also provides a "time-slice" profile of glass bottle manufacturers. Nine makers' marks on 62 bottle bases could be identified using the classic reference work by Julian Toulouse (1971). The most common was the "A.B.Co." mark used by the American Bottle Company of Chicago, Illinois, between 1905 and 1916 (Toulouse 1971:30). It occurred 32 times, or 52% of the total. . The next most common was the "AB" mark used by Adolphus Busch of Belleville, Illinois, between 1904 and 1907 (Toulouse 1971:26), with 13 occurrences at 21% of the total. Two other marks each composed between 5 and 10% of the total: the "M.B. & G. Co." mark used by the Massillon Bottle and Glass Company of Massillon, Ohio, between 1900 and 1904 (Toulouse 1971:348), and the "R & Co." mark used

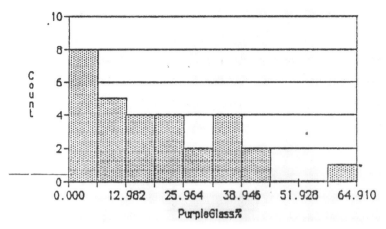

Fig. 4. Histogram of "purple" bottle glass assemblages at Gold Bar.

on whiskey bottles by Roth and Company of San Francisco between 1879 and 1888 (Toulouse 1971:438). The rest of the maker's marks appear relatively infrequently. Included are the "W.F. & S. Co." mark used by William Frantzen and Son of Milwaukee between 1900 and 1920 (Toulouse 1971:536); the "P.C.G.W." mark used by the Pacific Coast Glass Works of San Francisco between 1902 and 1924 (Toulouse 1971:416); the "O.B.C." mark used by the Ohio Bottle Company of Newark, Ohio, during its short 11–month life span in 1904 and 1905 (Toulouse 1971:399); the "M.B. Co." mark used by the Muncie Glass Company of Muncie, Indiana, between 1895 and 1910 (Toulouse 1971: 346); and the "I.G.Co." mark used by the Illinois Glass Company of Alton, Illinois, between 1880 and 1900 (Toulouse 1971: 264).

One of the time-honored "index fossils" of turn-of-the-century archaeological sites is amethyst-colored or "purple" glass (Hunt 1959). The documentary history of the bottle glass industry shows without question that manganese oxide, which changes glass color to amethyst upon exposure to sunlight, was used to bleach glass between 1880 and 1917. It is worth considering, however, whether the percentage of "purple glass" in archaeological assemblages changes chronologically during this period. If this is the case, it might be possible to date the assemblage simply by calculating the percentage. The 30 house-site features at the Gold Bar camp sites make it possible to test this theory; all the sites are known to have been occupied at about the same period of time—within the four-year period from 1905 to 1909. Figure 4 is a histogram showing the dis-

Table 2. Statistical description of Gold Bar "purple" bottle glass

Data File: Goldbar

Variable: Purple Glass %	Observations: 30
Minimum: 0.00000	Maximum: 64.90000
Range: 64.90000	Median: 15.90000
Mean: 19.12667	Standard Error: 2.78255
Variance: 232.277	Standard Deviation: 15.241
Coefficient of Variation: 79.683	Kurtosis: 1.14993
Skewness: 1.00441	

tribution of purple glass percentages in the 30 assemblages; table 2 is a statistical description of the population.

There is clearly extreme variability from one assemblage to another, suggesting that it is unlikely that quantifying purple-glass percentages will help in dating. The table, however, does suggest that the percentage of purple glass may be useful in identifying household activities because of the correlation between bottle color and bottle contents. Most of the bottles in early-20th-century mining camps contained beer, whiskey, or wine, few of which were bleached colorless and were therefore not susceptible to "purpling." Colorless glass containers were used more often as wide-mouthed fruit and vegetable jars and to hold medicines and other items for "family" consumption. For this reason, varying percentages of purple glass may reflect functional differences in the kind of activities taking place at the house site, not the date of occupation.

THE TIN CAN ASSEMBLAGE

The second abundant artifact category at early-20th-century mining camps is tin cans. Much like glass bottles, tin can technology experienced a rapid change in the late 19th and early 20th centuries (Busch 1981; Rock 1984). Until the late 19th century, virtually all tin cans were made with a "hole-in-cap" and soldered-seam technology. In 1888 Max Ams invented a "locking" double-seam for cans. The locking seam was first put into production in 1897 but was not that common until the early part of the 20th century (Busch 1981:102). By the turn of the century, evaporated milk cans were using locking side-seams with a "match-stick" filler hole to replace the hole-in-cap can. And in 1904 the Sanitary Can Company was organized to manufacture by machine an airtight can that used all locking seams and no solder. Sanitary cans rapidly replaced the earlier can technologies.

Table 3. Tin can assemblage from Gold Bar townsite

Type	Count
I. Milk cans (stamped ends with vent hole, crimped side seams)	
1. 3″ diameter and 4″ tall	63
II. Vegetable/fruit cans	
1. Stamped ends with hole and cap, crimped side seams	
a. 3.5″ diameter and 5″ tall	11
b. 3″ diameter and 4.5″ tall	26
c. 4″ diameter and 4.75″ tall	17
d. 2.5″ diameter and 4″ tall	1
2. Stamped bottom, crimped top, lapped/soldered side seam	
a. 3″ diameter and 4.5″ tall	1
III. Meat Cans	
1. Stamped ends with vent hole, lapped side seam	
a. 4″ diameter and 2.5″ tall	1
IV. Sanitary Cans	
1. 3″ diameter and 4.5″ tall	39
Total	158

Small milk cans and "personal"-sized fruit and vegetable cans, mostly distributed in dumps next to the boarding houses, dominate the Gold Bar can assemblage (table 3).

In contrast to dumps at the Reward Mine in Arizona (Teague 1980) and some northern California logging and mining camps (Rock 1984:106), Gold Bar trash dumps do not contain many large Number 10 tin cans. The technology used to manufacture the Gold Bar cans is varied. Fruit and vegetable cans with stamped ends, locked side-seams, and a hole-in-cap filler hole make up about 34% of the total. And milk cans with stamped ends, locked side-seams, and "matchstick" or "vent" holes make up another 40%. Sanitary cans compose about 25% of the total. The remaining one percent of the cans includes miscellaneous technologies. The assemblage suggests that the 1905–1909 period was a technological transition for the canning industry supplying the Gold Bar mines, which was most likely located in California. James Rock's observations that by 1910 California canners had begun using the sanitary can and that it dominated the industry by 1911 support such an interpretation (1984:106).

NAILS

Finally, nail technology changed during this period as wire nails replaced cut nails (Nelson 1968, Adams 2002). Late-19th-century sites, however, usually contain a combination of cut and wire nails in varying percentages. Exactly when wire nails completely replaced cut nails at the local level on the western mining frontier is unknown. The nail assemblage from Gold Bar adds important information: all the nails from this 1905–1909 site are wire.

The Archaeology of Mining Households

Most mining households were coresidential in the sense that the members all lived under the same roof. Documentary accounts suggest that the most common coresidential households consisted of large bunkhouse or boarding groups, families, and small single-sex groups. The 1900 federal population census for the Cortez Precinct in the Cortez Mining District, for example, enumerated 28 households. Of these, nine are nuclear-family households; three are extended-family households; one is a single-parent household; two are family with boarder households; four are all-male boarding houses, including a "hotel" with 19 residents; six are single-male households; two are single-female households; and one is an all-female partner household. The archaeological image of coresidential households comes mostly from the reconstruction of "house-site groups." Morphological patterns of such groups involve size, age, and sex, as illustrated by the Original Bullfrog camp discussed previously. The activities of house-site groups can also be reconstructed from the associated features and artifact assemblages.

In some cases, the coresidential household in mining camps also includes the same people who distribute and consume wages, food, and other materials. That is especially true of family households. But the two "activity spheres" of coresidence and distribution-consumption do not always include the same group of people, nor do the two necessarily share the same geographical location. The Chinese "sojourner household," for example, is a wage-pooling and distribution network that crosscuts the coresidential household and extends across two continents. And the all-male boarding house may actually include two separate buildings—one used as a bunkhouse for sleeping and the second a dining hall where food is consumed. This separation of activities may be visible only in the archaeological record, in which the two localities would have quite different archaeological assemblages. In fact, this distinction seems to have been true for the Gold Bar Mine in Death Valley National Park (Hardesty 1987a).

For the most part, production activities are strongly related only to the morphology of the all-male boarding households. Here, household size fluctuated with the time demands of mining or milling, greatly increasing with bonanza periods and plummeting with borrascas (periods of very low ore productivity). Other production activities do not seem to have had much effect on how the household was organized. Most food production, for example, took place outside the mining district and was imported to company stores, where household members purchased food. The gardening that did occur was usually on a small-scale and not at all related to household morphology.

Most coresidential households in mining camps were all-male or single-sex groups that had no group responsibilities for reproduction, childrearing, and related activities. Nor did they provide a social context within which personal possessions, names, or anything else could be transmitted from generation to generation. The activities of reproduction and inheritance that did take place in mining camps were mostly limited to family households, which varied in frequency from rare in early stages of camp development to maybe 50% of the camp later on. Only in nuclear-family households did the activities of reproduction, inheritance, coresidence, production, and distribution-consumption closely coincide with the same group of people.

Coresidential households with no reproductive or inheritance functions, however, were often crosscut by nonresidential world-system families with these roles. The large all-male households residing in bunkhouses and boarding houses, for example, included members of families with a spouse and offspring still in the "old country." One very common example of such a world-system interaction on the 19th-century mining frontier is the Chinese sojourner from a separated or mutilated family (Sui 1952; Lee 1960:203; Sung 1967:155). Maintenance of the geographically dispersed family depended on the wages flowing through the materials network connecting the mining camp with China. The 1900 census of the Garrison Mine precinct in the Cortez Mining District, for example, enumerated three large all-male Chinese households, two with 9 persons each and one with 20. Of these, individuals listed as "married," and presumably having a spouse and offspring in China, made up 67%, 33%, and 15%, respectively, of the total household.

Archaeologically visible house remains, privies, and trash dumps combine with county tax assessment rolls, newspaper accounts, and federal census schedules to bring to life household social formations at both Shoshone Wells and Gold Bar. There are five general types of mining households: single-person, mutual aid, family, occupational, and work groups (Hardesty 1992). Single-person households are associated with residential structures occupied by only one individual engaged in domestic activities. Mutual aid households consist of

A small group of people living together temporarily to share housing and domestic chores, for mutual protection, for friendship, and to pool resources. Coresidential groups of two to five males are typical. Social relationships within mutual aid households generally are structured by the rules of ownership and seniority rather than by the principles of kinship, class, and gender. (Hardesty 1992:186)

Family households are organized around coresidential nuclear-or extended-family groups. Occupational households consist of coresidential social groups (either family or nonfamily members) who jointly operate or work at a business such as a saloon, store, or brothel. Finally, work groups are boardinghouses or bunkhouses:

The bunkhouse is a coresidential household for workers usually operated by mining companies. Bunkhouse activities are mostly limited to coresidence and recreation or leisure, with culinary activities taking place in a separate dining hall or cook house. Boardinghouses also are organized around work groups, but include the activities of food preparation, distribution, and consumption. (Hardesty 1992:188)

The Simeon Wenban Household at Shoshone Wells

The local mining settlement of Shoshone Wells includes several distinctive household formations. One is associated with Simeon Wenban. He probably built his house in 1884; the house first shows up on the Lander County tax rolls in 1885 (p. 140), and only the "lot with improvements" is mentioned in the 1884 rolls (p. 261). Written accounts describe the house as a large two-story redwood building with high ceilings and a porch, surrounded by an irrigated lawn and locust trees—a created garden in the Victorian sense. (See Mark Leone's [1984]description of gardens from the Georgian period). The house also included running water from a gravity-fed water system, among other amenities (Murbarger 1963:34). Although the house was torn down in the 1950s (Molly Knudtsen 1983, pers. comm.), the existing site contains a substantial archaeological record of the building and its occupants. The site is marked by a low stone foundation somewhat less than 56 feet long and 23 feet wide; its long axis

Table 4. Artifact assemblage from Wenban's house site

Group	Class	Type	Unit 22	Unit 29	Unit T6
Domestic	Tableware	Ironstone, undecorated	7	1	89
		Ironstone, decorated			
		Gold line			1
		Tan/cream			
		Leaf transfer			1
		Blue transfer			11
		Green transfer			3
		Red transfer			1
		Black transfer			7
		Black woven edge			2
		Brown transfer			8
		Polychrome transfer			1
		Pink/gold			5
		Unglazed earthenware	29		29
		Stoneware, polychrome			1
		Stoneware, white			2
		Chinese wares, Swatow	9		
		Jian You	177		42
		Four Seasons	28		2
		Celadon	6		
		Incised			4
		"Wings" design			1
		Porcelain			
		Miniature tea cup			1
		Tea cup handle			1
		Floral design			33
		Butterfly design			1
		Blue, undecorated			1
		White, undecorated	1		40
		Lattice design			1
		Polychrome transfer			2
		Handpainted gold band			2
		Blue/white transfer		3	1
		Glass tumbler fragments			10
	Containers, Bottles	Brown	73	4	596
		Amber	70		141
		Olive	70	1	721
		Purple	3		189
		Green	16		
		Blue-green	3	7	155

(continued)

Table 4. Artifact assemblage from Wenban's house site (continued)

Group	Class	Type	Unit 22	Unit 29	Unit T6
Domestic	Containers, Bottles	Pale green		1	950
		Colorless	9	6	404
		Blue			19
		Emerald			50
		Milk	6	1	18
		"Black"	13		124
		Beer	2	1	11
		Champagne	1		3
		Ink			1
		Pate			1
		Condiment			1
		Whiskey			3
		Soda	1		
		Lea and Perrins	1		1
	Containers, Cans	Fish		3	
		Hole-in-top, soldered seam	1		8
		Milk, sanitary		2	
		Crimped seam, hole-top			7
		Sanitary			4
		Key-opened lids			2
		Can-opener lids		1	6
		Screw-on cap (bottle)			
		Unidentified fragments			23
	Pots				
	Buckets				
	Furnishings	Toilets, white ceramic		4	
Construction					
	Fasteners	Cut nails	36	117	247
		Wire nails	6		37
		Tacks			
		Screws			
		Bolts			
		Door hardware	1		
	Windows	Glass fragments			
	Materials	Plaster			
		Sheet metal			
		Shingles			
		Tar			
		Wire cloth			
		Wood lath			

(continued)

Table 4. Artifact assemblage from Wenban's house site (continued)

Group	Class	Type	Unit 22	Unit 29	Unit T6
Personal	Toiletries	Combs			
		Toothbrushes			
	Gaming	Chinese gaming pieces			
	Toys	Doll fragments			7
		Marbles			1
	Tobacco	Ceramic pipes			1
		Tobacco tins		1	
	Opium	Opium tins	21	2	
	Ornaments	Glass beads			
	Cash	Ch'ien lung (1736–1795)			
		K'ang His T'ung Pao			
		1900s United States dime			
		1871–P United States dime	1		
Weapons	Firearms	Cartridges	4		23
	Arrows	Projectile Points			
	Fishing	Fishhook			
Animals	Livery	Mule shoes	·		
		Harness			
Writing	Pencils	Leads			
Refuse	Bone	Bos			1
		Rodent			
		Unidentified			6
	Seeds	Pinyon Pine			
Clothing		Rivets, brass			
		Fabric			1
		Buttons	1		4
		Glass collar studs			1
		Suspender buckles			
		Hairpin, wire			
		Safety pin			1
		Shoe screw	1		

is oriented approximately northwest-southeast. In the southeastern end of the building is a stone-lined cellar about 22 feet square. Artifacts located in and around the foundation suggest that the mansion had plaster cornices, redwood siding, a red-brick chimney, a picket fence, and a shake-shingled roof. Test pits within the house foundations, however, failed to turn up much information about the Wenban family. The area was quite obviously kept rather free of trash.

The trash dump from Wenban's mansion, however, was located alongside a stream running about 75 meters downhill or to the northeast of the house. A test excavation of the dump revealed a thin sheet deposit ranging from 10 to 30 centimeters in thickness with no obvious stratigraphy. Table 4 lists the artifacts recovered from a surface collection of the feature.

The quantity and proportion of "luxury" artifacts are clearly much higher here than in comparable "family household" sites elsewhere in the Cortez Mining District. The presence of women and children alone cannot explain the differences among the artifact assemblages coming from the Shoshone Wells household sites. Luxury ceramics from the Wenban assemblage included a large number of decorated ceramics of Euroamerican manufacture, such as French porcelain from Limoges, Haviland, and Sarreguemines. Excavations uncovered cut crystal, etched glass, a pate container, a glass collar stud, and carved mother of pearl as well. Wenban had three daughters who at one time may have used the dolls represented by six fragments from the dump. Other toys included a tricycle or small bicycle fork and wheel and a cat's eye marble.

Chinese Households at Shoshone Wells

Several households at Shoshone Wells were associated with Chinese miners working in the Cortez Mining District. The Cortez district was one of the few places on the American mining frontier to use Chinese hardrock miners after the 1860s. Sometime between 1869 and 1873, Simeon Wenban replaced the "turbulent and riotous" Cornish and Welsh miners previously employed in the district with, as he called them, the "less quarrelsome," and undoubtedly less costly, Chinese miners (Bancroft 1889:18). No documentary record of the size of the Chinese population could be found. Popular histories, however, suggest that Wenban employed several hundred Chinese miners and mill workers (Bancroft 1889; Murbarger 1963). Both the documentary and the archaeological records suggest that the Cortez Chinese population lived in three places: Shoshone Wells, Upper Cortez next to the Tenabo Mill, and at the Garrison Mine above the mill. Rossiter Raymond, United States commissioner of mining statistics from 1868 to 1875, observed in 1871 that several mines in Southern California had used Chinese hard-rock miners for years, especially in Merced, Mariposa, and Tuolumne counties (Raymond 1871:4). In Nevada they were reputed to have been used at one time at the Red Mountain mines in Silver Peak and in 1870 in the Morey district (Raymond 1871:3). In Raymond's introduction to the 1871 report on mining west of the Rocky Mountains, he argued strongly in favor of using Chinese hard-rock miners in spite of strong national sentiment to the contrary (Raymond 1871:4–6). Nevertheless, the exclusionary policies of miners' unions prevented the use of Chinese labor in most mines, limiting their activity to the placer deposits that had been abandoned. Only 240 adult males, or less than eight percent of Nevada's Chinese population, were listed in the 1870 federal population census as engaged in mining (Rohe 1982:15–16). The percentage increased to just below 10% in the 1880 census and to about 15% in 1890 (Rohe 1982:16). Nearly all the Chinese miners in Nevada during this time pursued placer mining, including as many as 3,000 in the Spring Valley or Paradise district between 1884 and 1895 (Rohe 1982:18). After 1890 the Chinese miners rapidly abandoned the Nevada frontier, leaving only a few by 1900.

Documentary Images

The Chinese miners in the Cortez Mining District are nearly invisible in the federal population census schedules for several reasons: (1) before 1880 no people with Chinese names show up in the Cortez district schedules, (2) the 1880 and 1890 census schedules for the Cortez district are missing, and (3) no people with Chinese names are listed in the 1910 census. Population schedules from the 1900 census, however, did survive and include several people with Chinese names. Two distinct settlements are suggested by the census—one near the Garrison Mine and one near the Tenabo Mill. The Garrison Mine settlement is visible in the archaeological record as a cluster of house sites on leveled terraces next to the mine's lower adits (image 107).

The Garrison Mine Precinct census schedules of Eureka County identify 45 people as having Chinese origins, all but one of whom is an adult male. They classify 38 of these as "mine laborers." The census enumera-

107. Residential locus at the Garrison Mine, Cortez
Mining District. (Photograph by author, 1983.)

tor also identifies six households, one occupied by a single adult female
and another serving as a store (table 5).

Each of the four remaining households includes several adult males,
ranging from 3 to 20 people.

The Cortez Precinct census from Lander County identifies 32 people
with Chinese origins organized into 11 households (table 6).

Of these, six are women: two "laundresses" living in single-person
households, two "seamstresses" living together in the same household,
and two wives living in family households. Two of the households appear
to be stores. Four households have only one adult male, one of whom is
a "barber," one a "cook," and the other two "mill laborers." Each of the
remaining two households consists of several adult males, all "mill laborers." The only other person of Chinese origin showing up in the 1900
census is a "cook" at the Upper Cortez boarding house.

Without question, the Cortez census data suggests the prevalence of
the traditional "sojourner" adult male household. Yet it is clear that at
least by 1900 both family and adult female households were part of ethnic Chinese communities even on the rural mining frontier. The two
Chinese settlements documented in the Cortez Mining District also ex-
hibit sizable disparities in sex composition. Only 2% of the Garrison

Table 5. The 1900 household census for the Garrison Precinct

Chinese Households

Household #99   3 persons: merchant and 2 storekeepers, all adult males and married

Household #104   9 persons (head and 8 partners): 8 mine laborers, one butcher; all adult males; 6 married and 3 single

Household #115   20 persons (head and 19 partners): 20 mine laborers; all adult males; 3 married and 17 single

Household #116   9 persons (head and 8 partners): 7 mine laborers, 1 tool packer, 1 blacksmith's helper; all adult males; 3 married and 6 single

Household #117   1 person: adult female, married, no listed occupation

Household #118   3 persons (head and 2 partners): 3 mine laborers; all adult males and single

Black Households

Household #126   3 persons (Maggie Johnson, head, plus her sister and a [Probably in Mill Canyon] white male partner): 2 mine owners, 1 with no listed occupation; 1 adult female widow, 1 married adult female, and 1 single adult male

Italian Households

Household #110   6 persons from one family (head, wife, 3 sons, 1 daughter): adult male head is ore miner, no listed occupations for the others

Household #113   3 persons from one family (head, wife, 1 daughter): adult male head is ore miner, no listed occupations for the others

Other Immigrant Households

Household #96   2 persons from one family (husband, wife): ore miner, ENGLAND

Household #100   4 persons from one family (husband, wife, daughter, sister): ore miner; SCOTLAND

Household #102   7 persons (head and 6 partners): 1 engineer and 6 ore miners; all adult males; 1 married and 6 single; SWEDEN, CANADA, 2 ITALY, PORTUGAL, 2 AMERICA

Household #93   1 person: married adult male, mine foreman, CANADA

Mine population was female, compared to almost 19% in Cortez. Aggregated census data can be quite misleading because it does not capture this kind of variability.

The 1900 federal population census schedules do not mention the settlement of Shoshone Wells by name, but it seemed reasonable to assume that it was included in the Cortez Precinct census. This turned out not to be true. No street addresses or other geographical information were included in the population schedules, making it impossible to tie census data to house sites in the archaeological record of Shoshone Wells. The

Table 6. The 1900 household census for the Cortez Precinct

Boarding House

Frank Engstrom (hotel keeper), his wife, and one 11–year-old daughter; 2 servants (1 Chinese male, 1 Indian female) and 1 waitress; 13 male boarders (all single, 10 American, 1 Canadian, 2 European: 2 mill laborers, 3 day laborers, 1 miner, 1 engineer, 1 teamster, 1 carpenter, 1 blacksmith, 1 physician, 1 mine carman)

Italian Households

Household #4	Adult male head, his wife, 2 immature daughters, 1 brother-in-law; rented house; day laborer
Household #5	Adult male head, 3 married male boarders; rented house; all day laborers
Household #9	Adult male head, his wife, 4 immature sons, 1 immature daughter; owned house; miner
Household #10	Adult male head, his wife, 2 immature sons, 1 immature daughter; no record of ownership or renting of house; miner
Household #12	Adult male head only; owned house; day laborer
Household #13	Adult male head, 2 adult single sons; owned house; all day laborers

Mexican Households

Household #11	Adult male head, his wife, 2 immature sons, 1 brother-in-law; rented house (in same cluster as Italian households #10, 12, 13); wood chopper (2 adult males)
Household #14	Adult male head only; owned house (in same cluster as Italian households #10, 12, 13 and Mexican household #11); wood chopper

Chinese Households

Household #15	Adult male head (married but no wife in household), one adult male partner with his wife, and one adult male boarder; owned house; storekeepers
Household #16	Adult male head only; owned house; barber
Household #17	Adult male head only; owned house; day laborer
Household #18	Adult female head only; owned house; laundress
Household #19	Adult single female, adult married female partner; owned house; seamstresses
Household #20	Adult male head, his wife, 2 married adult male boarders; owned house; storekeepers
Household #21	Adult single female only; owned house; laundress
Household #22	Adult married male only; owned house; mill laborer
Household #23	Adult married male head, 8 adult male boarders (some married and some single); owned house; all mill laborers
Household #24	Adult married male head, 6 adult male boarders; owned house; all mill laborers
Household #28	Adult single male only; rented house; cook

(continued)

Table 6. The 1900 household census for the Cortez Precinct (continued)

American Households

Household #2   Adult married male and wife; rented house; mill foreman

Household #3   Adult married male and wife; rented house; store keeper

Household #27   Adult married male and wife, 2 immature sons, 1 daughter; rented house; miner

Black Households

Household #7   Adult single male, his mother, his single sister, and a single female guest; rented house; assayer, nurse, dressmaker

Household #8   Adult married male, his wife, 3 immature sons, 1 immature daughter; rented house; day laborer, dressmaker

Canadian Households

Household #6   Adult married male, his wife, and 2 immature sons; rented house; engineer, 1 son is a farm laborer, NOVA SCOTIA

European Households

Household #25   Adult married male and his wife; owned house; blacksmith IRELAND

Household #26   Adult married male, his wife, 2 immature sons, 2 immature daughters; rented house; mill laborer, SCOTLAND

Lander County tax assessment rolls after 1885, however, do refer to Shoshone Wells when describing the property of some of the residents of the Cortez district. Armed with the names of several people identified as residents of Shoshone Wells, some of whom had Chinese names, the research team went to the federal population schedules for 1900 with the intention of adding details about household organization. Surprisingly, not one of the names appeared on the census. Clearly, the census enumerator had not visited Shoshone Wells, rendering it invisible in the population census. For this reason, nothing can be said about the household organization of the Chinese hard-rock miners who lived there.

The tax rolls, however, became an important source of information in identifying the residents of some of the house sites at Shoshone Wells. There is little information regarding the settlement inhabitants before 1885. Before that date Simeon Wenban appears as a resident of Cortez but not specifically of Shoshone Wells. In 1885 the rolls for the first time not only detail Wenban's "dwelling house, office, store, and barn" at Shoshone Wells (1885, p. 140) but also mention a Chinese resident of Cortez named Ah Ho, who owns a "china cabin at Cortez" (Lander County Tax Assessment Rolls, 1885, p. 60). Until the late 1880s, in fact, people with

Table 7. Shoshone Wells property owners with Chinese surnames

Property Owner	First Appearance	Last Appearance
Ah Ho (How)	1885	1889
Sam Kee	1886	1890
Quong Hing	1886	1902
Sing Kong Woo Co.	1900	1905
Ah Fong (Upper Cortez?)	1886	1886
Yow Gim (Upper Cortez?)	1886	1886
Lun Que	1889	1889
Chow Ho	1889	1889
Sing Hop	1889	1889
Wah Hing and Co.	1900	1902

Chinese names appear in the Lander County tax rolls not as residents of Shoshone Wells but simply as owners of a "china cabin at Cortez." The first Chinese taxpayers in the Cortez Mining District probably lived at Shoshone Wells, however, since most of them appear later as property owners in the settlement. According to the 1889 tax rolls, for example, Ah Ho had "an adobe house at Shoshone Wells 1 door north of Sam Kee's store" (Lander County Tax Assessment Rolls, 1889, p. 1), suggesting that he probably lived in Shoshone Wells at an earlier date.

Table 7 gives the names of the Chinese taxpayers living at Shoshone Wells between 1886 and 1902.

The list includes two storekeepers: Sam Kee and Qwong Hing. Both of them show up in the 1886 tax rolls, but not until 1889 were their names associated with stores. The location of the two stores is the key to interpreting the archaeological record of Shoshone Wells. Both appear to have been situated in the "road cluster," along with all the other buildings showing up in the tax rolls. The 1889 tax rolls identified Sam Kee's store as being on "main street one door south of the house of Ah How [sic]" (Lander County Tax Assessment Rolls, 1889, p. 101). Ah Ho's home was described elsewhere as an adobe house (Lander County Tax Assessment Rolls, 1889, p. 1). The only adobe house site on the main street of Shoshone Wells with archaeological evidence of a Chinese occupation is Structure 13. If this is where Ah Ho's house once stood, then Structure 14 next door must be the site of Sam Kee's store. Two observations confirm this conclusion: (1) there is archaeological evidence of a Chinese occupation in this structure, and (2) the structure is one door south of what must have been Ah Ho's house site, Structure 13. Ah Ho's adobe house becomes an important reference point for determining the location of several other homes from the tax rolls. The 1889 Lander County tax rolls, for example, place the adobe house of Ho Chow on Main Street between Ah Ho's house and the adobe house of Que Lun (Lander County Tax Assessment Rolls, 1889, p. 53). These three adjacent adobe houses on Main Street were perhaps Structures 11, 12, and 13 in the archaeological record.

The Que Lun house, the northernmost in the row according to the tax rolls, is the next key documentary reference point. The records place Qwong Hing's store just behind it (Lander County Tax Assessment Rolls, 1889, p. 94). If the Que Lun house is Structure 11, then Qwong Hing's store would be Structure 10. All these structures seem to offer surface indications of a Chinese occupation, but they have not been excavated. Another possible site for Que Lun's house, however, is Structure 9, a partially standing adobe structure. In some ways, the tax rolls and the archaeological record provide better support for this interpretation. The tax rolls describe Que Lun's house as an adobe building "one door south of D. S. Truman's frame house" (Lander County Tax Assessment Rolls, 1889, p. 94), which fits the archaeological record of Structure 33. If so, Qwong Hing's store would be associated in some way with Structures 8 and 34. And this identification fits the tax roll data somewhat better than the first interpretation. Qwong Hing's store, for example, was located "one door south of Antonio Montero's frame house" (Lander County Tax Assessment Rolls, 1889, p. 94), which fits the archaeological record of Structure 7 or the complex of sites in that area.

Archaeological Images

The archaeological record suggests that the Chinese population at Shoshone Wells lived both in the bottomland cluster and in the road cluster. In an effort to understand the settlement more fully, a University of Nevada–Reno archaeological program operated at the site during the summers of 1981, 1982, and 1983 (Hardesty and Hattori, 1982, 1983b, 1984). When excavations concluded, the team had located and mapped most of the house sites in the settlement. In addition, it had test-excavated several of the house sites, including Structures 18, 20, 22, and P-4 in the bottomland cluster and Structures 13, 14, 35, 42, and 43 in the road cluster. This sample provides an archaeological image of the Chinese miners living at Shoshone Wells in the late 19th century.

The team discovered several low-rock foundations—probably from wooden-frame houses—arranged around what seemed like a walk-in well, similar to those on the hillside toward the upper edge of Shoshone Wells. Preliminary excavation of the well, however, suggested that it is in fact a deep dugout structure that may have been a "joss house" (temple) or similar building. Whatever its use, the dugout (Structure P-4) was apparently the central focus of the cluster. The archaeological records of Structures 18, 20, and 22 in this group have been sampled.

In 1983 Structure 22 was excavated. The house site is small, only about four meters per side. Structure 22 was sampled just with a single one-meter-square test pit, but the stratigraphic sequence is still reasonably clear. The upper level of fill in the structure includes large amounts of charcoal and artifacts. Beneath the artifact layers near the walls are pockets of melted adobe overlying a hard-packed earthen floor—stratigraphically, the lowest cultural layer. Several postdepositional stages are suggested by the stratigraphic sequence. The melted adobe probably represents the weathering of caulking between the stone foundation and wooden walls after the building was abandoned. The building was then periodically used for trash disposal, as suggested by the large quantities of artifacts dumped on the floor but overlying the melted adobe. Finally, the building was burned, as suggested by the charcoal and burned artifacts in the highest stratigraphic layer.

Table 8 is a profile of the artifact assemblage recovered from Structure 22.

Without question, the assemblage suggests a Chinese occupation. The artifact types with the highest numbers are Chinese ceramics, while opium tins, Chinese bottles, and a folding brass key for a Chinese lock also appear (image 108).

Of the Chinese ceramics, over 80% are brownware or Jian You, commonly used as food containers. Glass bottles of Western origins make up the next most abundant artifact type in the assemblage. Most of these are probably beer, whiskey, and wine or champagne bottles, along with one Lea and Perrins Worcestershire sauce bottle and one J. C. Ayer's patent medicine bottle. It is possible, of course, that the bottles were deposited by non-Chinese residents of Shoshone Wells; however, Western

Table 8. Artifact assemblage from Structure 22

Group	Class	Type	Frequency
Culinary	Tableware	Ironstone, undecorated	7
		Unglazed earthenware	29
		Swatow	9
		Jian You	177
		Four Seasons	28
		Celadon	6
		Porcelain, white undecorated	1
	Bottles	Brown glass	73
		Amber glass	70
		Olive glass	70
		Purple glass	3
		Green glass	16
		Blue-green glass	3
		Colorless glass	9
		Milk glass	6
		"Black" glass	13
		Beer (glass)	2
		Wine/ghampagne (glass)	1
		Soda (glass)	1
		Lea and Perrins Worcestershire (glass)	1
Construction	Fasteners	Cut nails	36
		Wire nails	6
		Door hardware	1
Personal	Opium	Brass containers	21
	Money	1871–P Dime (U.S.)	1
Weapons	Firearms	Cartridges	4
Clothing	Buttons	Porcelain	1
	Shoes	Screw	1

alcoholic beverage bottles are commonly associated with imported Chinese material culture elsewhere in the West at Virginia City, Lovelock, and Old Sacramento.

The deposition date for the trash dump in Structure 22 is estimated to be in the 1880s. An 1871–P dime in the assemblage provides a good *terminus post quem* date; the coin, however, is well worn (AG-40), suggesting that the deposit has a considerably later date. The occurrence of wire nails, though in a very small percentage (14%), suggests a date sometime before 1900. House sites from Gold Bar that date between 1905 and 1909 based on documentary sources have only wire nails. Additional support for the 1880s date comes from the occurrence in the assemblage of only

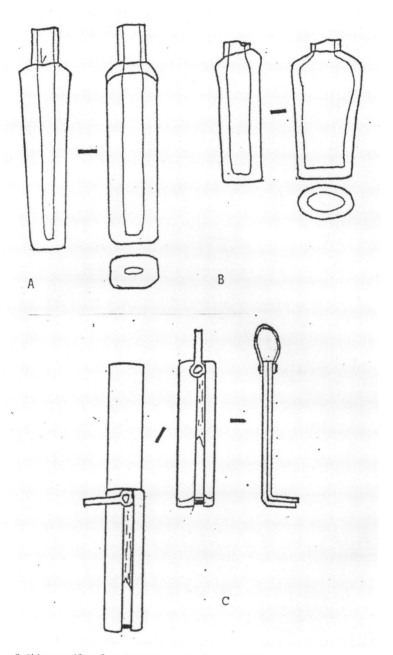

108. Chinese artifacts from Structure 22. (Hardesty and Hattori 1984, figures 1 and 3.)

Table 9. Artifact assemblage from Structure 18

Group	Class	Type	S	L1	L2	L3	L4	L5	L6	L7	L8	L9	U	Total
Domestics	Tableware	Jian You		1			1	1	4	2	12	8	1	30
		Swatow	1		1					2	1	1		7
		Porcelain				1						1		2
	Containers	Can, hole-top	3	1										4
	Lamps	Chimneys						1						1
	Drawer Knob	Porcelain											1	1
	Mirrors	Fragment					1							1
	Fuel	Kerosene can	3											3
	Other	Milk Glass									1			1
		Brass Lid	1											1
Construction	Fasteners	Cut nails			5	1	9	70	41	10	19	13	12	180
		Wire nails						1	2	1	1		1	6
		Wrought nails								1	1			2
		Unidentifiable							2	3	10	8	3	26
	Tacks	Tacks										2		2
	Spikes	Spikes										1		1
	Windows	Glass			2	1	5	65	41					114
	Tools	Files								1				1
	Blacksmith	Slag								2		5		7
	Washers	Brass									1			1
	Hinge	Hinge										1		1

(continued)

Table 9. Artifact assemblage from Structure 18 (continued)

Group	Class	Type	S	L1	L2	L3	L4	L5	L6	L7	L8	L9	U	Total
Personal	Clothing	Buttons								1	1	1		3
	Opium	Pipe stem				1								1
	Gaming	Chinese mark				1								1
	Firearms	Cartridge, .22								1				1
Animal	Maintenance	Nail, horseshoe				1			6	5	22	9	2	45
Unknown	Glass	Turquoise								10				10
		Colorless	7		2	2					15	9	13	48
		Amber	1					1	3				1	6
		"Black"		1				1	1			3		6
		Yellow								1				1
		Green								1	27	20	1	49
	Wood	Fragment		1		1	2	2	3	1	2	3	1	16
	Leather	Fragment	4											16
	Bone	Fragment	1	1						2	22	4	1	31
	Lithics	Bifaces			1						1			2
		Chert flakes	3		1	5	2	4		2	4	8	3	32
	Metal	Wire	2					1		6				9
		Lead fragment						1						1
		Unknown	1			1	2	1	10	10	3	2	1	31

handblown bottles with applied finishes, "WRA Co." and "UMC" cartridge cases, and a "Dixie Plug Cut Tobacco" tin.

The second house site in the "bottomland cluster" with archaeological evidence of a Chinese occupation is Structure 18. The site is visible as low rock foundations that probably once supported a wooden-frame house. The team dug a one-meter-square test pit into the structure, and while it did not reveal any floors or occupational surfaces, the stratified deposits contained artifacts throughout.

The composite artifact assemblage from Structure 18 is listed in table 9.

Again, the assemblage suggests a Chinese occupation. With the exception of nails and window glass, Chinese ceramics occur in the highest numbers, while other artifact types include an opium pipe and Chinese gaming pieces. Of the Chinese ceramics, over 80% are once again brownware or Jian You. No decorated ceramics other than Swatow were located, even though other Chinese house sites at Shoshone Wells contained the Four Seasons type. And again, following nails, window glass, and ceramics, glass bottles of Western origins make up the next most abundant artifact type in the assemblage. The presence of glass-lamp chimney fragments, "pearl oil" or kerosene cans, and cast-iron stove fragments suggests the adoption of western technology for domestic heating and lighting. Unlike the other Chinese house sites at Shoshone Wells, Structure 18 has archaeological evidence of horseshoeing, with many horseshoe nails and slag from a forge. The occupation date for Structure 18 is estimated to be in the 1880s. No good time markers are in the artifact assemblage, but the very low percentage of wire nails (3%) supports such an interpretation.

The third house site in the bottomland cluster to be tested is Structure 20, another low rock foundation for a wooden-frame building. Excavation of a one-meter-square test pit into the structure revealed an archaeological record quite similar to that of Structure 18. No living surfaces could be identified, but the stratified deposits contained artifacts throughout. The composite artifact assemblage from Structure 20 is listed in table 10.

Again, the artifact types with the highest numbers are Chinese ceramics, but archaeologists also uncovered an opium pipe fragment, several opium tins, Chinese gaming pieces, and a Chinese coin. In contrast to many of the other Chinese house sites at Shoshone Wells, only 40% of the Chinese ceramics are brownware or Jian You. The decorated ceram-

Table 10. Artifact assemblage from Structure 20

Group	Class	Type	Surf	L2	L3	L4	L5	L6	U	Total
Domestics	Tableware	Jian You	4	14	7	1	3		11	40
		Four Seasons	4		21				5	30
		Swatow	4	2	5	1	1		1	14
		Celadon	1						1	2
		Grey, incised			1					1
		Yellow, incised	1							1
	Containers	Ceramic bottles	1							1
		Cans, hole-in-top	2		2	1				5
	Refuse	Domestic pig				6			2	8
		Peach pits	2							2
		Pinenut shells		1					3	4
	Stoves	Cast-Iron parts	1							1
Construction	Fasteners	Cut nails	14	61	85	11	14	11	22	218
		Wire nails					1			1
		Wrought nails			17					17
	Washers	Brass				1				1
	Windows	Glass	1		16				1	18
	Roofing	Metal sheets	5							5
		Wood shingles	3							3
	Plaster	Fragment	1		4			1	1	7
Personal	Clothing	Suspenders		1						1
		Canvas/rubber boots			1					1

									Total
Opium	Tins	9	1	1	2					13
	Pipe bowl	1								1
	Incense?									
Gaming	Chinese mark									
Firearms	Cartridge, .32 "H"	1								1
	Cartridge, .410	1								1
	Cartridge, .44 UMC	1			1					2
Other	Harmonica	1								1
Animal										
Maintenance	Nail, horseshoe							1		1
	Curry comb	1								1
Unknown										
Glass	Turquoise		1	8	1	1		2		13
	Colorless	19	28	23	5	7	24	20		126
	Amber	2	3					3		8
	"Black"	2	1	3		1		1		8
	Purple	6					1	2		9
	Green	7	4	4	1		14	1		31
Wood	Fragment	7	1	24	4	2	3	4		45
Leather	Fragment	1		3			1			5
Bone	Fragment	19	11	27	10	17	35	5		124
Lithics	Chert flakes	2				1				3
Metal	Wire	1	2							3
	Unknown	31	2	22	1	2	8	2		68
Other	Lead foil	1		3				2		6
	Cork	1								1

ics include a relatively high percentage of Four Seasons (35%), along with smaller percentages of both Swatow and Celadon types. Glass bottles of Western origin are again the second-most common artifact after nails. And the use of Western technology for domestic heating is suggested by the presence of cast-iron stove fragments. Based on the very low percentage of wire nails in the artifact assemblage (less than 1% of the total number of nails), Structure 20 was most likely occupied in the 1880s. No good time markers are included in the assemblage.

THE ROAD CLUSTER

The second major group of house sites at Shoshone Wells with a significant archaeological record of a Chinese occupation is in the road cluster. Both partly standing adobe-block buildings and low rock foundations are included in this group. The archaeological records of Structures 13 and 14 were sampled. Structure 14 is a low rock foundation from what was probably once a wooden-frame building. The foundation was formed by digging into the hillside to a depth of about one-half meter and then lining the sloping walls with cobblestones. As with Structure 22, the stratigraphic sequence of this house site suggests its use for trash disposal after abandonment. While there is no archaeological evidence of burning, the large number of nails (over 600) in the artifact assemblage implies that the building disintegrated or was dismantled in place rather than moved.

Table 11 is a profile of the artifact assemblage recovered from Structure 14.

The large numbers of imported Chinese ceramics and opium tin suggest a Chinese occupation. Of the Chinese ceramics, almost 90% are brownware or Jian You. The assemblage from Structure 14, unlike the others with Chinese artifacts, includes a large number of ironstone pottery fragments, including a few decorated types. What this means is unclear. Some artifacts in the assemblage, like combs and porcelain doll fragments, suggest occupation by women and children. The combined use of Chinese and Western ceramics may point to a marriage between Chinese and Euroamericans or both Chinese and Euroamerican households dumping trash in the same place. There is a third possibility: there may have been more variation than expected in the extent to which Chinese households adopted Western material culture. Nails and then glass

Table 11. Artifact assemblage from Structure 14

Group	Class	Type	L1	L2	L3	L4	Total
Domestics	Tableware	Jian You	2	67	8		77
		Four Seasons	1	1	1		3
		Celadon		6			6
		Ironstone, white	6	146			151
		Ironstone, painted		3	3		6
		Unknown		24	3		27
	Containers	Cans, hole-in-top	1	4			5
	Cooking	Pot/pan	2				2
Construction	Fasteners	Cut nails	1	370	23		394
		Wire nails		206	9		215
		L-Head nails		39	2		41
		Tacks	1		1		2
	Screws	Wood screw	7				7
	Windows	Glass	2	36	4		42
	Brick	Fragment		2			2
	Tools	Miscellaneous		3			3
Personal	Clothing	Button		5			5
		Cloth		29	1		30
		Shoe, leather	40				40
		Shoe, rubber			4		4
	Opium	Tins		33			33
		Pipe		1			1
	Firearms	Cartridge	6				6
		Bullet	2				2
Animal	Maintenance	Nail, horseshoe		2			2
Unknown	Bottles	Glass	15	437	41	1	484
	Bone	Fragment	19	108	3		130
	Barrels	Hoop	5				5

bottles of Western origins are again the most abundant artifact types. And, again, most of the bottles were used for beer, whiskey, and wine or champagne, along with pickled food jars, pharmacy bottles, and canning jars. No Chinese bottles were located.

The deposition date for the trash dump in Structure 14 is estimated to be in the 1890s. No good time markers are included in the assemblage. Because 33% of the nails are made of wire, the structure most likely dates later than Structure 22 but is still considerably earlier than 1905, when the nails at Gold Bar were made exclusively of wire. The John Edwards/England maker's mark on the base of an ironstone plate, similar to one used by that company between 1880 and 1900 (Godden 1964:figure 1451),

Table 12. Artifact assemblage from Structure 13

Group	Class	Type	Total
Domestics	Tableware	Jian You	105
		Four Seasons	8
		Celadon	4
		Ironstone, undecorated	11
		Grey incised stoneware	1
		Majolica	1
		Polychrome stoneware	1
		Unglazed redware	2
	Containers	Tin cans, hole-in-top	2
		Tin cans, soldered side-seam fragments	13
	Lamps	Chimneys, glass	1
	Stoves	Cast-iron fragments	5
	Fuel	Kerosene can	3
Construction	Fasteners	Cut nails	45
		Wire nails	10
		L-Head nails	3
		Unidentifiable	59
		Wood screw	1
		Cut spike	1
	Windows	Glass fragments	11
	Brick	Fragment	4
	Plaster	Fragment	9
Clothing	Button	Porcelain	2
	Gloves	Cotton fragments	3
	Boots	Canvas/rubber fragments	2
	Other	Unidentified fragment (silk?)	10
Personal	Opium	Ceramic pipe bowl	10
	Money	Chinese coin (Kang His T'ung Pao, 1662–1772)	1
Animal	Maintenance	Nail, horseshoe	2
		Horseshoe	1
		Harness	1
Unknown	Glass	Aqua	1
		Green	1
		Amber	1
		Colorless	33
		"Black"	5
		Unidentifiable	66

handblown bottles with applied finishes, and "WRA Co." and "UMC" cartridge cases all support a 1880–1900 date for Structure 14.

Next to Structure 14 is a partially standing adobe-brick building designated as Structure 13. The structure was tested in 1981 and 1982 with two adjacent one-meter-square pits in its northeast corner. Excavations from the surface to a depth of about one-half meter revealed only melted adobe from a collapsed wall. At this level, the team located an artifact-rich charcoal layer, apparently from the building's final occupation. Unlike some of the other structures, Structure 13 has no evidence of postoccupational trash dumping. The test pit went to a depth of 1.15 meters, with no sign of an earlier occupation.

Table 12 is a profile of the artifact assemblage recovered from Structure 13.

The presence of imported Chinese ceramics and an opium pipe fragment suggests a Chinese occupation. Of the Chinese ceramics, about 65% are brownware or Jian You. Four Seasons and undecorated ironstone pottery are the most common Chinese tableware. It is difficult to draw conclusions from their presence because both types occur in such small quantities. The artifact assemblage from Structure 13 includes a large fragment of a rubber boot with a canvas top, suggesting that miners at Shoshone Wells used western mining footwear rather than traditional Chinese footwear. The other Chinese house sites contained similar, but smaller, boot fragments. And the presence of glass-lamp chimney fragments, "pearl oil" or kerosene cans, and cast-iron stove fragments in the assemblage once again implies that the inhabitants adopted western technology for domestic heating and lighting. The deposition date for the Chinese occupation of Structure 13 is estimated to be in the 1880s. No good time markers occur in the assemblage. Because wire nails make up only 13% of the nail total, the structure is probably about the same age as Structure 22, which had 14% wire nails.

Households at Gold Bar

The documentary images of the Gold Bar and Homestake camps depict several household types, including boarding houses, bunkhouses, and a superintendent's bungalow. The mention of 18 school-age children in 1908 is also evidence of family households. The artifact assemblages and the layout of the house-site features suggest that these and other

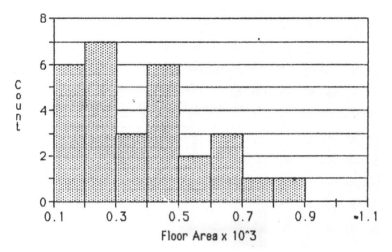

Fig. 5. Histogram of house-site floor areas at Gold Bar.

household types are archaeologically visible, making it possible to give historical details about the demography and social organization of the community. The archaeological definition of households at Gold Bar is based mostly on a number of factors: artifacts that are specific indicators of gender and age, such as toys and decorated ceramics; activity indicators, like artifacts related to blacksmithing or assaying; differences in the number of artifacts in the household assemblages; and differences in assemblage diversity.

Variability in Household Layout

The layout of house-site features at the Gold Bar settlement varied mostly in floor area and floor plan. The orientation of the house sites was consistently northeast-southwest, with only a couple of exceptions. All house sites followed square or rectangular floor plans, although there was a lot of size variation in each of the two plans. The distribution of floor areas among the 30 house sites is shown in the histogram in figure 5; table 13 is a statistical description of the same population.

The house sizes can be grouped into four clusters: (1) very large houses with floor areas over 1,000 square feet, of which there is one example (6–12); (2) large houses with floor areas between 700 and 900 square feet, with three examples (6–4, 6–16, and 6–22); (3) medium-sized houses with floor areas between 400 and 700 square feet, of which there are 12 examples (6–2, 6–3, 6–6, 6–9, 6–10, 6–13, 6–14, 6–15, 6–17, 6–21, 6–24, and

Table 13. Statistical description of Gold Bar house floor areas

Data File: Gold Bar
Variable: Floor Area
Minimum: 91.00000
Range: 1013.00000
Mean: 411.26667
Variance: 72113.099
Coefficient of Variation: 65.296
Skewness: 1.16908

Observations: 30
Maximum: 1104.00000
Median: 350.00000
Standard Error: 49.02826
Standard Deviation: 268.539
Kurtosis: 0.92892

6–25); and (4) small houses with floor areas of less than 400 square feet, with 14 examples (6–1, 6–5, 6–7, 6–8, 6–11, 6–18, 6–19, 6–20, 6–23, 6–26, 6–28, 6–29, 6–30, and 6–31).

Variability in Artifact Assemblages

The artifact assemblages associated with the house-site features at the Gold Bar settlement varied mostly in size, diversity, and activity pattern.

ASSEMBLAGE SIZE

Figure 6 is a histogram showing the distribution of artifact assemblage sizes among the 30 house sites. Table 14 is a statistical description of the same population.

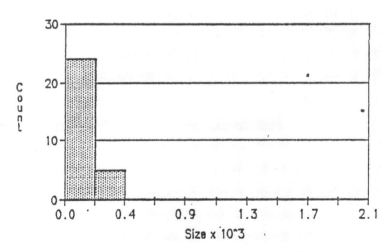

Fig. 6. Histogram of artifact assemblage sizes at Gold Bar.

Table 14. Statistical description of Gold Bar artifact assemblages

Data File: Gold Bar	
Variable: Size	Observations: 30
Minimum: 0.00000	Maximum: 2132.00000
Range: 2132.00000	Median: 113.00000
Mean: 188.30000	Standard Error: 68.74977
Variance: 141795.941	Standard Deviation: 376.558
Coefficient of Variation: 199.97771	Kurtosis: 26.79080
Skewness: 5.05196	

What caused the observed variation? Some studies have suggested that the amount of time a house site was occupied is positively correlated with the size of the domestic assemblage (Zeier 1986:20). The assumption is that more domestic and personal artifacts enter the archaeological record if a house is occupied for a longer period of time. Construction artifacts are excluded, assuming that the number of artifacts in this category is more closely related to building material than time of occupancy; however, a correlation between time and the number of repair-related artifacts may invalidate the assumption. Because it was impossible to establish the length of occupancy of the Rochester house sites in Pershing County, Nevada, no significant conclusions were reached when the theory was first applied (Zeier 1986: 136). Unfortunately, this is likely to be a common problem rather than an exception; written records that would give good chronological information are seldom available for mining-camp house sites. Researchers can only study the relationship between length of occupancy and the size of artifact assemblages at house sites properly in the exceptional instances when good archival data are available for households on the mining frontier. In any case, duration of occupancy is probably not a significant factor in varying assemblage sizes at the Gold Bar settlement. The camp was occupied for less than four years before abandonment, making it unlikely that the length of occupations among the house sites would have varied by more than a few months.

A second variable that may affect assemblage size is the size of the household group. Other things being equal, the size of the artifact assemblage for a given activity is expected to increase as a group expands in size; thus, one-person households at Gold Bar should have the smallest domestic assemblages, while boarding houses or bunkhouses should have the largest. The archaeological team was unable to locate any written accounts of household sizes at the Gold Bar settlement. For this reason, group size was estimated archaeologically from the area of the leveled terraces or platforms upon which the houses once stood. No attempt has been made to estimate the actual or absolute size of the group living in each house; however, it is assumed that some kind of direct relationship between floor area and group size exists.

All of this, of course, rests on the assumption that the per capita deposition rate in a mining camp is about the same from one household to another. At Gold Bar, there is little documentary or archaeological evidence of significant differences in rates of deposition brought about by such things as inequalities in wealth or social status. Without question, however, rates of artifact deposition do differ from one activity to another at Gold Bar. Specialized buildings such as bunkhouses do not appear to be associated with culinary activities, for example, and are therefore expected to have rather low depositional rates in comparison to house sites where food storage, preparation, and consumption took place. Boarding houses, by contrast, will likely have large trash dumps, reflecting the preparation and consumption of meals for and by large groups of miners. Charles Zeier (1986:133–134) notes also that the size of the artifact assemblage is significantly greater in "family" house sites than in "nonfamily" house sites at the Rochester mining camp in central Nevada. Zeier argued that some household organizations would perform more tasks than others and that more tasks imply a greater number of artifacts in the archaeological record. For this reason, there should be larger artifact assemblages in family house sites than in others. Unfortunately, there is often no documentary information that would allow the identification of family households in the archaeological record of mining camps. Still, family households can be identified through the use of gender and age "index artifacts" such as toys and items of dress.

ASSEMBLAGE DIVERSITY

Figure 7 is a histogram showing how assemblage diversity is distributed among the 30 Gold Bar house site features. Table 15 is a statistical description of the same population.

What were the factors in the observed variation? Zeier suggested time, size, and household organization as possible causes (1986:20). Differences in length of occupancy were not significant at Gold Bar, however.

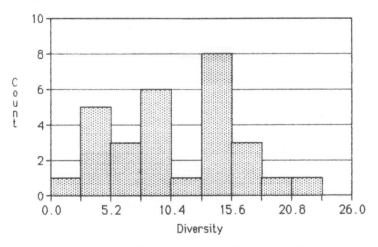

Fig. 7. Histogram of artifact assemblage diversity at Gold Bar.

Variation in household organization may play a more significant role in determining artifact diversity. A household in which more tasks were performed would seem to yield greater numbers of, and more diverse, artifacts. For reasons already mentioned, however, good statistical studies of the correlation between household organization and artifact diversity cannot be accomplished without independent documentary data. Assemblage size is another possible cause of diversity. Figure 8 is a simple linear regression showing the sizes at Gold Bar.

Since the relationship may not be linear, the two variables have been logarithmically transformed. The correlation coefficient is 0.67, significant at the 0.05 level and comparable to Zeier's (1986:136) results at Rochester. This is not a strong correlation, but it is stronger than any other

Table 15. Statistical description of Gold Bar assemblage diversity

Data File: Gold Bar
Variable: Diversity   Observations: 30
Minimum: 0.00000   Maximum: 26.00000
Range: 26.00000   Median: 10.50000
Mean: 11.13333   Standard Error: 1.10457
Variance: 36.6023   Standard Deviation: 6.04998
Coefficient of Variation: 54.34117   Kurtosis: -0.11642
Skewness: 0.45036

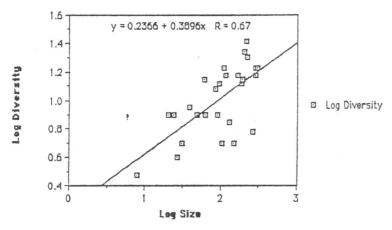

Fig. 8. Simple linear regression of assemblage diversity on assemblage size at Gold Bar.

relationship tested with the Gold Bar data. It is uncertain why this correlation exists.

ACTIVITY PATTERNS OF HOUSE-SITE ASSEMBLAGES

The artifact categories suggest that assemblages from the Gold Bar house-site features may reflect different kinds of activities as well as have various sizes and degrees of artifact diversity. A more detailed examination of these differences can enhance the identification of household types from the archaeological record. Figures 9 and 10 are histograms showing how the categories of ceramics and bottle glass (given as percentages) are distributed among the 30 Gold Bar house-site features. Tables 16 and 17 are statistical descriptions of the same populations.

The assemblages appear to fall into several distinctive clusters, each of which suggests a particular kind of household organization. Cluster 1 has no ceramics, or very low percentages of ceramics, together with high percentages of bottle glass. The total size of the assemblage, however, is usually quite small. The virtual absence of pottery may mean that the household members were eating at boarding houses rather than cooking for themselves, or that the occupants were eating directly from tin cans. This type of assemblage is found with both small and large floor sizes, indicating a range of household group sizes. The small floor size suggests a household of one or two adult males, while the larger floor size implies that the building was a bunkhouse for several people. Cluster 2 has relatively high percentages of undecorated ceramics and tin

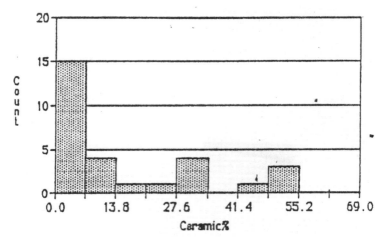

Fig. 9. Histogram of ceramic percentages at Gold Bar.

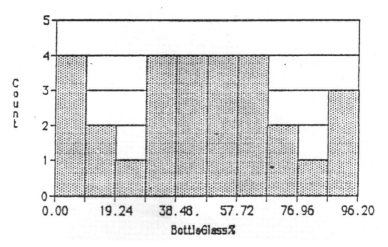

Fig. 10. Histogram of bottle glass percentages at Gold Bar.

cans, together with lots of bottle glass. The assemblage size is usually larger than Cluster 1, and the associated floor sizes range from medium to large houses. Cluster 2 suggests a large household with adult males who cook, probably a boarding house. The third cluster has very large numbers of bottle glass but virtually no pottery, probably representing a saloon. Finally, Cluster 4 has decorated ceramics and toys, suggesting a family with women and children.

Table 16. Statistical description of Gold Bar ceramics

Data File: Gold Bar
Variable: Ceramic %
Minimum: 0.00000
Range: 69.00000
Mean: 16.20667
Variance: 424.5503
Coefficient of Variation: 127.13668
Skewness: 1.08435

Observations: 30
Maximum: 69.00000
Median: 6.15000
Standard Error: 3.76187
Standard Deviation: 20.60462
Kurtosis: 0.02966

Table 17. Statistical description of Gold Bar bottle glass

Data File: Gold Bar
Variable: Bottle glass %
Minimum: 0.00000
Range: 96.20000
Mean: 47.33667
Variance: 793.83689
Coefficient of Variation: 59.52069
Skewness: -0.01042

Observations: 30
Maximum: 96.20000
Median: 47.65000
Standard Error: 5.14405
Standard Deviation: 28.17511
Kurtosis: -0.81778

Household Classification

Variability in house-site features and associated artifact assemblages suggest several household patterns. They include family households, bunkhouses, boarding houses, saloons, all-male domestic households, and special-purpose households. Differences in floor size, the size of the artifact assemblage, the diversity of the artifact assemblage, and the activity pattern of the artifact assemblage all define household patterns.

FAMILY HOUSEHOLDS

Three house sites at Gold Bar are associated with artifact assemblages having both decorated ceramics and toys: Features 6–6, 6–10, and 6–11. Of these, Features 6–10 and 6–11 may be part of the same household complex, with 6–11 being an outbuilding. In addition, both Features 6–19 and 6–15 have some decorated ironstone pottery, although no toys were located. The number of house sites identified archaeologically as family households, however, seems small for the 18 school-age children mentioned in written accounts of 1908 (Latschar 1981:145). Two other house sites were associated with artifact assemblages that had high percentages of undecorated ironstone pottery but no toys or decorated ceramics: Feature 6–15 and Feature 6–26. Both of these features were most likely also family household sites. The absence of decorated ceramics in some family household sites but not others may reflect differences in wealth. Perhaps there is some evidence of variation in social status in the archaeological record of Gold Bar. Certainly, the artifact assemblages of Features 6–10 and 6–11 stand out from the others in both size and diversity. What all this suggests is that there were either six or seven family households in the settlement, which would be more consistent with the documentary evidence.

BUNKHOUSES

John Latschar (1981:99) cites newspaper accounts from November 1905 of a bunkhouse for 14 miners at Gold Bar, along with a boarding house and a superintendent's bungalow. Again, historical photographs provide no specific information that might be used to identify the bunkhouses. Two large tents shown in a November 1905 photograph suggest some kind of special use. The two-room tent oriented northwest-southeast appears to be on the site of Feature 6–4, and the other tent, oriented in the same direction, is on or near the site of Feature 6–30. Of the two, only the Feature 6–4 tent shows up in a June 1906 photograph, now sitting next to a new large wooden-frame building. No artifacts are associated with Feature 6–4, perhaps supporting its designation as a bunkhouse. Feature 6–30 is associated with a small artifact assemblage that has no ceramics, a few tin food cans, bottle glass, and bedsprings, most likely the remains of a bunkhouse.

Newspaper accounts mentioned three additional bunkhouses at Homestake camp. In late 1905 the Homestake Consolidated Mining Company began the construction of a bunkhouse (Latschar 1981:125). The bunkhouse does not stand out in any of the early photographs; it could have been any one of the tents shown in the Homestake camp area in a June 1906 photograph. In February 1907 newspaper accounts mentioned the construction of another bunkhouse and boarding house by the Homestake-King Consolidated Mining and Milling Company (Latschar 1981:131). And in late 1907 yet another bunkhouse was built to house 15 men who had been hired to work at the Homestake-King Mill (Latschar 1981:135). The only obvious bunkhouse or boarding house in a January 1908 photograph is a large wooden-frame building that appears to be on Feature 6–16. No ceramics are in the associated artifact assemblage, but excavations did uncover two large tin can dumps. The absence of ceramics makes it unlikely that the building was a boarding house where food was consumed, although the large number of tin cans suggests food preparation. Another bunkhouse site is suggested both by the floor area and the artifact assemblage of Feature 6–2. Nothing appears at this site in historical photographs until January 1908. The large rectangular wooden-frame building that shows up in an early 1908 photograph looks like a bunkhouse, an interpretation that is supported by the absence of ceramics and the small size of the associated artifact assemblage. Finally, given the large size (638 square feet) of Feature 6–14 as well as an artifact assemblage that includes no ceramics but lots of bottle glass, the feature is probably the bunkhouse site.

BOARDING HOUSES

The earliest written account of a boarding house at the Gold Bar appeared in November 1905 (Latschar 1981:99). Unfortunately, the building could not be located in any of the historical photographs. The boarding house site, however, may have been Feature 6–21, which has an artifact assemblage with a high percentage of undecorated ironstone pottery and which may be present in the November 1905 photograph. Latschar (1981:104) located a newspaper account of a large boarding house for 60 miners being built in 1906. Feature 6–3, which first shows up as a large rectangular wooden-frame building next to the Feature 6–4 bunkhouse in the June 1906 photograph, is the most likely candidate. The associated artifact assemblage, with its high percentage of undecorated ironstone pottery, supports such an interpretation.

The account mentions only one boarding house at Homestake camp. With 63 men employed by the Homestake-King Consolidated Mining and Milling Company, the building must have been at least as large as the one at Gold Bar camp that fed 60. The most likely candidate is Feature 6–12, which has both a large floor area and an artifact assemblage that includes a high percentage of undecorated ironstone pottery.

SALOON

The archaeological team identified Feature 6–17, just across the road from the mine designated Feature 11, as Gold Bar's saloon. The key evidence was the artifact assemblage, which was heavily dominated by bottle glass and crown bottle caps. No mention of this saloon, which is far below Gold Bar camp, could be located in written accounts.

ALL-MALE DOMESTIC HOUSEHOLDS

Using artifact assemblages, the team identified several house sites at Gold Bar as households consisting entirely of adult males. With the exception of the superintendent's bungalow, which appears in the November 1905 photograph, all these households are invisible in the documentary record. The bungalow, however, which was built on the site of Feature 6–1, suggests a pattern of the associated artifact assemblage: a small amount of undecorated ironstone pottery, bottle glass, and male personal items such as pocket tobacco cans and snuff cans. Small all-male households were likely established at the following 12 house sites: Features 6–1, 6–5, 6–8, 6–18, 6–20, 6–22, 6–23, 6–24, 6–28, 6–29, 6–30, and 6–21.

SPECIAL PURPOSE BUILDINGS

Three house sites at Gold Bar are either too small to be a house or have unique artifact assemblages suggesting some other use. Feature 6–13 is associated with an artifact assemblage that indicates blacksmithing. Both Features 6–7 and 6–25 may have been outbuildings.

Global Networks

In *The Bandeirantes*, R. M. Morse describes the mining frontier in western South America as "a web or archipelago of patches" (Hennessy 1978:17), with each patch or island a place where ore deposits have been located. Miners colonized the island, surrounded by what to them was a social and cultural wilderness, and transformed the environment into a mining landscape. This island structure describes the geographical and ecological characteristics of mining frontiers in Nevada and the American West. Mining islands range in size from small localities to regions covering several square miles, and they have variable and changing boundaries that reflect technology, social and cultural context, history, and geology. Each island is, in effect, a case study of the "sensitivity" of geographical places as a habitat for human occupation, and researchers can study them using the methods of cross-cultural comparison (Kirch 1997).

Mining islands in Nevada and the American West were linked into a vast transportation, communications, demographic, and economic network on a global scale. Materials, people, and information circulated throughout the networks. Immanuel Wallerstein (1974, 1980) refers to such a structure as a "modern world system." A world system is a large-scale social system that can exist independently, has a complex division of labor, and is socially and culturally diverse (Sanderson and Hall 1995:96). Historically, the most common type of world system is the world empire, a large-scale social system integrated by military force, like the Inca Empire or the Roman Empire. In contrast, the world economy, another type of world system, is organized around loose networks of economic production and exchange and incorporates more or less independent and sovereign nation-states (Sanderson and Hall 1995:96). The modern world system is a distinctive variety of world economy based on capitalism that may have emerged in the 1500s in Europe or even earlier in China and Mesopotamia. In Wallerstein's view, the structure of a modern world system is built on relations of economic exchange ranging between cores—geographical centers of surplus accumulation and economic and political power—and peripheries, marginal regions of primary production and extraction with little surplus accumulation and power. In contrast, Eric Wolf (1982) located the structure of modern world systems in the relations of production, including labor, surplus, and wealth. Wolf (1982:75) considered the key component to be the "mode of production," which he defined as "a specific historically occurring set of social relations through which labor is deployed to wrest energy from Nature by means of tools, skills, organization, and knowledge."

Material Networks

One network circulated materials, including the supplies needed to support mining operations and the bullion from the mines. How such networks operated is clear from both documentary and archaeological data. For the Cortez Mining District in central Nevada, documentary records of purchases made by the Cortez Company, Ltd.—918 store invoices between 1891 and 1893—reveal how the district was tied into global marketing networks (invoices and account books, Special Collections, Getchell Library, University of Nevada, Reno; Mine Records, Churchill County Museum and Archives). Table 18 shows where the commodities were purchased.

Table 18. Geographical origins of Cortez Store invoices, 1891–1893

Location	Companies	Invoices
Auburn CA	1	4
Aurora IL	1	1
Beowawe NV	3	19
Boca CA	1	4
Denver CO	1	1
Elko NV	6	14
Indianapolis IN	1	1
Newcastle CA	2	44
Ogden UT	2	14
Omaha NE	2	25
Reno NV	2	49
Sacramento CA	15	473
San Francisco CA	26	253
Uintah UT	1	
West Oakland CA	1	6

The vast majority (726 or 79.1%) of purchases originated in the California commercial centers of Sacramento and San Francisco; most of the others came from the rest of California, Nevada, and Utah. A few purchases, however, were made as far away as Omaha, Denver, Indianapolis, and Aurora, Illinois. Of the 918 invoices in the collection, 500 (54.4%) came from just five companies: Baker and Hamilton, Sacramento (hardware); Booth and Company, Sacramento (food); Brown Brothers and Company, San Francisco (clothing); Cahn, Nicklesburg Company, San Francisco (shoes); and D. Dierssen Company, Sacramento (food).

Table 19 lists all the companies from which the Cortez store purchased commodities between 1891 and 1893, along with the number of invoices for each.

Several things about the materials interaction spheres on the mining frontier seem clear from the invoices. Virtually nothing was purchased from local producers. Beowawe is the only local place listed in the invoices, and it was the closest shipping point along the Central Pacific Railroad to the Cortez mines. Some purchases were made in Elko, Nevada, a town about 60 miles away. Still, the "effective" sphere within which most materials were distributed was regional in scale: most of the marketing "nodes" were in California, between 300 and 500 miles away. The heavy and expensive mining and milling machinery, which does not appear in the Cortez store invoices, also originated for the most part within this

Table 19. List of suppliers to the Cortez Store, 1891–1893

Company	Location	Invoices
Adams, L.S.	Sacramento CA	1
Allison Coupon Company	Indianapolis IN	1
Augora Robe and Glove Co.	Unknown	1
Auburn Cooperative Fruit Co.	Auburn CA	4
Baker and Hamilton	Sacramento CA	91
Bartlett and Ostreicher	Elko NV	3
Benson and Company	Beowawe NV	5
D. Block and Company	San Francisco CA	1
Boca Brewing Company	Boca CA	4
Henry Bohm	Unknown	1
Booth and Company	Sacramento CA	235
James Brain	Elko NV	1
John Breuner Company	Sacramento CA	17
Brown Bros. and Company	San Francisco CA	52
Buckingham and Hecht Co.	San Francisco CA	2
M.E. Bushee	Unknown	1
Cahn, Nicklesburg Company	San Francisco CA	67
J. Calegaris, Druggist	San Francisco CA	1
California Bottling Company	San Francisco CA	4
D.G. Camarinos	San Francisco CA	1
F.S. Chadborne	Unknown	1
Cudahy Packing Company	Unknown	1
Dallemand and Company	San Francisco CA	8
D. Dierssen Company	San Francisco CA	55
F. Dittenhoefer	Unknown	1
Abner Doble Company	San Francisco CA	4
Samuel Dye, Wholesaler	Uintah UT	1
L. Elkins and Company	Sacramento CA	1
Elko-Tuscarora Mercantile Co.	Elko NV	2
Fairchild, Grace, and Co.	Ogden UT	8
Fallaway Bros. and Dingwall	Denver CO	1
Friedlander, Koch, and Co.	San Francisco CA	3
Goldberg, Bowen, and Co.	San Francisco CA	1
Hall, Luhrs, and Company	Unknown	1
M. Heller and Sons	San Francisco CA	3
S.M. Henley	Elko NV	1
M.W. Hodkins	West Oakland CA	6
Holbrook, Merrill, and Stetson	Sacramento CA	3
Iler and Company	Omaha NE	2
Jones, Mundy and Co.	San Francisco CA	2
George D. Kellogg	Newcastle CA	17
Kline and Company	San Francisco CA	2

(continued)

Table 19. List of suppliers to the Cortez Store, 1891–1893 (continued)

Company	Location	Invoices
Langley and Michaels	San Francisco CA	21
Leak Glove Company	San Francisco CA	3
B.F. Leete Company	Reno NV	19
Levi Strauss and Co.	San Francisco CA	8
William Lewis Company	San Francisco CA	12
Liebe Bros. and Co.	San Francisco CA	1
Livermore Warehouse Co.	Unknown	1
Locke and Lavenson	Sacramento CA	12
Main and Winchester	San Francisco CA	4
Malm and Steel	San Francisco CA	1
Matson, Abbott and Barnes	Ogden UT	6
Jacob Miller and Son	Aurora IL	1
Miscellaneous Stage Companies	Beowawe NV	13
J.F. Muller, Doctor	Elko NV	1
Murphy, Grant and Co.	San Francisco CA	41
Paxton and Gallagher Co.	Omaha NE	23
Clarence Nelson, Sadler	Sacramento CA	8
Reno Creamery	Reno NV	30
Rosenthal, Feder and Co.	San Francisco CA	6
Sacramento Glass and Crockery	Sacramento CA	4
George Shreve Company	San Francisco CA	2
W.T. Smith Company	Elko NV	6
Southern Pacific Railroad	Beowawe NV	1
W.R. Strong and Co.	Sacramento CA	31
Sullivan, Kelly and Co.	Sacramento CA	4
R.A. Swain and Co.	Sacramento CA	5
Triest and Company	San Francisco CA	2
Truman, Hooker and Co.	Sacramento CA	3
Waterhouse and Lester	San Francisco CA	1
Whittier, Fuller and Co.	Sacramento CA	3
Wilmerding and Company	Unknown	1
W.J. Wilson and Company	Newcastle CA	27

regional sphere. The 1864 Cortez Company Mill, for example, the first in the district, was equipped with a steam engine from the Vulcan Iron Works in San Francisco, a steam boiler from the Coffey and Risdon Company in San Francisco, and stamp mills framed in part with California timber (*Reese River Reveille*, 7 May 1864:1). San Francisco, in fact, grew up in part as a manufacturing center for the milling and mining equipment used on the Nevada mining frontier.

But this documentary image of global marketing networks mostly reflects the retailing and wholesaling distribution nodes. The archaeological image of global marketing networks is more oriented toward the "production" networks created by the locations of commodities manufacturing. In the archaeological record, the durable embossing on bottles and cans usually gives information about the manufacturer, not the distributor. And, as Adams (1976) has shown for the town of Silcott, Washington, these interaction spheres are national and international in scale. The trash dumps at the Gold Bar Mine in Death Valley National Park offer a good example (Hardesty 1987a). Identifiable makers' marks on glass bottles include those of the American Bottle Company of Chicago; Adolphus Busch of Belleville, Illinois; the Massillon Bottle and Glass Company of Massillon, Ohio; Roth and Company of San Francisco; William Frantzen and Son of Milwaukee; Pacific Coast Glass Works of San Francisco; Ohio Bottle Company of Newark, Ohio; the Muncie Glass Company of Muncie, Indiana; and the Illinois Glass Company of Alton, Illinois. Quite obviously, the archaeological record reveals the "eastern" orientation of the production interaction spheres, while the documentary record shows the "western" orientation of the distribution spheres. Both perspectives are correct, but each one captures only part of the story. It is impossible to overestimate the importance of using documentary and archaeological data interactively to understand adequately the dynamics of the Nevada mining frontier.

Population Networks

The mining frontier in the American West was also integrated into a global population network, as the 1900 federal population census for the Cortez Mining District reveals. The schedules for the Garrison Mine Precinct identify a group of 156 people living next to and mostly working in the Garrison Mine, the largest in the district at that time. Several nationalities and ethnic groups were present. Of these, the largest number of people (79) was American-born, with 32 born in Nevada. The others had migrated from the states of Pennsylvania, Maryland, Missouri, California, Maine, Michigan, Ohio, Vermont, Utah, New Jersey, Kentucky, Indiana, Georgia, Texas, Louisiana, Mississippi, New York, Wisconsin, Illinois, and Iowa. There were two African Americans in this group. Forty-five had emigrated from China. Twenty-five of the Garrison Mine residents came from countries in Europe, including Italy, Scotland, Ireland, England, Portugal, Sweden, Switzerland, Finland, and Germany. Two of them were from Mexico, one from Australia, and four from Canada. Without question, the Nevada mining frontier was linked into a world-wide migratory system.

The group had a high male-to-female sex ratio, as is typical of mining populations. Of the 156 people, only 44 (28.2%) were female. The high ratio, however, was due in part to the very low percentage of females among the Chinese settlers, of whom only one was a woman. Twenty-eight of the American-born residents, or 35.4%, were female, including both of the African Americans. And of the 32 European, Mexican, Australian, and Canadian immigrants, 15 (46.8%) were female. The percentage of children in the Garrison Mine population was low as well, again typical of mining frontier camps. Twenty-four of the 156 Garrison mine residents, or 15.4 percent, were children under the age of 15. Again, however, the demographic profile was greatly affected by the 45 Chinese miners, none of whom had children living at the settlement.

Information Networks

Finally, world-system structures are created by the exchange of information, ideas, and symbols. The completion of the transcontinental telegraph in 1861 made possible the rapid transmission of information. Perhaps the most important consequence of the telegraph was that it created a much larger pool of capital for the frontier mines via the regional, national, and international stock market. The organization of the San Francisco Stock and Exchange Board on 1 September 1862, for example, was the direct result of the development of the Comstock Mining District. The completion of the transcontinental railroad in 1869 complemented, in the materials sphere, the telegraph revolution in the information sphere. In many ways, the two spheres worked together to create ecological structures. The transmission of technical information about mining into the frontier mines was facilitated by the rapid bulk transport of books and machinery via railroad.

Victorian culture is probably the best-documented ideological system linking the mining frontier with the heartland of America and Europe during the late 19th and early 20th centuries (Baker 1978; Hardesty and Hattori 1983a). Victorianism emerged out of a new "industrial social order" that revolutionized 19th-century Europe and America. The new social order was brought about by the rise of industrialism, urbanism, and large corporations, all of which required dramatic changes in work habits and social relations (Howe 1975, 1976; Trachtenberg 1982). Perhaps the most visible expression of the new industrial order was an urban middle class carrying a Victorian ideology. Victorian ideology was marked by a compulsive work ethic; punctuality; a worldview dominated by rationality, order, and natural laws of morality; temperance; the cult of domesticity; knowledge and self-cultivation; didacticism; and conspicuous consumption (Howe 1975, 1976). All these things reinforced the regularity, discipline, and hierarchical structure of the new work place; they also encouraged industrial mass production and provided the ideological rationale for the new urban middle class.

Both the documentary and archaeological records show clearly that Victorian ideology was carried onto the mining frontier. The archaeological record of Victorian culture on the mining frontier is most visible in the layout of settlements and in trash dumps. George Teague (1980:140–145, 149–153), for example, argued that the apparent shift in the layout of the Vekol Hills camp in southern Arizona from a rather haphazard to a more rigid, linear plan reflected the influence of Victorian culture. And John W. Reps (1975, 1979) provided documentary evidence of the widespread use of the "universal grid" layout in mining towns, which may be related to the Victorian emphasis on rationality and order, especially in the case of corporate "company towns" (Allen 1966). Signs of both conspicuous consumption and temperance are visible in the trash dumps of mining camps. During the late 19th century, nothing reflected the Victorian value of conspicuous consumption more than the emergence of mass advertising to market products on a large scale (Trachtenberg 1982:135–139). The most important change in advertising occurred when marketers began advertising mass-produced goods for daily use instead of a few luxury goods (Trachtenberg 1982:137). Archaeologically, the change is documented on the mining frontier by the appearance of large trash dumps made up largely of glass bottles and tin cans. The same trash dumps also record what in some cases may be the Victorian value of temperance. Teague (1980:140) perhaps finds evidence of this ideological change in the Vekol Hills settlements. During the late 19th and early 20th centuries, the number of glass bottles containing alcoholic beverages in the trash dumps declined dramatically. The observable change may be attributable either to an actual decline in drinking or to a shift in where drinking took place.

4. Conclusions
Understanding Variability and Change on the Mining Frontier

The mining rushes and subsequent mining created and transformed a series of mining frontiers in Nevada and the American West. They varied in detail but shared many social and cultural patterns that reflected similar environmental adaptations. They exhibited flexible and quickly changing social formations and sociotechnical systems, rapid environmental change and the formation of distinctive landscapes, and an island structure that best describes the geographical and ecological characteristics of mining frontiers in the American West and elsewhere. Starting with the premise that the mining frontier is a unique environmental setting, evolutionary theory offers a significant approach to understanding variability and change in mining-related settlement-systems, social networks, and sociotechnical systems (Hardesty 1985a, 1985b, 1986c).

The mining frontier as an ecological theater has two distinctive characteristics. First, it is a network of islands. Second, the theater is marked by boom-bust cycles. At the level of individual mining district islands, boom-bust cycles are usually tied to the geological vagaries of the ore body. At the level of island networks, however, the boom-bust cycles are best viewed as correlated episodes or "punctuations" of world-system technological or economic changes (Hardesty 1985a: 215). How miners coped with boom-bust cycles, on the one hand, and with the island structure of the frontier, on the other, is therefore of substantial interest within the interpretive framework of evolutionary theory.

How evolutionary mechanisms and processes work on mining frontiers is illustrated by Patrick Kirch's (1980, 1997) model of cultural adaptation on islands. The model makes four assumptions: (1) human behavior is expressed in some way in the archaeological record, (2) human behavior is variable, (3) the behavioral variants are reproduced differentially, and (4) adaptation occurs as those behavioral variants that cope with the problems of the ecological theater become more abundant through differential reproduction. For purposes here, the feature systems of mining technology, settlement, and households express behavioral variants through the documentary and archaeological record. The process of adaptation on the mining frontier therefore means the differential reproduction of particular kinds of feature-systems. Some become more abundant, some less so.

Kirch's model portrays the process of adaptation as a predictable sequence of three stages. The first stage occurs when colonists with pre-adapted behavior enter a new environment. It is a stage of low variability and poor adaptation to new problems. After the initial colonization of the new habitat, the settlers enter a coping stage of adaptation. During this second, problem-solving stage, experimentation and innovation is encouraged, thereby increasing both behavioral variability and, by definition, the intensity of selection acting upon the system. The final stage occurs when the colonists have adapted their behavior to the environment. Following unsuccessful experiments, directional selection has retained only the solutions to the critical environmental problems; as a result, the settler's behavior has low variability but a much better environmental fit.

Coping Strategies

Miners use two kinds of adaptive or coping strategies to solve the problems of the mining frontier. Opportunistic strategies can be defined as rules of conduct for maximizing resource gains. They might be applied for short-term mining of an unexpectedly abundant ore body or a sudden market opportunity. The most common opportunistic strategies are expansion into a new geographical area; resource intensification, including greater capital investment in land and labor and increasing resource specialization; and pooling (like partnerships, cooperatives, or sharing of tools and labor) to muster more resources (Bennett 1969, 1976). Several abrupt shifts in the behavior of colonists usually occur as the opportunistic strategy is put into effect, such as revolutionary changes in settlement pattern and household organization. Kirch's (1980, 1997) model of cultural adaptation also suggests that opportunistic strategies will reduce the amount of variability in the behavior of settlements and households because the most effective strategies are adopted quickly. At the same time, population growth should rapidly increase. Mining booms are expected to cause revolutionary shifts in opportunistic coping strategies.

The concept of opportunity cost may be the key to understanding opportunistic strategies (Hardesty 1986d). Expansion into a new niche occurs when "the benefit/cost ratio of staying in the old niche is less than the opportunity benefit/opportunity cost ratio of shifting to a new niche" (Hardesty 1986d:13). How to measure the costs of moving into a new niche is a problem. Certainly it involves the expense, however measured, of coping with or removing competitors, who in western mining districts were often the Native Americans living in the area. And it includes the cost of equipment and labor used to develop the mine. Capitalization is therefore one of the key parts of opportunistic strategies in mining areas.

Data from the Cortez Mining District illustrates how opportunistic strategies brought about changes in mining technology (Hardesty and Edaburn 1982). Here, the first miners carried with them a pre-adapted and standardized technology developed on the Comstock Lode. The Cortez Gold and Silver Mining Company Mill, for example, the first in the district, used a Washoe process pan amalgamation technology imported from the same San Francisco foundries supplying the Comstock mills. Included in the highly standardized milling technology was a 40–horsepower steam engine from the Vulcan Iron Works, a Coffey and Risdon steam boiler, eight 700–pound California stamps, settling tanks, twelve Knox amalgamating pans, and two wooden agitators (*Reese River Reveille* 7 May 1864:1). But the imported technology was a failure (Bancroft 1889:12). Experimentation demonstrated that roasting with salt was required before the complex ores would release the precious metals (Bancroft 1889:12; Oberbillig 1967:30). In 1865 the Cortez Mill adopted the new Reese River process by adding four reverberatory furnaces for the chloridizing roast (Bancroft 1889:12; *Reese River Reveille* 8 May 1867:1). The opportunity cost of the technological change, however, was quite high. Not only were the new furnaces expensive, but the Reese River process requires large amounts of salt, which had to be delivered from outside the district. Higher mill yields, either through more ore production from the mines or by increasing the efficiency with which the mill extracted bullion from the ore, had to compensate for the additional cost. The addition of more amalgamation equipment later made the mill more efficient, allowing all four furnaces to be used to best advantage (*Reese River Reveille* 8 July 1867:1). Even with these changes, however, the opportunity costs could not be met. By 1868 the Cortez Company, which operated the mill, stopped its mining operation, and the Cortez district was nearly deserted (Raymond 1869:82; Hague 1870[3]:406). But the discovery of a large ore body at the Garrison Mine changed all that. Simeon Wenban, the mine owner, purchased the Cortez Company Mill to process the ore from the new mine. The mill was enlarged and reopened by 1870 (Emmons 1910:101). This realization of a new mining opportunity represented a successful leap to a new ecological niche. The mill continued operations until 1886, when Wenban built a new mill next to the mine.

Taking advantage of new mining opportunities, however, is sometimes less important than surviving sudden, unpredictable changes in the environment. Perhaps the best example comes from the ore body itself. Despite the geological constancy of the ore body in most mining districts, it is a constantly changing environment to a miner with little knowledge of its variability; he must search for it as if blindfolded. Not until the 20th century was modern exploratory technology, including drilling and remote sensing, available to greatly facilitate the collection of information about an ore body before mining. Many ore bodies are distributed randomly below the ground, making mining something like the movement of passengers on a lifeboat drifting aimlessly toward an island. And if ore body outcrops are rare, the tracking process is even more difficult. Each new ore body poses unique mining and milling problems. For this reason, mining as an adaptive process involves tracking a very complex and variable environment. Resiliency and flexibility are much more effective ways of coping with environmental problems under such circumstances (McCay 1981). Strategies include finding new markets, cutting costs, and geographical contraction. Kirch's (1980, 1997) model also suggests that a resiliency strategy—experimenting with ways to cope with the conditions of intensified stress—may increase variability in behavior among mining settlements and households. And overall population size is expected to decline. Failing to cope with the sudden loss of a resource opportunity leads to a rather rapid shift to a new niche or to abandonment of the area.

In the Cortez Mining District, resiliency strategies were built around changes in tools and the organization of labor to minimize mining and milling costs (Hardesty and Edaburn 1982). The Russell lixiviation technology installed at Wenban's 1886 Mill, for example, used calcium sulfide instead of sodium sulfide (Egleston 1887:529–531). Wenban was able to quarry limestone from an outcropping next to the mill and make lime from a nearby kiln, so that lime could be obtained for next to nothing. The use of Krom rolls at the same mill was another manifestation of cutting costs in the adaptive strategy. Krom rolls do not grind ores as finely as other methods, but they are cheaper to buy, less costly to maintain, and do not require a building because they are self-contained (Eissler 1898:213–217). Finally, Krom rolls reduce the cost of ore extraction because they can grind more metals—the base metals zinc, copper, and lead as well as gold and silver.

The second part of the resiliency strategy is cutting the cost of mining the ore body through labor. Perhaps the most unique innovation was the nearly exclusive use of immigrant Chinese miners by the Tenabo Mill and Mining Company in the Cortez Mining District. The company's paternalistic relationship with the miners sustained the mining operation even when the ore environment was at its worst. If the mine suddenly entered a period of borrasca (very low ore production), the miners were willing to work for nothing but subsistence until the crisis was over because of their loyalty to the company. Another labor innovation was the contract and tribute system used by the Manhattan Silver Mining Company in the Reese River Mining District. Miners worked for a percentage of what they found as opposed to a set wage. The contract and tribute system allowed the expansion of mining into a large number of ore bodies through only small investments. Not only did the system cut labor costs by eliminating strikes and high wages, but it also reduced the risk to the company of a sudden borrasca in single mines.

A Coevolutionary Model of Adaptive Change

The cornerstone of Darwinian evolution is the individual organism and the material conditions in which it survives (Rindos 1984). Adequately incorporating the "individual" into evolutionary interpretations of social and cultural behavior, however, has posed a problem (Deiner 1980). Ian Hodder (1986) has made the same point for archaeology in general. A coevolutionary model of change and variability that is built around the individual can apply to the mining frontier (Hardesty 1985b). The model is outlined here as an example of yet another approach to asking questions about mining sites.

Human behavior is creative; it can rapidly create new ecological theaters through principles and ideologies that "transform nature into culture" (Bennett 1976; Bargatsky 1984; Hardesty 1985b, 1986d). Each new theater has a distinctive pattern of differential fitness. Individuals with the highest fitness values in the pattern have the greatest chance of increasing their behavior over time at the expense of those with lower fitness values. The result is evolutionary change in the direction of the behavior stipulated by the initial cultural baggage, a classic example of a positive-feedback loop in a coevolutionary relationship.

Explaining the beginning of a new evolutionary direction in this feedback loop is a critical problem in such a model. Paul Deiner (1980) argues that unique historical events are "kickers" that drastically change the ideologies controlling social institutions and technologies—political upheavals or revolutions, technological innovations, military conquests, and religious movements, for example. The new ideologies instantly create new ecological theaters. On the 19th-century mining frontier, such leaps often took place on the heels of (1) technological innovations like the railroad, the telegraph, and new milling or mining techniques; (2) geological events such as the discovery of new ore bodies; (3) economic events like changes in the market prices of precious metals; and (4) ideological events such as the spread of Victorianism. The sudden leap to a new ecological plateau or structure creates another pattern of differential fitness, changing the sorting process and bringing about a new direction of evolutionary change. Evolution on the mining frontier can be viewed, then, as a sequence of historically unique quantum leaps working in tandem with a rather mechanical process of selection.

Perhaps the most important measurement of adaptive change through selection is Darwinian fitness, simply the ratio of the reproductive rate of a particular variant to that of the variant that is being reproduced at the highest rate. A measurement of the fitness of genetic variants, for example, uses the number of biological offspring in the ratio. But the evolutionary study of nongenetic variants is more complicated. How the behavior of individuals is differentially reproduced has generated considerable controversy (Durham 1976; Chagnon and Irons 1979; Rindos 1984). Biographies of individuals, however, may offer the best information about the adaptive process, a topic that could integrate such diverse areas as ethnography, history, time-geography, and life history studies in biology. Certainly, documentary accounts of individuals on the mining frontier are common (Bancroft 1889; Hughes 1957; Walton 1960; Fell 1982). The individual is less visible in the archaeological record. Individuals, however, can basically cope with the ecological theater because of their membership in social groups. This suggests that the household, which is more visible, may be the closest archaeological link to evolutionary theory.

Richard Mazess (1975) proposes several domains of secular fitness in individuals, including physical performance, nervous system functioning, growth and development, nutrition, reproduction, health, cross-tolerance and resistance, affective functioning, and intellectual ability. A similar approach is taken here. Fitness is anything related to the survival, persistence, and reproductive success of individuals and their behavior on the mining frontier of 19th-century and early-20th-century America. When evaluating evolutionary change, however, only relative success is important (Rindos 1984:38–44). For this reason, things that create differences in persistence, survival, and reproduction are the best indicators of fitness domains. Anything that increases or decreases competition with others, for example, would be an appropriate fitness domain. On the mining frontier, opportunism—the ability to move rapidly into different ecological niches—was one of the most important ways in which this was accomplished and is therefore a significant fitness domain. Other fitness domains include things that increase or decrease the effectiveness of exploiting resources on the mining frontier. Work capacity, health and nutrition, mining knowledge and experience, organizational resources (such as household strategies or corporations at the world-system level), and capitalization are but a few of these domains.

The fitness of social variants is measured similarly by their relative rate of reproduction. For example, the fitness of a type of household, such as a large single-sex coresidential group, can be measured by combining documentary and archaeological information about its frequency over time in a mining settlement. Types of household organization are expected to vary in fitness because of their greater or lesser success in coping with boom-bust cycles and other environmental stresses on the mining frontier. Large single-sex coresidential households may be the most fit as a resilience strategy for coping with extreme boom-bust fluctuations. Certainly it is possible to document the relative rate at which such households are being reproduced in different boom-bust environments and use the data to test such a proposition.

An illustration of the coevolutionary model comes from the Comstock Mining District. During the 1850s, individuals or small groups explored Gold Canyon and worked the placers in what might best be called a prospector structure. The prospector structure includes (1) the use of a nonindustrial technology like Long Toms and simple arrastras that can be handled by single individuals or small groups; (2) low capitalization, usually no more than a grubstake; (3) a dispersed control structure centered on individual miners; (4) low potential yield from the placers; and (5) low spatial autocorrelation of the placers being worked—that is, historical events on each of the placer islands on the frontier were more or less independent of one another. Prospector structures were defined further by the relative absence of large-scale communication and transportation networks that could create regional, national, and world systems, such as the railroad and telegraph. As a result, the Comstock was isolated from the outside world. And even though Mexican and Chinese nationals worked the placers, they did not participate in the world systems, as did the Chinese Six Companies that were later to dominate the Comstock.

The prospector structure has significant implications for patterns of individual fitness. Leveling mechanisms like readily accessible placers, the low yields and dispersion of placers, cheap, low-technology industry, and low capitalization acted to limit greatly the extent of mining success or failure. The minimal differences in fitness are reflected further in the demographic and social organization of the typical mining camp within the prospector structure: it was of small size, had an egalitarian social structure, was inhabited mostly by adult males, and had little variation from one household to another.

The discovery in 1859 of the Comstock Lode at the head of Gold Canyon set in motion a series of changes that created a dramatically new ecological theater. The Comstock Lode was a deeply buried ore body containing large amounts of silver and gold that could not be exploited with the technology, ideology, and capitalization of the prospector structure. In the 1860s the corporate industrial structure rapidly replaced the prospector structure. The corporate model included (1) high capitalization; (2) industrial technology with specialized mining and milling tools and processes; (3) high spatial autocorrelation, with extensive networks of ore bodies integrated into large regional, national, and world systems that tended to change together rather than separately (Hardesty 1985a); (4) high potential yields; and (5) a centralized control structure. Revolutions in communications and transportation integrated the Comstock into world systems and further defined the industrial structure. One manifestation of the world-system structure was the introduction of Victorian ideology into the control structure. Another was the expansion of the Chinese Six Companies network into the Comstock.

The sudden shift from the prospector to the corporate industrial structure dramatically changed the pattern of differential fitness underlying evolutionary change on the Comstock. Perhaps its greatest impact was increasing differences in mining success among individuals. Differences in mining knowledge and experience, capitalization, ethnicity, and ideology all played a role. Individuals such as William Sharon, James G. Fair, John W. Mackay, and William C. Ralston operated especially well within this ecological structure mostly because of greater wealth and corporate resources, and they took over the highly centralized control structure. Victorian ideology increased differential fitness even more by promoting self-improvement and self-sacrifice, didacticism, and compulsive behavior stressing hard work (Howe 1976), all of which widened the gap between those at the top of the control structure and those at the bottom. The "rich get richer" positive-feedback loop continued to affect the human populations in the Comstock corporate industrial structure until the 1880s. By this point, miners had removed the main body of the lode, leaving the remainder virtually inaccessible because of the heat and water encountered at great depths. This decade ushered in a new ecological structure focused on mechanized placer mining, carving out yet another evolutionary pathway on the Comstock.

References Cited

Abbe, Donald R.

1985 *Austin and the Reese River Mining District: Nevada's Forgotten Frontier.* University of Nevada Press, Reno.

Adams, William H.

1976 Trade Networks and Interaction Spheres—A View from Silcott. *Historical Archaeology* 10(2):99–112.

2002 Machine Cut Nails and Wire Nails: American Production and Use for Dating 19th-Century and Early-20th-Century Sites. *Historical Archaeology* 36(4):66–88.

Alanen, Arnold J.

1979 Documenting the Physical and Social Characteristics of Mining and Resource-Based Communities. *The Association of Preservation Technology Bulletin* 11(4):49–68.

Allen, James B.

1966 *The Company Town in the American West.* University of Oklahoma Press, Norman.

Angel, Myron (editor)

1881 *History of Nevada.* Thompson and West, Oakland CA.

Arrington, Leonard J.

1958 *Great Basin Kingdom: An Economic History of the Latter Day Saints, 1830–1900.* Harvard University Press, Cambridge. Reprinted 1993 by the University of Utah Press, Salt Lake City.

1979 *The Mormons in Nevada.* Las Vegas Sun, Las Vegas NV.

Ashbaugh, Don

1963 *Nevada's Turbulent Yesterday: A Study in Ghost Towns.* Westernlore Press, Los Angeles CA.

Baker, Stephen

1978 Historical Archaeology for Colorado and the Victorian Mining Frontier: Review, Discussion, and Suggestions. *Southwestern Lore* 44(4):11–31.

Bancroft, Hubert H.

1889 *History of the Life of Simeon Wenban.* Chronicles of the Kings. The History Company, San Francisco CA.

Bargatsky, T.

1984 Culture, Environment, and the Ills of Adaptationism. *Current Anthropology* 25(4):399–415.

Bennett, John W.

1969 *Northern Plainsmen: Adaptive Strategy and Agrarian Life.* Aldine Press, Chicago IL.

1976   *The Ecological Transition: Cultural Anthropology and Human Adaptation.*
       Pergamon Press, New York NY.

Bonham, Harold
1969   *Geology and Mineral Deposits of Washoe and Storey Counties, Nevada.*
       Nevada Bureau of Mines and Geology, Bulletin 70, Mackay School of Mines,
       University of Nevada, Reno.

Braudel, Fernand
1940   Preface to *La Méditerranéen et le monde Méditerranéen á l'époque de Phillippe II.*
(1980) Armand Colin, Paris. Reprinted 1980 in *On History,* Sarah Matthews,
       translator, by University of Chicago Press, Chicago IL.

Briuer, L., and Clay Mathers
1996   *Trends and Patterns in Cultural Resource Significance: An Historical Perspective
       and Annotated Bibliography.* U.S. Army Corps of Engineers, Alexandria VA.

Brown, Ronald C.
1979   *Hard-Rock Miners: The Intermountain West, 1860–1920.* Texas A&M University
       Press, College Station.

Browne, J. Ross
1871   *Adventures in the Apache Country: A Tour Through Arizona and Sonora,
       with Notes on the Silver Regions of Nevada.* Harper and Brothers, New York NY.

Brumfiel, Elizabeth
1992   Distinguished Lecture in Archaeology: Breaking and Entering the
       Ecosystem—Gender, Class, and Faction Steal the Show. *American
       Anthropologist* 94(3):551–568.

Buchler, Ira R., and Henry A. Selby
1968   *Kinship and Social Organization: An Introduction to Theory and Method.*
       Macmillan, New York NY.

Busch, Jane
1981   An Introduction to the Tin Can. *Historical Archaeology* 15(1):95–104.

Calkins, F. C.
1944   *Outline of the Geology of the Comstock Lode District.* U.S. Geological Survey,
       Open File Report.

Canuto, Marcello A., and Jason Yaeger (editors)
2000   *Archaeology of Communities: A New World Perspecive.* Routledge, London,
       England

Carter, Anthony T.
1984   Household Histories. In *Households: Comparative and Historical Studies
       of the Domestic Group,* Robert McC. Netting, Richard R. Wilk, and Eric J.
       Arnould, editors, pp. 44–83. University of California Press, Berkeley.

Cassel, John F.
1863   Book of Records of the Cortez Mining District, Lander County, Nevada
       Territory. Special Collections, Getchell Library, University of Nevada, Reno.

Chadwick, Robert
1982   Montana's Silver Mining Era: Great Boom and Bust. *Montana* 32(2):16–31.

Chagnon, Napoleon A., and Willian Irons (editors)
1979   *Evolutionary Biology and Human Social Behavior: An Anthropological Perspective.*
       Duxbury Press, North Scituate MA.

Churchill County Museum and Archives.
1893   Mine Records. Churchill County Museum and Archives, Fallon NV.

Clow, Richmond L.
2002   *Chasing the Glitter: Black Hills Milling, 1874–1959.* South Dakota State Historical Society Press, Pierre SD.

Cook, Sherburne F.
1972   *Prehistoric Demography.* Mccaleb Module 16. Addison-Wesley, Reading PA.

Couch, Bertrand F., and Jay A. Carpenter
1943   *Nevada's Metal and Mineral Production.* University of Nevada Bulletin 37(4), Geology and Mining Series, No. 38.

Crumley, Carole
1994a   Historical Ecology: A Multidimensional Ecological Orientation. In *Historical Ecology: Cultural Knowledge and Changing Landscapes,* Carole L. Crumley, editor, pp. 1–16. School of American Research Press, Santa Fe NM.

Crumley, Carole (editor)
1994b   *Historical Ecology: Cultural Knowledge and Changing Landscapes.* School of American Research Press, Sante Fe NM.

Davies, J. Kenneth
1984   *Mormon Gold: The Story of California's Mormon Argonauts.* Olympus Publishing Company, Salt Lake City UT.

Deetz, James
1988   American Historical Archaeology: Methods and Results. *Science* 239(4838):363–367.

Deiner, Paul
1980   Quantum Adjustment, Macroevolution, and the Social Field: Some Comments on Evolution and Culture. *Current Anthropology* 21(4):423–443.

Delyser, Dydia
1999   Authenticity on the Ground: Engaging the Past in a California Ghost Town. *Annals of the Association of American Geographers* 89(4):602–632.

De Quille, Dan [William Wright]
1876   *The Big Bonanza.* American Publishing Company, Hartford CT. Reprinted 1974 by Nevada Publications, Las Vegas.

Dorr, John V. N.
1936   *Cyanidation and Concentration of Gold and Silver Ores.* Mcgraw-Hill Book Company, New York NY.

Drinker, Henry S.
1883   *A Treatise on Explosive Compounds, Machine Rock Drills, and Blasting.* John Wiley and Sons, New York NY.

Durham, William
1976   The Adaptive Significance of Cultural Behavior. *Human Ecology* 4(2):89–121.

Egleston, Thomas
1887   *Metallurgy of Silver, Gold, and Mercury in the United States,* 2 vols. John Wiley and Sons, New York NY.

Eissler, Manuel
1898   *The Metallurgy of Silver: A Practical Treatise on the Amalgamation, Roasting and Lixiviation of Silver Ores Including the Assaying, Melting and Refining of Silver Bullion,* 4th edition. Crosby, Lockwood and Son, London, England.

Elliott, Russell R.

1966 *Nevada's Twentieth-Century Mining Boom: Tonopah, Goldfield, Ely.* University of Nevada Press, Reno. Reprinted 1988 by the University of Nevada Press, Reno.

Emmons, William H.

1910 *A Reconnaissance of Some Mining Camps in Elko, Lander, and Eureka Counties, Nevada.* U.S. Geological Survey, Bulletin 408, Washington DC.

Engineering and Mining Journal

1910 *Engineering and Mining Journal* 8 January, 22 January. Hill Publishing Company, New York NY.

1911 *Engineering and Mining Journal* 1 April. Hill Publishing Company, New York NY.

1927 Cortez Stamp Mill at Tenabo, Nev., changed to Flotation Plant. *Engineering and Mining Journal* 124(5):188. Hill Publishing Company, New York NY.

Fell, James E.

1982 *Arthur Redman Wilfley, Miner, Inventor, and Entrepreneur.* Western Business History Research Center, Colorado Historical Society, Louisville CO.

Fetherling, George

1997 *The Gold Crusades: A Social History of Gold Rushes, 1849–1929,* revised edition. University of Toronto Press, Toronto, Canada.

Francaviglia, Richard V.

1997 *Hard Places: Reading the Landscape of America's Historic Mining Districts.* University of Iowa Press, Iowa City.

Getchell Library

1893 Invoices and account books. Special Collections, Getchell Library, University of Nevada, Reno.

Gianella, Vincent

1936 *Geology of the Silver City District and the Southern Portion of the Comstock Lode, Nevada.* University of Nevada Bulletin 30(9), Nevada Bureau of Mines and Mackay School of Mines, University of Nevada, Reno.

Gilluly, James, and Harold Masursky

1965 *Geology of the Cortez Quadrangle, Nevada.* U.S. Geological Survey, Bulletin 1175, Washington DC.

Godden, Geoffrey A.

1964 *Encyclopaedia of British Pottery and Porcelain Marks.* Crown Publishers, New York NY.

Godoy, Ricardo A.

1985 Mining: Anthropological Perspectives. *Annual Review of Anthropology* 14:199–217.

1990 *Mining and Agriculture in Highland Bolivia.* University of Arizona Press, Tucson.

Goin, Peter, and C. Elizabeth Raymond

2004 *Changing Mines in America.* Center for American Places, Santa Fe NM.

Goody, Jack (editor)

1958 *The Domestic Cycle in Domestic Groups.* Cambridge Papers in Social Anthropology, No. 1. Cambridge University Press, Cambridge.

Hague, James D.

1870 The Cortez District. *U.S. Geological Exploration of the Fortieth Parallel,* Vol. 3. Professional Papers of the Engineer Department, U.S. Army, No. 18. Washington DC.

Hall, Martin, and Stephen W. Silliman (editors)

2006　*Historical Archaeology.* Blackwell, Malden MA.

Hammel, Eugene

1972　The Zadruga as a Process. In *Household and Family in Past Times: Comparative Studies in the Size and Structure of the Domestic Group over the Last Three Centuries in England, France, Serbia, Japan and Colonial North America, with Further Materials from Western Europe,* Peter Laslett and Richard Wall, editors, pp. 335–374. Cambridge University Press, Cambridge, England.

Hammel, Eugene, and Peter Laslett

1974　Comparing Household Structure Over Time and Between Cultures. *Comparative Studies in Society and History* 16:73–109.

Hardesty, Donald L.

1981　Recovery of Historical Archeological Data in Bullfrog Claim and Mining Sites, Nye County, Nevada, Death Valley National Monument. University of Nevada, Reno, and the National Park Service, San Francisco.

1985a　Evolution on the Industrial Frontier. In *The Archaeology of Frontiers and Boundaries,* Stanton W. Green and Steve M. Perlman, editors, pp. 213–229. Academic Press, Orlando FL.

1985b　Evolutionary Thinking in Historical Archaeology: Suggestions from the Industrial Frontier. Paper presented at the 1985 Annual Meeting of the Society for American Archaeology, Denver CO.

1986a　Bonanza! The Comstock Lode and California. In *Silver in the Golden State: Images and Essays Celebrating the History and Art of Silver in California,* Edgar W. Morse, editor, pp. 57–83. Oakland Museum History Department, Oakland CA.

1986b　Evaluation of Cultural Resources at the Gold Bar Mine, Death Valley National Monument. Report to Columbus Mines, Inc., Reno NV.

1986c　Industrial Archaeology on the American Mining Frontier: Suggestions for a Research Agenda. *Journal of New World Archaeology* 6(4):47–56.

1986d　Rethinking Cultural Adaptation. *The Professional Geographer* 38(1):11–18.

1987a　Cultural Resources Data Recovery at the Gold Bar Mine, Death Valley National Monument. Report to Columbus Mines, Inc., Reno NV.

1987b　Evaluation of Cultural Resources in the Bullfrog/Montgomery-Shoshone Area. Report to St. Joe Gold Corporation, Tucson AZ.

1987c　Evaluating Site Significance in Historical Mining Districts. Paper presented at the 1987 Annual Meeting of the Society for Historical Archaeology, Savannah GA.

1992　The Miner's Domestic Household: Perspectives from the American West. In *Sozialgeschichte des Bergbau im 19. und 20. Jahrundert: Beiträge des Internationalen Kongresses zur Bergbaugeschichte Bochum, Bundesrepublik Deutschland, 3–7* (Toward a Social History of Mining in the 19th and 20th Centuries), Klaus Tenfelde, editor, pp. 180–196. Verlag C. H. Beck, München, Germany.

1998　Power and the Industrial Mining Community in the American West. In *Social Approaches to an Industrial Past: The Archaeology and Anthropology of Mining,* A. Bernard Knapp, Vincent C. Pigott, and Eugenia W. Herbert, editors, pp. 81–96. Routledge, London, England.

2001　Issues in Preserving Toxic Wastes as Heritage Sites. *The Public Historian* 23(2):19–28.

2006   Industrial Archaeology, Landscapes, and Historical Knowledge. In *Monitoring Science and Technology Symposium: Unifying Knowledge for Sustainability in the Western Hemisphere*, Celedonio Aguirre-Bravo, Patrick J. Pellicane, Denver P. Burns, and Sidney Draggan, editors, pp. 514–517. Proceedings RMRS-P-000. Fort Collins CO: U.S. Department of Agriculture, Forest Service, Rocky Mountain Research Station.

2007   Historical Evaluation of the Billie Borate Mine, Death Valley, California. Report to American Borate Company, Virginia Beach VA.

Hardesty, Donald L., and Sharon Edaburn

1982   Technological Systems on the Nevada Mining Frontier. Paper presented at the 1982 Annual Meeting of the Society for Historical Archaeology, Philadelphia PA.

Hardesty, Donald L., and Valerie Firby

1980   Managing Archaeological Resources on the Comstock. Heritage Conservation and Recreation Service, National Architectural and Engineering Record, Washington DC.

Hardesty, Donald L., and Don D. Fowler

2001   Archaeology and Environmental Changes. In *New Directions in Anthropology and Environment: Intersections*, Carole L. Crumley, editor, pp. 72–89. Altamira Press, Walnut Creek CA.

Hardesty, Donald L., and Eugene M. Hattori

1982   *Archaeological Studies in the Cortez Mining District, 1981.* Bureau of Land Management, Technical Report No. 8, Reno NV.

1983a   An Archaeological Model of Victorianism on the Nevada Mining Frontier. Paper presented at the 1983 Annual Meeting of the Society for Historical Archaeology, Denver CO.

1983b   *Archaeological Studies in the Cortez Mining District, 1982.* Bureau of Land Management, Technical Report No. 12, Reno NV.

1984   *Archaeological Studies in the Cortez Mining District, 1983.* Bureau of Land Management, Battle Mountain District, Battle Mountain NV.

Hattori, Eugene M., Donald L. Hardesty, and Alvin Mclane

1984   Additional and Updated Cortez History. In *Archaeological Studies in the Cortez Mining District, 1983*, Donald L. Hardesty and Eugene M. Hattori, pp. 46–53. Bureau of Land Management, Battle Mountain District, Battle Mountain NV.

Hattori, Eugene M., and Marna Thompson

1987   Using Dendrochronology for Historical Reconstruction in the Cortez Mining District, North-Central Nevada. *Historical Archaeology* 21(2):60–73.

Heikes, V.C.

1927   Reduction Mills in Nevada in 1925. *Information Circular* 6028, U.S. Bureau of Mines. Washington DC.

Hennessy, Alistair.

1978   *The Frontier in Latin American History.* University of New Mexico Press, Albuquerque.

Hezzelwood, G. W.

1930   Mining Methods and Costs at the Consolidated Cortez Silver Mine, Cortez, Nevada. *Information Circular* 6327, U.S. Bureau of Mines. Washington DC.

Hill, James M.

    1912   *The Mining Districts of the Western United States*. U.S. Geological Survey, Bulletin 507, Washington DC.

Hine, Robert V.

    1980   *Community on the American Frontier: Separate But Not Alone*. University of Oklahoma Press, Norman.

Hine, Robert V., and John Mack Faragher

    2000   *The American West: A New Interpretive History*. Yale University Press, New Haven CT.

Hodder, Ian

    1986   *Reading the Past: Current Approaches to Interpretation in Archaeology*. Cambridge University Press, Cambridge, England.

Holliday, J. S.

    1999   *Rush for Riches: Gold Fever and the Making of California*. University of California Press, Berkeley.

Horton, Robert C., and Francis Church Lincoln

    1964   *Outline of Nevada Mining History*, 2 pts. Mackay School of Mines, University of Nevada, Reno.

Hovis, Logan

    1992   Historic Mining Sites: A Typology for the Alaskan National Parks. National Park Service, Alaska Regional Office, Anchorage.

Howe, Daniel W.

    1975   American Victorianism as a Culture. *American Quarterly* 27:507–532.

    1976   Victorian Culture in America. In *Victorian America*, Daniel Walker Howe, editor, pp. 1–19. University of Pennsylvania Press, Philadelphia.

Hughes, Richard B.

    1957   *Pioneer Years in the Black Hills*. A. H. Clarke Co., Glendale CA.

Hughes, Thomas P.

    1983   *Networks of Power: Electrification in Western Society, 1880–1930*. Johns Hopkins University Press, Baltimore MD.

Hunt, Charles B.

    1959   Dating of Mining Camps with Tin Cans and Bottles. *Geotimes* 3(8):8–10, 34.

Hyde, Charles K.

    1998   *Copper for America: The United States Copper Industry from Colonial Times to the 1990s*. University of Arizona Press, Tucson.

Ingalls, Walter R.

    1907   The Silver-Lead Mines of Eureka, Nevada. *The Engineering and Mining Journal* 84(23):1051–1058.

Isenberg, Andrew C.

    2006   *Mining California: An Ecological History*. Hill and Wang, New York NY.

Jackson, W. Turrentine

    1963   Treasure Hill. University of Arizona Press, Tucson. Reprinted 2000 by the University of Nevada Press, Reno.

James, Ronald M.

    1994   *Temples of Justice: County Courthouses of Nevada*. University of Nevada Press, Reno.

1998   The Roar and the Silence: A History of Virginia City and the Comstock Lode. University of Nevada Press, Reno.

Jones, Olive

1971   Glass Bottle Push-Ups and Pontils. *Historical Archaeology* 5:62–73.

Jones, Olive, and Catherine Sullivan

1989   The Parks Canada Glass Glossary for the Description of Containers, Tableware, Flat Glass, and Closures, revised from 1985 edition. Canadian Parks Services, Ottawa.

Kelly, Roger E., and Marsha C. Kelly

1983   Arrastras: Unique Western Historic Milling Sites. *Historical Archaeology* 17(1):85–95.

Kirch, Patrick

1980   The Archaeological Study of Adaptation. In *Advances in Archaeological Method and Theory*, Vol. 3, Michael B. Schiffer, editor, pp. 101–156. Academic Press, New York NY.

1997   Microcosmic Histories: Island Perspectives on 'Global' Change. *American Anthropologist* 99(1):30–42.

Knapp, A. Bernard, Vincent C. Piggot, and Eugenia W. Herbert (editors)

1998   Social Approaches to an Industrial Past: The Archaeology and Anthropology of Mining. Routledge, London, England.

Kral, Victor E.

1951   Mineral Resources of Nye County. University of Nevada Bulletin 45(3), Geology and Mining Series, No. 50.

Küstel, Guido

1863   Nevada and California Processes of Silver and Gold Extraction. F. D. Carlton, San Francisco CA.

Lander County Tax Assessment Rolls

1884   Lander County Tax Assessment Rolls. Battle Mountain NV.

1885   Lander County Tax Assessment Rolls. Battle Mountain NV.

Laslett, Peter, and Richard Wall (editors)

1972   Household and Family in Past Time: Comparative Studies in the Size and Structure of the Domestic Group over the Last Three Centuries in England, France, Serbia, Japan and Colonial North America, with Further Materials from Western Europe. Cambridge University Press, Cambridge, England.

Latschar, John

1981   A History of Mining in Death Valley National Monument, Vol. 2, Pt. 1. Historic Preservation Branch, Pacific Northwest/Western Team, Denver Service Center, National Park Service, Denver CO.

Lee, Rose Hum

1960   The Chinese in the United States of America. Hong Kong University Press, Hong Kong.

Legislature of the State of Nevada

1891   Report of the Surveyor General of the State of Nevada. In *Appendix to the Journals of the State Senate and Assembly*, 25th Session. State Printing Office, Carson City NV.

1911   Report of the State Inspector of Mines. In *Appendix to the Journals of the State Senate and Assembly*, 25th Session, Vol. 2. State Printing Office, Carson City NV.

1939   Report of the State Inspector of Mines. In *Appendix to the Journals of the State Senate and Assembly*, 39th Session, Vol. 1. State Printing Office, Carson City NV.

1941   Report of the State Inspector of Mines. In *Appendix to the Journals of the State Senate and Assembly*, 40th Session, Vol. 1. State Printing Office, Carson City NV.

1943   Report of the State Inspector of Mines. In *Appendix to the Journals of the State Senate and Assembly*, 41st Session, Vol. 1. State Printing Office, Carson City NV.

Leone, Mark

1984   Interpreting Ideology in Historical Archaeology: The William Paca Garden in Annapolis, Maryland. In *Ideology, Power, and Prehistory*, Daniel Miller and Christopher Tilley, editors, pp. 25–35. Cambridge University Press, Cambridge, England.

Lincoln, Francis C.

1923   *Mining Districts and Mineral Resources of Nevada*. Nevada Newsletter Publishing Company, Reno. Reprinted 1982 by Nevada Publications, Las Vegas.

Lingenfelter, Richard E.

1986   *Death Valley and the Amargosa: A Land of Illusion*. University of California Press, Berkeley.

Little, Barbara J., and Paul Shackel

1989   Scales of Historical Anthropology: An Archaeology of Colonial Anglo-America. *Antiquity* 63(240):495–509.

Lord, Eliot

1883   *Comstock Mining and Miners*. U.S. Geological Survey, Washington DC. Reprinted 1959 by Howell-North, Berkeley CA.

Lorrain, Dessamae

1968   An Archaeologist's Guide to Nineteenth Century American Glass. *Historical Archaeology* 2: 35–44.

MacFarren, H. W.

1912   *Text Book of Cyanide Practice*. McGraw Hill, New York NY.

Mann, Michael

1986   *The Sources of Social Power, volume 1, A History of Power from the Beginning to A.D. 1760*. Cambridge University Press, Cambridge, England.

Mathews, M. M.

1985   *Ten Years in Nevada: Or, Life on the Pacific Coast*. University of Nebraska Press, Lincoln.

Mazess, Richard

1975   Human Adaptation to High Altitude. In *Physiological Anthropology*, Albert Damon, editor, pp. 167–209. Oxford University Press, New York NY.

McCay, Bonnie

1981   Optimal Foraging or Political Actors? Ecological Analyses of a New Jersey Fishery. *American Ethnologist* 8:358–382.

McClelland, Linda Flint, J. Timothy Keller, Genevieve P. Keller, and Robert Z. Melnick

1999   Guidelines for Evaluating and Documenting Rural Historic Landscapes. National Park Service, *National Register Bulletin 30*, Washington DC.

Miller, Alfred S.

1900   *A Manual of Assaying: The Fire Assay of Gold, Silver, and Lead, Including Amalgamation and Chlorination Tests*. John Wiley, New York NY.

Miller, George, and Catherine Sullivan

1984 Machine-Made Glass Containers and the End of Production for Mouth-Blown Bottles. *Historical Archaeology* 18 (2):83–96.

Mining and Scientific Press

1920 *Mining and Scientific Press* 29 May. San Francisco CA.

Molinelli, Lambert

1879 *Eureka and Its Resources: A Complete History of Eureka County, Nevada, Containing the United States Mining Laws, the Mining Laws of the District, Bullion Product and Other Statistics for 1878, and a List of County Officers.* H. Keller and Company, San Francisco CA. Reprinted 1982 by the University of Nevada Press, Reno.

Morse, Kathryn Taylor

2003 *The Nature of Gold: An Environmental History of the Klondike Gold Rush.* University of Washington Press, Seattle.

Murbarger, Nell

1963 The Last Remaining Light. *True West* (January-February):32–34.

Murdock, George P.

1949 *Social Structure.* Macmillan Co., New York NY.

Myrick, David

1963 *Railroads of Nevada and Eastern California, Volume 2, The Southern Roads.* Howell-North Books, Berkeley CA.

Naramore, Charles, and C. G. Yale

1910 *Gold, Silver, Copper, Lead and Zinc in the Western States and Territories in 1908.* U.S. Geological Survey, Washington DC.

Nash, June

1979 *We Eat the Mines and the Mines Eat Us: Dependency and Exploitation in Bolivian Tin Mines.* Columbia University Press, New York NY.

Nelson, Lee H.

1968 Nail Chronology as an Aid to Dating Old Buildings. *American Association for State and Local History Technical Leaflet* 48, *History News* 24(11), Nashville TN.

Netting, Robert McC., Richard R. Wilk, and Eric J. Arnould

1984 Introduction. In *Households: Comparative and Historical Studies of the Domestic Group*, Robert McC. Netting, Richard R. Wilk, and Eric J. Arnould, editors, pp. xii–xxxviii. University of California Press, Berkeley.

Nevada Historical Society Collection.

n.d. Nevada in Maps. Nevada Historical Society Collection, Division of Museums and History, Nevada Department of Cultural Affairs, Reno NV.

Nicoletta, Julie

2000 *Buildings of Nevada.* Oxford University Press, New York NY.

Noble, Bruce, and Robert Spude

1992 Guidelines for Identifying, Evaluating, and Registering Historic Mining Properties. National Park Service, *National Register Bulletin* 42, Washington DC.

Oberbillig, Ernest

1967 Development of Washoe and Reese River Silver Processes. *Nevada Historical Society Quarterly* 10(2):3–43.

Owens, Kenneth N.

2002 Gold-Rich Saints: Mormon Beginnings of the California Gold Rush. In *Riches*

Storms, William H.

1909   *Timbering and Mining: A Treatise on Practical American Methods.* McGraw-Hill, New York NY.

Sui, Paul C.

1952   The Sojourner. *American Journal of Sociology* 58:34–44.

Sung, B. L.

1967   *Mountains of Gold.* Macmillan, New York NY.

Teague, George A.

1980   *Reward Mine and Associated Sites: Historical Archeology on the Papago Reservation.* National Park Service, Western Archeological Center Publications in Anthropology, No. 11, Tucson AZ.

1987   The Archaeology of Industry in North America. Doctoral dissertation, University of Arizona, Tucson.

Tingley, Joseph, Thomas Lugaski, and Alvin McLane

2001   Discovery of Mining Camps in South-Central Nevada. *The Mining History Journal* 8:18–29.

Todd, Arthur C.

1967   *The Cornish Miner in America.* Glendale, Clark, New York NY.

Toulouse, Julian

1971   *Bottle Makers and Their Marks.* Thomas Nelson, Inc., Camden NY.

Trachtenberg, Alan

1982   *The Incorporation of America: Culture and Society in the Gilded Age.* Hill and Wang, New York NY.

Twitty, Eric

2002   *Riches to Rust: A Guide to Mining in the Old West.* Western Reflections Publishing Company, Montrose CO.

Van Bueren, Thad M.

2004   The "Poor Man's Mill:" A Rich Vernacular Legacy. IA: *The Journal of the Society for Industrial Archaeology* 30(2):5–24.

Van Saun, Edwin

1910   Cyaniding at the Montgomery-Shoshone Mill. *The Engineering and Mining Journal* (22 January 1910):217–219.

Vanderburg, William O.

1936   *Placer Mining in Nevada.* Nevada Bureau of Mines and Geology, Bulletin 27, Reno NV.

1937   Mines of Clark County. In Formation Circular 6964, U. S. Bureau of Mines. Washington DC.

1938   Reconnaissance of Mining Districts in Eureka County, Nevada. *Information Circular 7022*, U.S. Bureau of Mines. Washington DC.

Wallerstein, Immanuel

1974   *The Modern World-System.* Academic Press, New York NY.

1980   *The Modern World System II.* Academic Press, New York NY.

Walton, Clyde C. (editor)

1960   *An Illinois Gold Hunter in the Black Hills; the Diary of Jerry Bryan, March 13 to August 20, 1876.* Illinois State Historical Society, Springfield.

Weed, Walter H.

1922   *The Mines Handbook*, Vol. 15. The Mines Handbook Company, Tuckahoe NY.

Weight, Harold, and Lucile Weight

1970   *Rhyolite, The Ghost City of Golden Dreams*, 5th edition. The Calico Press, Twentynine Palms CA.

Weight, Lucile

1950   The Chinese Ghost of Cortez. *Westways* 42(2):10–11.

Whitehall, H.R.

1875   Biennial Report of the State Mineralogist for 1873 and 1874. Appendix to the Journal of the Senate, Seventh Session. Carson City NV.

Whitley, Colleen (editor)

2006   *From the Ground Up: A History of Mining in Utah*. Utah State University Press, Logan.

Wilk, Richard R., and Robert McC. Netting

1984   Households: Changing Form and Functions. In *Households: Comparative and Historical Studies of the Domestic Group*, Robert McC. Netting, Richard R. Wilk, and Eric J. Arnould, editors, pp. 1–28. University of California Press, Berkeley.

Wilson, Rex L.

1981   *Bottles on the Western Frontier*. University of Arizona Press, Tucson.

Wolf, Eric R.

1982   *Europe and the People Without History*. University of California Press, Berkeley.

Wright, Ira L.

1930   Milling Methods and Costs at the Black Hawk Concentrator, Hanover, New Mexico. *Information Circular* 6359, U.S. Bureau of Mines. Washington DC.

Wyman, Mark

1979   *Hard Rock Epic: Western Miners and the Industrial Revolution, 1860–1910*. University of California Press, Berkeley.

Young, Otis

1970   *Western Mining; An Informal Account of Precious-Metals Prospecting, Placering, Lode Mining, and Milling on the American Frontier from Spanish Times to 1893*. University of Oklahoma Press, Norman.

1975   Philipp Deidesheimer, 1832–1916, Engineer of the Comstock. *Historical Society of Southern California* 57(Winter):361–369.

Zanjani, Sally

1992   *Goldfield: The Last Gold Rush on the Western Frontier*. Ohio University/Swallow Press, Athens OH.

2002   *The Glory Days in Goldfield, Nevada*. University of Nevada Press, Reno.

Zeier, Charles

1986   Archaeological Investigations at Rochester Heights and Nearby Historic Settlements, Pershing County, Nevada. Report to Coeur-Rochester, Inc., from Intermountain Research, Silver City NV.

1987   Historic Charcoal Production Near Eureka, Nevada: An Archaeological Perspective. *Historical Archaeology* 21(1):81–101.

Index

Page numbers in italics refer to illustrations

Adams, William H., 175
adaptation. *See* coevolutionary model of
    adaptive change; coping strategies
Adelberg and Raymond manuscript
    collection, 3
adits, 38, 40, 42, 43, 45, 53. *See also* shafts
adobe houses, 121, 122, 124–25, 146–48,
    156, 159. *See also* house sites
Adolphus Busch, 130, 175
aeration tanks. *See* agitation tanks
African Americans, 120, 175, 176
agitation tanks, 86, 89–91, *91*, 97, 99, 100
agitators, 78, 79, 93, 181
Agricola, 107
Ah Ho, 145–47
air compressors, 41, *41*, 60–61, 63, 103
Alaska, xiii, 12, 38, *39*
Alder Gulch MT, xiii
Allis-Chalmers ball mills, 95–99, *97*. *See*
    also ball mills
Allis-Chalmers gyratory crushers, 67, 95.
    See also gyratory crushers
Allis-Chalmers tube mills, 69, 95–99. *See*
    also tube mills
all-slime mills, 69. *See also* slimes
Alton IL, 131, 175
amalgamating tables or plates, 70, 93
amalgamation mills, 117. *See also*
    amalgamating tables or plates;
    amalgamation pans; pan
    amalgamation; patios
amalgamation pans, 14, 77–78, *77*, 93,
    181. *See also* pan amalgamation; pans
    and bateas
Amargosa City camp, 114
Amargosa River, 117

American Bottle Company, 130, 175
American City settlement, 1
American Flat, 22
Ams, Max, 132
andesites, 33
Anglo-European community, 119–22, 156.
    See also British immigrants; Cornish
    miners; European immigrants
animals, 42, 49, 111
anvils, 66
Appalachian gold fields, 80
archaeological records, 15–28; adaptive
    change in, 184–85; on Consolidated
    Cortez Mill, 99–104; cultural
    adaptation model in, 179–80; of
    Eureka smelters, 105; feature systems
    of, 16–20; on Gold Bar Mine, 59;
    location of mining sites in, 21–23; of
    material networks, 175; of mining
    households, 134–70; of mining
    settlements, 118–34; of mining-
    settlement systems, 109–17; of
    mining site formation and structure,
    20–21; multiple images of past in,
    23–28; of Shoshone Wells house sites,
    147–59; of Shoshone Wells stores,
    146–47; of underground mining, 46; of
    ventilation systems, 52; on Victorian
    ideology, 177. *See also* assemblages;
    feature systems; house sites; mining
    landscapes; trash dumps and scatters
architecture, 12–15, 23–28. *See also*
    buildings and structures
Arctic Canyon, 11
Arctic Mine, 45, *45*, 100–103, 111
Arctic Tunnel, 43, 99
argentite. *See* silver sulfide
Arizona, 17, 34, *36*, *37*, 133, 177

arrastras, 17, 17, 18, 65, 65, 186
artifacts. *See* assemblages
assaying, 20, 70, 104–7, 160. *See also*
    beneficiation
assemblages: in archaeological study
    of households, 134; at Gold Bar
    settlement, 128–34, 159–70; as
    reflection of wealth and social status,
    168; at Shoshone Wells settlement,
    121, 148–59, 149, 150–52, 154–55, 157,
    158; variability at Gold Bar settlement,
    161–70, 161, 162, 164, 165, 166, 167;
    at Wenban's house site, 137. *See also*
    archaeological records; ceramics;
    glass bottles; households; ironstone
    pottery; nails; tin cans; trash dumps
    and scatters
Aurora IL, 172
Aurora settlement, 1
Austin NV, 3, 7
Austin settlement, 1
Australia, 176

bailing out, 53
Baker and Hamilton, 172
ball mills, 65, 69, 95–99, 97, 117
Bancroft, Hubert H., 3, 83
The Bandeirantes (Morse), 170
Bannack MT, xiii
barrel chlorination, 79–80
batholiths, 32–33. *See also* volcanic rock
Beatty camp, 114, 115
Belleville IL, 130, 175
beneficiation: architecture for, 12–14;
    chemical methods, 73–104; crushing
    and grinding methods, 64–70;
    definition of, 29, 64; simple collection
    methods, 70–73. *See also* assaying;
    chemical beneficiation; crushing and
    grinding; smelters and smelting
Beowawe, 172
Bertrand Mill, 80–83
Bewick-Moering Syndicate of London, 111
Bickford slow-match fuses, 41
Big Bend National Park, 12
Billie Mine Portal, 13, 14

Bi-Metallic Mine, 115
Bingham Canyon Copper Mine, 36
biographies, 184–85. *See also* diaries
Bisbee AZ, 36, 37
Bishop CA, 15
Black Hawk Flotation Mill, 72–73, 73, 99
Black Hills. *See* South Dakota
blacksmith shops, 57, 58, 58, 160, 170
Blake's jaw crusher, 67, 68, 87. *See also* jaw
    crushers
blanket-and-pipe replacement bodies, 34
blanket sluices, 79. *See also* sluices and
    sluicing
blanket tables, 70. *See also* amalgamating
    tables or plates
blast furnaces, 104, 105
blasting, 41
Blue Bird Mill, 83
boarding houses: archaeological records
    of, 134, 135; at Gold Bar settlement,
    58, 59, 126, 159, 163, 168–70; as part
    of architectural record, 15. *See also*
    bunkhouses; single-sex households;
    work group households
Bodie CA, 9, 10, 13, 16, 30, 49
Bodie Standard Mill, 12
Boise Basin ID, xiii
Bonanza Mountain, 113–16
Bonanza NV, 114
bonanza ores, 33
bonanza periods, 135. *See also* boom-bust
    cycles
boom-bust cycles, 179, 181–83, 185. *See
    also* bonanza periods; borrascas
booming, 36
Booth and Company, 172
Boron CA, 36
borrascas, 135, 183. *See also* boom-bust
    cycles
boundaries, 8–10
British Columbia, xiii
British immigrants, 113, 120, 175. *See also*
    Anglo-European community; Cornish
    miners; England
British investment, xiv
Brown Brothers and Company, 172

Browne, John Ross, 3, 4
Bruckner cylinders, 81, 81, 85, 111
Bruckner furnaces, 83, 85
Brumfiel, Elizabeth, 109
bucket-line dredges, 38. *See also* dredging
    technology
buddles, 71. *See also* concentrators
buildings and structures: at Cortez
    Company Camp, 112; as part of
    architectural record, 12, 14–15; as
    part of landscape, 8; special purpose
    at Gold Bar settlement, 170. *See also*
    architecture; blacksmith shops;
    boarding houses; bungalows;
    bunkhouses; households; house sites;
    powerhouses; saloons
bulldozing, 36
Bullfrog Gold Bar Mining Company, 55
Bullfrog Goldfield Railroad, 115
Bullfrog Miner, 7, 126
Bullfrog Mining District: amalgamation
    in, 70; boom in, xv; census records
    for, 7; fire insurance map of, 87; "glory
    hole" in, 35; Gold Bar Mine in, 55;
    hoist engine in, 25; Homestake-King
    Mill site in, 92; settlement-systems in,
    113–17
Bullfrog Mountain, 55
Bullfrog NV, 114–16
bullion, 78, 83, 84, 89, 99, 105, 171, 181
bullion furnaces, 99
Bullion Mine, 52, 53
bullion recovery buildings, 103
bullwheels, 16
bungalows, 126, 159, 168, 170
Bunker Hill screens, 95
bunkhouses, 15, 126, 134, 135, 159, 163,
    168–69. *See also* boarding houses;
    single-sex households; work group
    households
Bureau of Land Management (BLM), 2, 4
Burleigh mechanical rock drill, 40, 41
Burm Ball Mine, 117. *See also* Original
    Bullfrog Mine
burros, 42

Butte MT, 83
Butters filter, 93
Butters Mill. *See* Charles Butters Mill

cages, 51, 52
Cahn, Nicklesburg Company, 172
calcium hyposulfite, 80
calcium sulfide, 82, 182
Caledonia Mine, Gold Hill, 41
California: architecture in, 12, 13;
    Chinese miners in, 141; chlorination
    in, 80; Cortez store purchases from,
    172, 174; history of mining in, xiii;
    miners from, 175; stamp mills in gold
    fields of, 66; surface mining in, 36;
    trash dumps in, 133. *See also specific*
    places in
California Mine, 53
California Pan Mill, 79
camshafts, 66, 66
Canadian immigrants, 113, 120, 176
canaries, 52
capitalization, 181, 185–87. *See also*
    economic events
Cariboo region (British Columbia), xiii
Carpenter, Jay A., 4
Carson City NV, 6
Carson Range, 15, 22
Carson River, xiv, 10, 22
Carson Valley farmlands, 10
cartographic sources, 2
case records, 4
cave-ins, 45
Cedar Hill, 26
census records: for Cortez district, 7, 113,
    119–20, 125, 134, 135, 141–43, 143–45,
    145–57, 175–76; for Garrison Mine,
    175–76; for Gold Bar settlement, 126,
    136; as information source, 7; on
    Nevada Chinese population, 141–43;
    in study of households, 28, 134–36. *See*
    also government records; population
    size
centralized control structure, 186–87
Central Mine, 53
Central Pacific Railroad, 172

ceramics: at Gold Bar settlement, 165–69, 166, 167; "luxury" in Wenban assemblage, 140; at Shoshone Wells settlement, 122, 148, 153, 156, 159. See also assemblages; ironstone pottery
charcoal, 19, 105, 107, 148, 159
charcoal ovens, 23
Charles Butters Mill, 84–87, 86
Chasing the Glitter (Clow), 29
Checklist of U.S. Public Documents, 4
chemical beneficiation, 73–104. See also beneficiation; chlorination; cyanide leaching technology; pan amalgamation; patios; Russell leaching technology; Von Patera
Chicago IL, 130, 175
children: archaeological evidence of, 135; at Garrison Mine, 176; at Gold Bar settlement, 128, 159, 160, 163, 166–68; at Shoshone Wells settlement, 140, 156
Chilean mills, 69, 87
Chinese community: census records on Nevada, 141; in coevolutionary model of adaptive change, 186; at Garrison Mine, 113, 175, 176; in resiliency strategy, 183; at Shoshone Wells, 27, 119–22, 125, 140–59, 150; sojourner households of, 134, 135, 142
Chinese economic system, 171
Chinese Six Companies, 186, 187
chlorination, 73, 79–80
Churchill County Museum and Archives, 2
chutes and chuteway raises, 46, 93
city directories, 8
classifiers, 69–70, 87, 93, 95–99. See also sizing screens
Clearwater River ID, xiii
clothing, 172. See also footwear
Clow, Richmond, 29
coevolutionary model of adaptive change, 183–87. See also evolutionary theory
Coffey and Risdon Company, 174, 181
coins, 149
Colorado, xiii, 80. See also Denver CO
Colorado Mining Company, xiv

Colorado River, xiv
communications buildings, 15. See also information networks
company records, 2–3
company stores, 135
company towns, 109, 118, 177
Comstock Lode: Butters Mill on, 86; chlorination at, 80; in coevolutionary model of adaptive change, 186; discovery of, xiii, xiv; landscape of, 8–10; square-sets on, 46; technology developed on, 181
Comstock Mining District: air compressor at Caledonia Mine in, 41; coevolutionary model for adaptation in, 185–87; Cornish pump at Union Shaft in, 54; cyanide leaching technology in, 87; drainage methods in, 53–55; geological formations in, 33, 34; hoisting systems in, 49, 51, 51, 52; location model for, 22; patios in, 74, 75; personal reminiscences of, 3; Sanborn fire insurance maps of, 1; and San Francisco Stock Exchange Board, 176; stamp mills in, 66, 66; underground workings in, 43; ventilation methods in, 52, 53
concentrators, 70–72, 91, 99, 117. See also Dorr thickening tanks; vanners
concrete machine pads, 59, 62–63, 63, 93, 107
Consolidated Cortez Mill, 96; conversion to oil flotation concentration plant, 99–103; cyanide leaching technology at, 94–104, 97, 98, 99; gyratory crushers at, 67; map of, 100; powerhouse at, 101, 102; tailings flow at, 99–100, 101; trash at, 20, 103–4, 103, 107
Consolidated Cortez Mine, 43, 44, 69
Consolidated Cortez Silver Mines Company (CCSMC), 11–12, 111–12
conspicuous consumption, 177
contamination, 10
Cook, Sherburne, 25
coping strategies, 180–83

copper, xiii, 32, 64, 70, 104, 183

copper amalgamating pans, 93. *See also* amalgamation pans

copper sulfate, 74, 77, 78

Cornish miners, 71, 122, 140. *See also* Anglo-European community; British immigrants

Cornish pumps, 12, 54, 55

corporate industrial structure, 186–87. *See also* industrial social order

"Cortez City" camp: establishment of, 110; plans for, 112

Cortez Company, Ltd.: camp as as gravity center, 112; end of operations at, 181; material network of, 171–75

Cortez Company Mill, 112, 174, 181

Cortez Gold and Silver Mining Company (CGSMC) Mill, 110–11, 181

Cortez Gold Mines, 112

Cortez Joint Stock Company, 110

Cortez Mines Limited, 2–3, 111. *See also* Tenabo Mill and Mining Company (TMMC)

Cortez Mining District: adit at Arctic Mine in, 45; Allis-Chalmers tube mill at, 69; Arctic Mine waste dump and tramway at, 30; census records for, 7, 113, 119–20, 125, 134, 135, 141–43, 143–45, 145–47, 175–76; Chinese in, 122, 140–41, 183; Consolidated Cortez Mill at, 96; coping strategies in, 181–83; cyanide leaching technology at, 94; feature systems in, 17–18; geographical area of, 23; government records of, 5, 6; household artifact assemblages in, 140; landscape of, 11; material network of, 171–75; "Nevada Giant Ledge" in, 33, 34; settlements in, 118–25, 118; settlement-systems in, 110–13; shrinkage system in, 45–46, 47; in sociotechnical systems in, 31; tax assessment rolls for, 120, 145–47; trash dumps in, 20; underground mining system in, 43. *See also* Cortez Precinct; Garrison Mine Precinct; Shoshone Wells settlement

Cortez Mountains, 11

Cortez NV: census records for, 7; leaching technology in, 83; miners at, 2, 119; Simeon Wenban as resident of, 145

Cortez Precinct, 7, 113, 120, 134, 142–47, 144–45. *See also* Cortez Mining District

Cortez store invoices, 171–72, 172–74

Couch, Bertrand F., 4

county records, 5–6. *See also* tax assessment rolls

Crescent Valley, 112

Cripple Creek CO, xiii, 80

cross-cuts, 43, 45

crucibles, 105, 106, 107

Crumley, Carole, 109

crushing and grinding, 64–70, 87, 95, 97. *See also* beneficiation; gyratory crushers; rock breakers

cultural adaptation model, 179–83

cultural identity, 109–10

cultural representations, 10–11

cupels, 105–7, 106

cupreous hyposulfite, 83

cut-and-pit mines, 8

cyanidation, 65, 72

Cyanidation and Concentration of Gold and Silver Ores (Dorr), 29

cyanide leaching technology: in Beatty, 117; at Charles Butters Mill, 84–87; at Consolidated Cortez Mine, 94–104; in Cortez Mining District, 111–12; description of, 83–104; at Homestake-King Mill, 91–94; at Montgomery-Shoshone Mill, 87–91; replacement of chlorination, 80; and square-set stoping, 45; at Tenabo Mill, 20, 31, 83; in United States, 84; at Wenban's mill, 11

cyanide vats, 30

Darwinian fitness. *See* fitness

Davis, J. R., 55

Dawes, T. D., 46

Dayton NV, 1

D. Dierssen Company, 172

Death Valley National Park, 12, 13, 15, 25, 28, 55, 62, 134–35, 175
Deidesheimer, Philipp, 43–45, 53
Deiner, Paul, 184
Deister concentration tables, 99. *See also* concentrators
Denver CO, 72, 172
Denver mine, 113, 115
De Quille, Dan, 3, 52
diaries, 3. *See also* biographies
dies, 66
differential reproduction, 180
dispersed control structure, 186
distribution nodes (retailing and wholesaling), 175
documentary records: adaptive change in, 184–85; of Chinese in Cortez district, 140–47; for Cortez district, 119–20; cultural adaptation model in, 180; of Gold Bar settlement, 125; of households, 134; for locating mining sites, 21, 22; of material networks, 171–75; of mining technology, 32; of Nevada mining history, 1–8; of Shoshone Wells settlement, 122; in studying mining past, 23–28; on Victorian ideology, 177
Dodge's jaw crushers, 67. *See also* jaw crushers
dolomite, 34
doodlebugs, 38
Dorr agitation tanks, 97, 99
Dorr classifiers, 70, 93, 95–99. *See also* classifiers
Dorr, John, 29
Dorr thickening tanks, 89, 90, 99
double jacking, 41
drafts, 52, 53
dragline dredges, 38. *See also* dredging technology
drainage methods, 53–55
dredging technology, xv, 36, 38
drift mining, 40
drifts, 43, 45, 46
drill holes, 35
drills, 40–41, 40, 61
dry-crushing mills, 31, 66, 67, 67

drying kilns, 76
dry-land dredges, 38. *See also* dredging technology
dry-set stone houses. *See* stone houses
dry washing, 36
dugout structures, 122, 124, 125, 148. *See also* house sites
dust catchers, 105
dynamite, 41

Eagle AK, 38, 39
Eagle Mountains, 36
Eclipse Development Company, 115
Eclipse mine, 115
ecological characteristics, 11, 170–71, 176, 179–80, 182–86
economic events, 179–84. *See also* capitalization
economic power networks, 109, 171
Egleston, Thomas, 29
El Dorado, xiii
Eldorado Mining District, xiv
electricity, 31, 115–16
electric motors, 93
elevation and flow sheet, 73
Elko NV, 172
Embrey tables, 71. *See also* concentrators
Emmons, S. F., 4
engineer-designed mine complexes, 8
Engineering and Mining Journal, 24, 29, 87, 88, 116
England, 84. *See also* British immigrants; British investment
environmental changes, 182
Esmeralda district, xiv
Esmeralda settlement, 1
ethnic diversity, 27, 119–22, 175, 187. *See also* world systems
Eureka and Palisade Railroad, 15
Eureka County (NV), 5, 113, 119–20, 141–42
Eureka Mining District, 104–5
Eureka (NV), xv, 23, 80–81, 104
European economic system, 171
European immigrants, 113, 175, 176. *See also* Anglo-European community

evolutionary theory, 179. *See also* coevolutionary model of adaptive change

extraction, 29, 34–35, 55–59. *See also* open-pit mining; surface mining; underground mining

extraction architecture, 12–13

Fagergren flotation cells, 72, 72, 99
Fairbanks and Morse generators, 102, 103
Fair, James G., 187
family households, 134, 135, 136, 140, 142, 159, 163, 167–68
feature systems: in cultural adaptation model, 180; description and analysis of, 16–20; of Gold Bar Mine, 56–57, 59; of Gold Bar settlement households, 167–70; at Homestake-King Mill, 93; of Homestake Mine, 59–63; layers of, 20–21; in locating mining sites, 23; of mining technology, 31–32. *See also* archaeological records
feedback loop, 184, 187
ferrous sulphate, 79
field survey strategy, 22
Finland, 175
fissure veins, 34
fitness, 183–87
floating bucket dredges, xv. *See also* dredging technology
flooding, 53
flotation, 65, 70, 72–73. *See also* Fagergren flotation cells; oil flotation technology
flotation mill (Beatty), 117
flux, 104, 105
food production and consumption, 134, 135, 163, 165, 169, 172
footwear, 159. *See also* clothing
Forman Shaft, Gold Hill, 50
Fort Churchill, 124
Fraser River, xiii
Frassetti, Joe, 6
free milling, 64
Freiberg barrels, 14
frothed rock ores, 70
frothing machines, 72

Frue vanners, 71, 71
funiculars, 15
furnaces. *See* blast furnaces; Bruckner furnaces; bullion furnaces; muffle furnaces; retort furnaces; reverberatory roasting furnaces; revolving furnaces or cylinders; Stetefeldt furnaces

gallows headframes. *See* headframe hoisting systems
gangue, 64, 71, 72, 81
Garrison (Number 1 level), 43
Garrison Mine, 5, 111, 113, 122, 141, 142, 175–76, 182
Garrison Mine Precinct, 113, 120, 135, 141–43, 143, 175–76. *See also* Cortez Mining District
gas hoists, 61
Geiger Grade Railroad, 15
gender, 160, 163. *See also* single-sex households; women
General Land Office, 4, 5
geographical boundaries, 10
geographical characteristics, 179
geographical clusters, 20–21, 119–22, 124, 125, 128, 146–59
geographical distribution, 21–23. *See also* world systems
geographical expansion, 180, 183
geological clusters, 120–22
geological distribution, 9
geological events, 184
geological formations, 32–34
geologists, 21
geology of ore bodies, 38, 179, 182
Georgia, 175
Germany, 175
ghost towns, 10
giant powder. *See* dynamite
Giant Powder Company, 41
"Giants," 12
"Giant" water nozzle, 39
glass bottles: cultural change reflected by, 177; at Gold Bar settlement, 126, 128, 130–32, 165, 166, 166, 167, 169, 170,

glass bottles (*continued*)
175; at Shoshone Wells settlement,
121, 122, 148–53, 156–59. *See also*
assemblages
glass, window, 107, 153
"glory holes," 35, 36
Godoy, Ricardo A., 110
gold: assaying of, 105, 107; in
beneficiation, 64, 65; in chlorination,
79, 80; in Comstock Lode, 186; in
cyanide leaching, 84, 89, 93; in
flotation, 72; found by Mormon
prospectors, xiv; in geological
formations, 32–34; history of mining,
xiii–xv; mining in Cortez district, 12;
recovery with amalgamating plates,
70; smelting of, 104, 105; surface
mining of, 36, 38; use of Krom rolls
on, 183
Gold Bar area, Homestake-King Mill at,
93, 115
Gold Bar Mill, 56, 128
Gold Bar Mine, 54, 56, 58, 59;
blacksmithing feature at, 57, 58;
extraction at, 55–59; hoisting system
at, 50, 56; main shaft at, 64; material
network of, 175; new shaft at, 57–59,
60; office buildings at, 58, 59; original
shaft at, 55–57, 57; rock-waste dumps
above, 63; sniping on property of, 60;
strike at, 113; study of households
at, 28; superstructure, 55, 56;
underground at, 48. *See also* Gold Bar
settlement
Gold Bar Mine camp, 126, 129; census
records for, 7; designation of, 128;
households at, 159; nails at house sites
at, 149; population estimate, 116. *See
also* Gold Bar settlement
Gold Bar settlement: activity patterns at,
134–35, 165–70; artifact assemblages
at, 128–34; census records for,
126, 136; deposition rates at, 163;
household groups at, 162–63;
household organization at, 163–65;
layout of, 128; length of house site

occupancy at, 162; map of, 127; social
archaeology of, 125–34; variability
in artifact assemblages at, 161–70,
161, 162, 164, 165, 166, 167; variability
in household layout at, 159–61. *See
also* Gold Bar camp; Gold Bar Mine;
Homestake camp
Gold Canyon, xiv, 22, 34, 186
Gold Center camp, 114, 115
gold chloride, 79
Goldfield Daily Tribune, 7
Goldfield News, 7
Goldfield NV, xiii, xv, 7, 9, 55, 80, 115
gold fields, 66
Gold Hill News, 7
Gold Hill NV, 1, 41, 50, 52
gold ores, 84
Gould and Curry Mill, 8, 66, 74
government records, 3–6, 28. *See also*
census records
Grass Valley, 11, 19, 118–19
gravity centers, 21–22, 112
grid pattern, 26, 26, 177
grinding. *See* crushing and grinding
grizzlies, 75–76, 93
ground sluicing, 36. *See also* sluices and
sluicing
Guanajuato, Mexico, 84
gyratory crushers, 67, 93, 95. *See also*
crushing and grinding

Hague, James, 3
Hamilton NV, xiv
hammers, 40–41
hand methods, 35, 36
hard rock deposits, 35
hard-rock miners, 140–41
Harper's New Monthly Magazine, 8
Harris, Frank "Shorty," 55, 113
Hazeltine, Ben, 55
headframe hoisting systems: description
of, 49–52, 50; at Forman Shaft, 51;
at Gold Bar Mine, 50, 55–58, 56; at
Homestake Mine, 60, 63; at Joshua
Tree National Park, 42. *See also* hoisting
works

heap leaching, 65, 112, 117

Hearst, George, 110

Heikes, V. C., 94–95

Hercules gasoline hoists, 57. *See also* hoisting works

heterarchical organizations, 109

Hine, Robert V., 110

Hing Wah and Company, 6

Historic American Engineering Record (HAER), 12

Hobo mine, 115

Ho Chow, 147

Hodder, Ian, 183

hoisting engines, 25, 59–60, 63

hoisting methods, 49–51. *See also* headframe hoisting systems; hoisting works

hoisting works, 38–40, 55–58, 56, 60, 61, 61. *See also* headframe hoisting systems; hoisting methods

"hole-in-cap" cans, 132, 133

Homestake camp: boarding houses at, 169; bunkhouses at, 168; designation of, 128; households at, 159. *See also* Gold Bar settlement

Homestake Consolidated Mining Company, 59, 60, 126–28, 168

Homestake-King Consolidated Mining and Milling Company, 168, 169

Homestake-King Mill, 92; bunkhouse for workers at, 169; closure of, 61, 116, 128; construction of, 128; cyanide leaching technology at, 91–94; erection of, 115; map of, 94; milling flow sheets from, 95

Homestake-King Mine, 61–62, 70, 116

Homestake Mine, 61; concrete machine pads at, 62–63, 63; feature systems of, 59–63; hoisting works at, 60–63, 61; map of, 62; operations at, 117; settlements at, 115

Homestake Mine and Mill, 128

Hop Sing, 6

horizontal passages. *See* adits; drifts

horizontal stratigraphy, 20

host rocks, 33

hotels, 134. *See also* boarding houses

household feature systems, 19–20

households: activity patterns in, 28, 134–35, 165–70; adaptive change in, 185, 186; architecture of, 15; Chinese at Shoshone Wells, 140–59; classification at Gold Bar settlement, 167–70; coping strategies in, 180; glass bottles in, 130, 132; at Gold Bar settlement, 159–70; in multiple-image study, 27–28; organization at Gold Bar settlement, 163–65; at Shoshone Wells settlement, 121; of Simeon Wenban, 136–40; types of, 136. *See also* assemblages; house sites; settlements; settlement-systems

house sites: archaeological records of Gold Bar, 126; archaeological records of Shoshone Wells, 147–59; assemblages from Wenban's, 137–39; classification at Shoshone Wells, 123–24; construction variability at Shoshone Wells, 122–25; dating of Gold Bar, 131–32; floor areas at Gold Bar, 160, 160–61, 161, 163, 165; at Garrison Mine, 113; groups of, 28, 134; horizontal stratigraphy of, 20; layout at Gold Bar, 128, 159–61; layout at Shoshone Wells, 120–22; map of Gold Bar, 127; at Shoshone Wells, 27; tax assessment records for Shoshone Wells, 145–47; variability of assemblages at Gold Bar settlement, 161–70, 161, 162, 164, 165, 166, 167. *See also* archaeological records; households; settlements; settlement-systems

Hughes, Thomas, 29–31

Humboldt County (NV), xiv

Humboldt district, xiv

hydraulic technology, xv, 36, 38, 39

Idaho, xiii

identification records, 4

ideological events and networks, 109, 176–77, 184, 186, 187. *See also* Victorian culture

Illinois, 130, 131, 172, 175
Illinois Glass Company, 131, 175
index artifacts, 131, 163
Index to Mining Locations, 5
Index to Tonopah Mining District
   Records, 5
Indiana, 131, 172, 175
Indianapolis IN, 172
Indian Springs NV, 116
indigenous peoples, xiii
industrial social order, 176–77. See also
   corporate industrial structure
industrial technology feature systems,
   19–20
Information Circulars, 24, 29
information networks, 176–77, 186. See
   also communications buildings
infrastructure architecture, 12, 15
Ingalls, Walter R., 105
Iowa, 175
Ireland, 175
iron, xiii, 32, 104
iron buckets, 48, 49, 53
ironstone pottery, 157–58, 167–70. See also
   assemblages; ceramics
Italian community, 27, 113, 119–22, 175

jacks, 40–41
Jackson, Robert, 84
jaw crushers, 64, 67, 68, 87
jigs, 71. See also concentrators
Jones, Nathaniel V., xiv
Joshua Tree National Park, 12, 36, 42, 65
joss houses (temples), 122, 148
journals, 3, 24, 29

Kaiser's Eagle Mountain Iron Mine, 36
Keane Wonder Mill, 12
Keane Wonder Mine, 15
Kelly, Marsha C., 17
Kelly, Roger E., 17
Kennecott Copper Mill (AK)
Kennecott copper mine (NV), 12, 36
Kentucky, 175
kickers, 184

kilns. See drying kilns; limestone quarry
   and kiln
Kinkaid Mill, 71
Kirch, Patrick, 179–83
K. K. Consolidated smelter, 104–5
Klondike Gold Rush, xiii
Knox amalgamating pans, 181. See also
   amalgamation pans
Kral, Victor E., 117
Krom rolls, 68, 69, 81, 111, 183
Krom's jaw crushers, 67. See also jaw
   crushers

labor, 171, 183. See also mill laborers; mine
   laborers
Ladd Mountain, 113, 114
Lake Gilbert, 11
Lake Mead, xiv, 17
Lake Tahoe, 15
Lander County (NV): census records
   for, 113, 119–20, 142–47; government
   records on, 5; tax assessment rolls for,
   6, 136, 145–47
Las Vegas and Tonopah Railroad, 115. See
   also railroads
Las Vegas Valley, xiv
Latschar, John, 168
Lavender copper pit, 36, 37
leaching. See cyanide leaching
   technology; heap leaching; leaching
   tanks; leaching vats; Russell leaching
   technology
leaching tanks, 88–89, 93, 117
leaching vats, 83, 85
lead, xiv, 72, 83, 104, 105, 183
lead acetate, 88
lead carbonate, 83
lead oxide, 105–7
lead-silver ores, xv
Leadville CO, xiii
legal records, 4
Lenox ore cars, 58. See also ore cars
lime, 88
limestone, 11, 104
limestone quarry and kiln, 18–19, 19,
   182–83

Lingenfelter, Richard E., 116
litigation, 5, 113–14, 116, 120
lixiviation. *See* leaching
location model, 21–22
"locking" double-seam cans, 132, 133
lode formations, 35–36
Loftus, J. P., 55
London, 111
Long Toms, 14, 36, 186
Lord, Eliot, 49
Louisiana, 175
Lovelock NV, 149
Lower Cortez, 112, 120. *See also* Shoshone
    Wells settlement
low-tech drainage methods, 53
low-tech hand-powered tools, 36, 40–41
low-tech hoisting methods, 49–51
lumber industry, 124. *See also* timbers

machinery purchases, 172–74
Mackay, John W., 187
Mackay School of Earth Sciences and
    Engineering, 95. *See also* Mackay
    School of Mines
Mackay School of Mines, 84. *See also*
    Mackay School of Earth Sciences and
    Engineering
Maine, 175
Main Street (Shoshone Wells), 147
Malakoff Diggings CA, 34, 39
Manhattan Mining District, xv, 38
Manhattan Post, 7
Manhattan Silver Mining Company, 3,
    183
A Manual of Assaying (Miller), 29
manway raises, 45–46. *See also* raises
Mariposa County CA, 141
Mariscal Quicksilver Works, 12
Marsac Mill, 83
Maryland, 175
Massillon Bottle and Glass Company,
    130, 175
Massillon OH, 130, 175
Matamoras Mill furnace, 105
"match-stick" filler hole cans, 132, 133
material networks, 171–76

Mathews, Mary McNair, 3
matte mixtures, 104
Mayflower Mill, 115, 116, 117
Mayflower Mine, 24, 113, 115, 117
Mazess, Richard, 185
McCoy, W. W., 104–5
McCully gyratory crushers, 93. *See also*
    gyratory crushers
mechanical methods, 36, 38, 41
Merced County CA, 141
mercury, 32, 36, 64, 70, 74, 77, 78
mercury amalgamation mills, 11
Merrill clarifying presses, 98, 99
Merrill slime press, 98
metallic sulfides, 32
*Metallurgy of Silver, Gold and Mercury in the
    United States* (Egleston), 29
Mexican community, 119, 120, 124–25,
    186
Mexican Mine, 53
Mexico, 17, 49, 74, 83, 84, 176
Michigan, 175
microenvironments, 11
military power networks, 109
Mill Canyon, 11, 112
Miller, Alfred, 29
Miller, George, 130
milling flow sheets, 76, 84, 88, 95
milling technologies, 45, 181–84
mill laborers, 113
mills, 65, 115, 116, 117. *See also specific mills*
mill tailings: at California Pan Mill, 79;
    in chlorination, 79; at Consolidated
    Cortez Mill, 99–100, 101; in cyanide
    leaching at Montgomery-Shoshone
    Mill, 87–89, 91; cyanide process used
    on, 84; at Homestake-King Mill, 93;
    in pan amalgamation, 78; as part
    of landscape, 9, 11–12; reworking at
    Mayflower Mine, 117; reworking in
    Cortez Mining District, 111. *See also*
    rock-waste mining dumps
Milwaukee WI, 131, 175
mine laborers, 113, 141
Mineral City settlement, 1
Mineral County (NV), xiv

Mineral Hill, 75
mineral patent survey plats, 2
Mineral Resources West of the Rocky
    Mountains, 4
Mineral Resources West of the United
    States, 4
miners. *See* hard-rock miners; labor; mill
    laborers; mine laborers
miners' unions, 141
Mining and Scientific Press, 24, 29
mining camps, 20, 25–26, 28, 110, 114,
    186. *See also* settlements; settlement-
    systems
mining claim markers, 8, 10
mining districts, 8
Mining Engineer's Handbook (Peele), 43
mining islands, 170–71, 179
mining landscapes, 8–12, 9, 35, 179. *See
    also* archaeological records
Mining Locations, 5
mining rushes, xiii, xiv–xv, 179
mining technologies and methods, xiii,
    23–24, 29, 31–32, 181–84, 186
Minnesota, 36
Miocene period, 22
Mississippi, 175
Missouri, 175
mode of production. *See* production
modern world systems, 171. *See also* world
    systems
Montana, xiii, 83
Montare, Antonio, 6
Monte Cristo Pan Mill, 79, 80
Montero, Antonio, 147
Montgomery NV, 113–14
Montgomery-Shoshone Consolidated
    Mining Company, 114
Montgomery-Shoshone Mill, 69, 87–91,
    87, 88, 89, 116, 117
Montgomery-Shoshone Mine, 2, 35,
    113–14, 117
Montrose, A., 6
Morey district, 141
Mormon Fort, xiv
morphology, 16–17, 25, 27–28, 134, 135
Morse, R. M., 170

mortar boxes, 66
Mount Cory (Nevada), 83
Mount Davidson, 26, 26
Mount Tenabo, 110–12, 118
mucking out, 41
Mud Springs NV, 116
muffle furnaces, 105
Mugginsville, 112. *See also* Shoshone Wells
    settlement
mule trains, 111
Muncie Glass Company, 131, 175
Muncie IN, 131, 175
Murdock, George P., 25
mutilation of mining sites, 20–21
mutual aid households, 136

nails, 107, 128, 133–34, 149, 153, 156–57,
    159. *See also* assemblages
Naramore, Chester, 3
Nash, June, 110
National Architectural and Engineering
    Record, 12
National Archives, 4, 5
National Bank claim, 113
National Park Service, 12. *See also* Death
    Valley National Park; Joshua Tree
    National Park
Native Americans, 181
neighborhoods. *See* ethnic diversity;
    geographical clusters
Networks of Power (Hughes), 29–31
Nevada Bureau of Mines and Geology,
    2, 4
Nevada-California Power Company, 15,
    115–16
Nevada Central Railroad, 15
Nevada Giant Ledge, 33, 34, 111
Nevada Giant ore body, 118
Nevada Legislature, 5
Nevada State Archives, 2, 6
Nevada State Historical Society, 2
Nevada State Historic Preservation Office
    Web site, 7
Nevada State Office, 2
Nevada Supreme Court, 5, 120
Newark OH, 131, 175

New Jersey, 175

New Mexico, 72–73, 73

newspaper accounts, 7, 22, 28, 118, 125–26, 135, 168, 169. *See also specific newspapers*

New York, 175

New York Public Library, 3

New Zealand, 84

Noble, Bruce, 29

"no man's land," 23

Nye County (NV), 5, 58, 93–94

occupational households, 136

O'Hara furnaces, 111

Ohio, 130, 131, 175

Ohio Bottle Company, 131, 175

oil flotation technology, 99–103, 111–12

Old Sacramento NV, 149

Oliver filters, 98, 99, 100

Omaha NE, 172

Ontario (Utah), 83

open-pit mining, 8, 9, 12, 36, 38, 112, 117. *See also* extraction; surface mining

Ophir Mill, 80

Ophir Mine, 49, 53–55

opportunistic strategies, 180–82

ore-bearing faults, 22

ore bins, 58, 91, 93

ore bodies, 21, 35, 38, 179, 182. *See also* ore deposits

ore cars, 42, 50, 58

ore deposits, 2. *See also* ore bodies

ore skips, 57–59

Original Bullfrog camp, 25, 114–16, 134

Original Bullfrog Mine, 113, 117. *See also* Burm Ball Mine

Osceola Mining District, xv, 38

Osceola Placer Mining Company, xv, 38

outliers, 10

Owens automatic bottle machine, 130

Owyhee Mountains, xiii

Pacific Coast Glass Works, 131, 175

pan amalgamation, 75–81, 79, 83–84, 110, 111, 181. *See also* amalgamation pans

pans and bateas, 36. *See also* amalgamation pans

Paradise district, 141

Park City UT, 83

patios, 14, 74, 74, 75

Peele, Robert, 43

Pennsylvania, 175

Pershing County NV, 162

Peru, 49

Pfaffenberger, Brian, 31

photographic record, 22–23, 35, 126, 128, 168–70

picks and shovels, 41

Pikes Peak, xiii

pine oil, 72, 99

pinyon-juniper woodlands, 10, 11

Pioneer Mill site, 25

Pioneer Mine, 115, 117

Pioneer NV, 115, 116

"Pioneer" section (Bullfrog Mining District), 113, 116–17

placer mining, xv, 141

placers, 34–36, 34, 38–40, 186, 187

Planchas de Plata, 34

planned mining, 43

Plattner, Karl Friedrich, 79

political power networks, 109

Pony Express stations, 124

pooling, 180

population networks, 175–76

population size, 181, 182. *See also* census records

Portuguese, 120, 175

potassium cyanide, 83–84

Potosi Spring, xiv

powerhouses, 101, 102, 103

power shovels, 36, 38

privies, 126, 135

problem domains, 31

production, 171, 175, 177

prospect holes, 35

prospector structure, 186–87

Prussia, 79

pulp, 70, 71, 74, 77, 78

"purple" bottle glass, 130–32, 131, 132

quartz, 32, 55
Queen Mill, 98
Qwong Hing, 146, 147

railroads, 15, 72, 77, 99, 111, 115, 172, 176, 184. *See also* transportation or circular networks
Rainbow Mountain, 113–14
raises, 43, 45–46
Ralston, William C., 187
"random" methods, 23
rat-hole system, 42, 43
Rawhide NV, xv, 48, 79, 80, 98
Raymond, Rossiter, 4, 141
Red Mountain mines, 141
Reese River, xiii, xiv
Reese River Mining District, 51, 124–25, 183
Reese River Process (pan amalgamation), 75, 76, 111, 181. *See also* pan amalgamation
Reese River Reveille, 7
refining technology, 29
Reinhart, N. P., 55
replacement bodies, 34
reproductive rates of variants, 184, 185
Reps, John W., 4–5, 26, 177
residential architecture, 12, 15. *See also* boarding houses; bunkhouses; households; house sites
resiliency strategies, 182–83, 185
resource intensification, 180
retort furnaces, 70, 78
reverberatory roasting furnaces, 110–11, 181
revolving furnaces or cylinders, 67, 67
Reward Mine, 133
Rhyolite, 2
Rhyolite Daily Bulletin, 125–26
Rhyolite Herald, 7, 125–26
Rhyolite NV, 7, 15, 69, 87, 114, 114, 115–17
rhyolites, 33
Riches to Rust (Twitty), 29
Richmond Consolidated Smelter, 104
riffles, 36

roads. *See* transportation or circular networks
Roberts Mining and Milling Company, 112
Rochester house sites, 162–64
Rock, James, 133
rock breakers, 65, 67, 69–70, 76. *See also* crushing and grinding
rock drills, 40–41
rockers, 36
rock matrix, 64, 66
rock waste, 45, 46. *See also* rock-waste mining dumps
rock-waste mining dumps, 8, 9, 35, 57, 59, 63, 103; at Arctic Mine, 30; reworking in Cortez Mining District, 111. *See also* mill tailings; rock waste; trash dumps and scatters
rod mills, 65, 69
rollers, 64
rotating mullers, 77
Roth and Company, 130–31, 175
Round Mountain Mining District, xv, 38
"Rush to Washoe," xiv
Russell, E. H., 83
Russell leaching technology, 11, 17–20, 31, 83, 84, 111, 182–83
Ruth NV, 36

Sacramento CA, 172
Sacramento Union, 7
safety cages, 51. *See also* cages
saloons, 126, 166, 170. *See also* temperance
salt, xiii, 11, 74, 76–78, 80, 181
Salt Lake City UT, 36, 72, 115
Salt Lake Valley, xiv, 99
Sam Kee, 146
sampling strata, 22–23
Sanborn fire insurance maps, 1–2, 87, 87, 116
sand leaching tanks, 88–89, 93
sands, 65, 87–88
sand tailings, 91. *See also* mill tailings
San Francisco CA, 7, 72, 111, 130–31, 172, 174, 175, 181
San Francisco Stock Exchange Board, 176

Sanitary Can Company, 132
sanitary cans, 132, 133
satellite imagery, 35
satellite settlements, 8. *See also*
    settlements
Schwab, Charles, 114
Scotland, 175
scrapers, 36, 38
screens. *See* Bunker Hill screens;
    classifiers; sizing screens
secondary accounts, 6
semidiesel engines, 103
settlements: coping strategies in, 180; in
    Cortez district, 118–25; at Gold Bar,
    125–34; in multiple-image study, 24–
    26; at Shoshone Wells, 121; Victorian
    culture in, 177. *See also* households;
    house sites; mining camps; satellite
    settlements; settlement-systems
settlement-systems: archaeology of,
    109–17; in Bullfrog Mining District,
    113–17; community concept in, 109–10;
    at Shoshone Wells, 121; variability in,
    110, 179–80, 182. *See also* households;
    house sites; mining camps; satellite
    settlements; settlements
settlers, 78, 78, 79, 79
settling out process, 78
settling tanks, 87, 91, 181
Seven Troughs district, xv
shafts: at Gold Bar Mine, 55–59, 57, 60,
    64; at Homestake Mine, 59, 60, 63; at
    Joshua Tree National Park, 42; open,
    10; in rat-hole system, 43; vertical, 38,
    40. *See also* adits
Sharon, William, 187
Shermantown NV, xiv
shoring, 59, 63
Shoshone Wells settlement: bottomland
    cluster at, 121, 147–56; census records
    for, 7, 136, 143; Chinese households
    at, 140–59, 146; description of,
    118–25; establishment of, 110; ethnic
    neighborhoods at, 27, 119–22; as
    gravity center, 112; hillside cluster at,
    121, 122; house site at, 27; layout of,

120–22; map of, 121; ravine cluster
    at, 121, 124, 125; road cluster at, 121,
    124, 125, 146, 147, 156–59; Simeon
    Wenban's household at, 136–40;
    tax assessment rolls for, 6, 143–47;
    Wenban cluster at, 27, 122. *See also*
    Cortez Mining District
shrinkage system of stoping, 45–46, 47
Silcott WA, 175
silver: assaying of, 105, 107; in
    beneficiation, 64; in Comstock Lode,
    186; in flotation, 72; in geological
    formations, 32–34; in leaching
    technology, 80, 89; mining in Cortez
    district, 12; in pan amalgamation,
    78; in patios, 74; production of
    Consolidated Cortez Silver Mines, 112;
    recovery with amalgamating plates,
    70; smelting of, 104, 105; use of Krom
    rolls on, 183
silver chloride, 34, 66, 75, 80, 81, 84
Silver City fault, 33
Silver City NV, 1
silver flotation mills, 72–73, 73
silver-gold sludge, 84
silver lodes, xiv
silver ores, 84
Silver Peak NV, 141
silver precipitate, 99
silver sulfide, 32, 34, 66, 73, 82, 84
simple collection methods, 70–73. *See
    also* amalgamating tables or plates;
    beneficiation; concentrators; flotation
Sinaloa, Mexico, 83
single jacking, 41
single-person households, 136
single-sex households, 134, 135, 170, 185.
    See also boarding houses; bunkhouses;
    gender
Sirena Mine, 84
Six-Mile Canyon, 22, 79, 87
sizing screens, 66–67. *See also* classifiers
slag: glassy, 105, 107; liquid, 104, 105
slime presses, 98
slimes, 65, 69, 87–89, 95. *See also* stock
    slime tanks

slopes, 43

sluices and sluicing, xv, 36, 38, 79

smelters and smelting, 70, 72, 89, 99, 104–5, 104. *See also* beneficiation

Smith, Jane F., 4

smoke ditches, 105

sniping, 36, 60

social architecture, 12, 15

social organization and interaction, 25, 109, 110, 118, 179, 186

social variants, 185

sociotechnical systems, 29–31, 179

sodium carbonate, 83

sodium cyanide, 84, 88–89

sodium hyposulfite, 80, 81, 83

sodium silver hyposulfite, 81–82

sodium sulfide, 182

soldered-seam cans, 132

sound waves, 35

South America, 170–71

South Dakota, xiii, 66, 80

Spain, 17

Spanish explorers, xiii–xiv

Spring Mountains, xiv

Spring Valley district, 141

Spude, Robert, 29

square-sets, 45, 46

stamp batteries, 66, 76, 91

stamp mills, 65–67, 67, 70, 79, 174

stamps, 64, 93, 111, 181

Standard Mill, 13

state mineralogist reports, 120

statistics, 5

status records, 4

steam boilers, 174, 181

steam engines, 49, 51, 174, 181

steam-powered pumps, 53–54

Stetefeldt furnaces, 75–77, 81, 82

Stewart, William M., 117

St. Louis Mine, 112

St. Louis mining camp, 110, 112

stock market, international, 176

stocks, 32

stock slime tanks, 93. *See also* slimes

stone houses, 122–24. *See also* house sites

stopes and stoping, 38, 45–46, 47, 57

Sullivan angle-compound type air compressors, 103. *See also* air compressors

Sullivan, Catherine, 130

Sunset Mining Company, 116

surface mining, 35–38, 52. *See also* extraction; open-pit mining

surplus, 171

Sutro Tunnel, 53

Sweden, 175

Switzerland, 175

tabular deposits, 33

Tahoe Basin, 10

tax assessment rolls, 5–6, 28, 120, 135, 145–47. *See also specific counties*

Taylor Mill, 75, 76–77, 76

Teague, George, 177

tectonic activity, 33

telegraph, 176, 184

temperance, 177. *See also* saloons

Tenabo Mill, 32; Chinese settlements near, 122, 141; and Cortez district settlements, 112, 113; effluent from, 100; feature systems of, 17–20, 19; geographical area of, 23; leaching technology at, 83, 85; milling flow sheet for Russell process at, 84; sociotechnical systems at, 31

Tenabo Mill and Mining Company (TMMC): Chinese miners at, 183; company records of, 3; construction of mill, 119; government records on, 5; in litigation, 120; and purchase of Cortez Gold and Silver Mining Company Mill, 111. *See also* Cortez Mines Limited; Tenabo Mill

tent camps, 114, 128, 168

Territorial Enterprise, 7

Tertiary period, 22, 33

Texas, 12, 175

textbooks, 24, 29

timber, 43, 45, 93, 174. *See also* lumber industry

time capsules, 46

time slice of life, 126, 130–31

tin cans, 128, 132–33, 133, 169, 177. See also
    assemblages
tipples, 15
Tok AK, 38, 39
Tonopah and Tidewater Railroad, 115
Tonopah District Records, 5
Tonopah Mining Districts, 5
Tonopah NV, xiii, xv, 55
Tonopah Sun, 114
Toquima Range, xv, 38
Toulouse, Julian, 130
townsite plats, 1–2, 26
townsite survey files, 4–5
Tramp Mine, 115–17
Tramps Consolidated Mining Company,
    115
tramways, 15, 30, 60, 63, 99–103. See also
    transportation or circular networks
transportation or circular networks,
    8, 15, 171, 186. See also railroads;
    tramways
Transvaal NV, 115
trash dumps and scatters: in
    archaeological study of households,
    135, 148, 149; at Consolidated
    Cortez Mill, 20, 103–4, 103, 107; in
    feature systems, 19–20; at Gold Bar
    settlement, 126, 133, 163, 175; at
    Homestake-King Mill, 93; at Shoshone
    Wells settlement, 120–22, 148, 149,
    156, 157, 159; Victorian culture in, 177;
    at Wenban's house site, 140. See also
    archaeological records; assemblages;
    rock-waste mining dumps
Treasure City NV, xiv
Treasure Hill, xiii–xv
Trent agitation tank, 91
Trommels, 70. See also classifiers
Truman, D. S., 147
trump-lines, 49
tube mills, 65, 69, 91, 95–99
Tuolumne County CA, 141
turquoise, xiii, xiv
Tuscarora NV, 67
Twitty, Eric, 29

underground mining: drainage methods
    in, 53–55; hoisting methods in,
    49–51; methods of, 41–43; of placer
    and lode formations, 35–36, 38–40;
    structure of, 21; ventilation methods
    in, 52–53; workings of, 40–49, 60. See
    also extraction
Union Shaft, 54, 55
Union Tunnel, 53
University of Nevada-Reno, 95, 147
University of Nevada-Reno Library, 2–3
Upper Cortez, 119, 120, 122, 141
urban centers, 118
urban middle class, 177
U.S. Borax mine, 36
U.S. Bureau of Mines, 2–4, 24, 29
U.S. Geological Survey, 4, 24
U.S. Geological Survey Cortez
    Quadrangle, 112
U.S. Mining Law (1866), 5
U.S. Treasury Department, 4
Utah, xiv, 36, 72, 83, 99, 115, 172, 175

Vanderburg, William O., xiv, 112
vanners, 71, 87. See also concentrators
Varney pans, 111
Veatch, Andrew A., 110
vein deposits, 33
Vekol Hills camp, 177
ventilation methods, 52–53
Vermont, 175
vertical shafts, 38, 40. See also shafts
Victorian culture, 27, 122, 176–77, 184,
    187. See also ideological events and
    networks
Virginia and Truckee Railroad, 15
Virginia City National Historic
    Landmark, 12
Virginia City NV: California Pan Mill
    in, 79, 79; Frue vanners in, 71; glass
    bottles at, 149; illustrations of Gould
    and Curry Mill in, 8; layout of, 26;
    mining landscapes in, 10; newspaper
    of, 7; ore-bearing faults and placers
    in, 22; personal reminiscences in, 3;
    Sanborn fire insurance maps of, 1;
    study of mining settlement in, 26

Virginia Evening Chronicle, 7
Virginia Range, 10
volcanic rock, 32–33, 122, 124
Von Patera, 80–83
Vulcan Iron Works, 174, 181

Wallerstein, Immanuel, 171
Wall Street Mill, 12
Washoe amalgamation pans, 14. *See also*
    Washoe Process (pan amalgamation)
Washoe City settlement, 1
Washoe Lake, 84
Washoe Process (pan amalgamation),
    14, 75, 79, 79, 110, 181. *See also* pan
    amalgamation
Washoe Valley, 15
water, 21, 22, 66, 74, 111, 116, 118–19
water skips, 53
water tanks, 93
wealth, 171
wells. *See* dugout structures
Welsh miners, 140
Wenban's 1886 Mill, 182–83; closure of, 11
Wenban, Simeon: at Cortez Gold and
    Silver Mining Company Mill, 110;
    employment of Chinese miners, 140;
    household at Shoshone Wells, 27, 119,
    122, 136–40; ownership of Tenabo Mill
    and Mining Company, 111; personal
    reminiscences of, 3; purchase of
    Cortez Company Mill, 182; tax records
    of, 6, 120, 145
Western Mining (Young), 24, 29
Western Shoshones, 118–19
wet-stamp mills, 66
Wheeler amalgamation pan, 77

whims, 49, 49, 53, 55, 56
Wilfley tables, 14, 71–72, 87
William Frantzen and Son, 131, 175
Williams salt marsh, 19
windlasses, 48, 49, 53
wind sails, 52
winzes, 43
Wisconsin, 131, 175
Wolf, Eric, 171
women, 134, 140, 142–43, 156, 166, 176.
    See also gender
Wonder Mining News, 7
wooden-frame houses, 122, 124, 125, 128,
    148, 153, 156. *See also* house sites
work ethic, 177
work group households, 136. *See also*
    boarding houses; bunkhouses
working drifts, 46. *See also* drifts
world systems, 121, 135, 170–77, 179,
    186–87. *See also* ethnic diversity;
    geographical distribution
World War II, 117
Wright, William. *See* De Quille, Dan

Yale, C. G., 3
Yedras Mill, 83
Yellow Jacket mine, 51
Young, Brigham, xiv
Young, Otis, 24, 29
Yung Look, 6

Zeier, Charles, 23, 163, 164
zinc, 72, 183
zinc boxes, 89, 91, 93
zinc shavings, 84

In the Historical Archaeology of the American West series

Mining Archaeology in the American West
A View from the Silver State
Donald L. Hardesty

To order or obtain more information on these or other University of
Nebraska Press titles, visit www.nebraskapress.unl.edu.